# The Complete
# Chessplayer

## Fred Reinfeld

A FIRESIDE BOOK
*Published by Simon & Schuster*
*New York London Toronto Sydney Tokyo Singapore*

**FIRESIDE**
Simon & Schuster Building
Rockefeller Center
1230 Avenue of the Americas
New York, New York 10020

Published in 1987 by Prentice Hall Press
First Fireside Edition 1992
Originally published by Prentice-Hall, Inc.

Manufactured in the United States of America

22  23  24  25

Library of Congress Catalog Card Number 52-10667

ISBN 0-671-76895-6

# INTRODUCTION

"Chess, like love, like music, has the power to make men happy." This was the dictum of Siegbert Tarrasch, one of the greatest chessmasters of all time, after fifty years of chessplaying.

Chess is an easy game to learn. It is also an easy game to master up to the point where it can yield enjoyment. Often when I come to a dead end in a chapter or an article, I simply drop my work and spend an hour or two with my chess books. Sometimes I play over a fine game, or glance at diagrams of interesting positions. I forget about the difficulties of my work; the mental fog lifts; and when I come back refreshed and invigorated, I find invariably that the stumbling block is gone, and that I can proceed with confidence and enthusiasm.

It would be stretching the truth to say that I worked out this process with my own unaided good sense. I learned about it from the late Ernst R. Behrend, who was president of the Hammermill Paper Company and, like all first-rate executives, knew how to make the most of his time. Whenever he came to New York on a business trip he would call me up for a chess session. During the time we were playing, all appointments and telephone calls were shunted aside as Mr. Behrend luxuriated in the relaxation that chess afforded him. His one regret about chess, he often told me, was that he hadn't learned it earlier in life. The delightful paradox of these meetings was that although he was the pupil and I was the teacher, I learned even more than he did.

I can honestly say that I have learned a great deal from chess: how to be patient, how to bide my time, how to see the other man's point of view, how to persevere in unpromising situations, how to learn from my failures.

Another great chessmaster, Tartakover, remarked once that "the winner of a game of chess is the man who makes the next-to-the-last mistake." What he meant was that chess is a contest in which there are often blemishes and imperfections on both sides. The search for perfection is a will-o'-the-wisp.

Yet many aspects of chess can be learned and applied with relative ease. That has been my reason for writing this book. There are techniques and methods for handling *typical* positions which can be applied on a great many occasions. Poor Watson always gaped at Sherlock Holmes because he did not see the reasoning behind Holmes's brilliant conclusions. It is the *underlying reasoning* in chess that I am concerned with, that I have tried to supply in this book.

When you read the chapters on tactical play, for example, you will become aware of the richness and scope of attacking play in chess. You will find at the same time that you can *control* these possibilities, you can produce them or prevent them, by familiarizing yourself with *a small number of motifs* which are applicable to *a great many positions.* Thus without devoting years to the game, or without engaging in intensive study, you will find that your enjoyment will be enormously enhanced at the very same time that your playing strength is substantially increased.

As you read this book you will also develop the expert's ability to plan. With the initial feeling of helplessness gone, you will find that each position has a definite character, that there are clues to that character, and that these clues help you to plan. The beginner feels like the sailors on the first voyage of Columbus: he doesn't know where he is heading, and he doesn't know what to do about it. But the beginner takes a mighty step forward when he learns how to appraise chess positions and how to make a plan based on that appraisal.

The ordinary player, then, who wants to play chess for fun, needs to get over the first hurdle—the feeling of despair that comes from not knowing how to appraise, how to plan, how to execute. I call this the "first" hurdle, but for some people it remains a lifetime hurdle because they do not avail themselves of a little study. How to appraise, how to plan, how to execute, these are the "how to's" with which this book is concerned.

Once you feel that you are the master of the chessmen—at least to some extent—you will be a match for your cronies, for the players in your circle. Having a feeling of assurance about your game will make it possible for you to extract to the full all the pleasure that chess can give. And that pleasure is considerable.

# CONTENTS

# MAJOR OPENINGS

# 1

# THE ELEMENTS

## THE CHESSBOARD AND CHESSMEN

Chess is a game played by two opponents, "White" and "Black," on a board of 64 squares. The board has eight vertical and eight horizontal rows of squares.

Each player has sixteen pieces at the beginning of the game:

| White | | Black |
|:---:|:---:|:---:|
| ♔ | one King | ♚ |
| ♕ | one Queen | ♛ |
| ♖ ♖ | two Rooks | ♜ ♜ |
| ♗ ♗ | two Bishops | ♝ ♝ |
| ♘ ♘ | two Knights | ♞ ♞ |
| ♙ ♙ ♙ ♙ ♙ ♙ ♙ ♙ | eight Pawns | ♟ ♟ ♟ ♟ ♟ ♟ ♟ ♟ |

At the beginning of the game the pieces are set up as shown in Diagram 1.

*All* of the squares are used in chess. The alternate light and dark coloring of the squares is a useful visual aid. The pieces on each side are also distinctively colored in order to avoid confusion. The light-colored pieces are called "White"; the dark-colored pieces, "Black." The light-colored squares are "white" squares; the dark-colored squares, "black."

White always moves first. In setting up the pieces for the beginning of a game, note that **White always has a white square at his nearest right-hand corner.**

In your study of this book, you will be dependent on the numerous diagrams for a full understanding of the text. You have been shown the diagram representation of each piece. Now let us assume that you

Diagram 1          Diagram 2

are a complete beginner; you have just purchased your chess set and you wish to set up your pieces in the position of Diagram 1.

Your King is the tallest piece of all, with a crown surmounted by a cross. Place him in the middle of each horizontal back row (horizontal rows are called "ranks"). The White King goes on a black square; the Black King, facing him at the other end of the board, goes on a white square. (Check this on Diagram 2.) The vertical row between the two Kings is called a file; the file on which the Kings are placed is called the King file.

Now take the next largest piece—the Queen, also crowned, with a little knob on top. Place the Queens in the middle of each back row. The White Queen goes on a white square to the left of the White King. The Black Queen goes on a black square adjacent to the Black King. The Queens are facing each other along the Queen file. Note the rule of Queen on color: **the White Queen on a white square, the Black Queen on a black square.**

Now compare the "real" Kings and Queens with the diagram symbols for the King and Queen. You should have no trouble recognizing them from now on.

Next come the Bishops. There are four of them, two White ones, two Black ones. They are rather squat, roly-poly figures, with a slit on top that reminds one somehow of a bishop's mitre. Place one White Bishop to the right of the White King; this is White's King Bishop, and he goes on a white square. The other Bishop goes on a black square to the left of the White Queen. The Black Bishops are placed on the opposite back row, facing their White colleagues. (Check this on

Diagram 2.) Thus White's King Bishop faces Black's King Bishop along the King Bishop file. White's Queen Bishop faces Black's Queen Bishop along the Queen Bishop file.

The Knights are easy: no one could miss the horses' heads! The Knights are placed next to the Bishops. After the two White Knights and the two Black Knights have been set up, the King Knights face each other along the King Knight file; the Queen Knights face each other along the Queen Knight file.

Next come the Rooks, four castle-shaped affairs with turrets. They are placed in the corners, the White Rooks on White's back row, the Black Rooks facing them from Black's back row. White's King Rook faces Black's King Rook along the King Rook file; White's Queen Rook faces Black's Queen Rook on the Queen Rook file.

Now you are left with the eight Pawns of each color. They are set up very easily: the White Pawns are placed on White's second rank; the Black Pawns are placed on Black's second rank. (See Diagram 1.)

With all the chessmen set up, you are invited to scrutinize the diagram symbols carefully until you are satisfied that you can identify them without reference to the actual pieces on the board. *Familiarize yourself thoroughly* with these diagram symbols so that they will be just as clear to you as the actual chessmen. To read diagrams easily is the mark of a good player; it helps you to learn rapidly and thoroughly, and to get a great deal of enjoyment out of the game. A few minutes' casual drill identifying the diagram pieces during, say, the first five reading periods devoted to this book will be of incalculable value in enhancing your playing skill.

In all chess diagrams, White's side is at the bottom of the diagram; Black at the top of the diagram. (See Diagram 1.) Hence White moves *up the diagram,* toward the top of the page. Black moves *down the diagram,* toward the bottom of the page.

Practice setting up the pieces in the opening position until you can do it quite rapidly. Remember: White's nearest right-hand corner is a white square; "Queen on color"; the pieces (other than Pawns) go on the first rank; the Pawns go on the second rank.

Now let us see how the chessmen move and what they can accomplish.

## HOW THE CHESSMEN MOVE AND CAPTURE

**The King** is the most important piece of all. Why this is so will be explained later on. His powers of moving are easy to describe. The King can move one square in any direction.

Diagram 3          Diagram 4

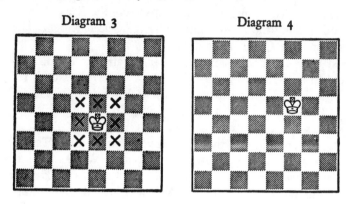

In Diagram 3, the King has eight possible moves: *horizontally,* left or right (two squares); *vertically,* up or down (two squares); *diagonally* (four squares). Diagonals, by the way, are rows of squares of the same color and extending in the same direction. The row of squares from the bottom left-hand corner to the top right-hand corner is a diagonal. The King's possible moves are indicated by crosses.

Diagram 4 illustrates a *diagonal move* made by the King from Diagram 3.

None of the chess pieces can move to a square occupied by one of their own men. Hence, in Diagram 1, neither King has a single move at his disposal!

The chessmen *capture* enemy pieces in accordance with the way the capturing piece moves. Thus, in Diagram 5, the King can capture the Bishop, but he cannot capture the Pawn. The Bishop is within the King's moving range. The Pawn is not within the King's moving range.

In Diagram 6 we see the position resulting from White's capture of the Bishop. This move is described as "King takes Bishop." In chess notation, this is written "KxB."

**The Rook,** like the King, can move *horizontally* (left and right), and *vertically* (up and down). But, unlike the King, the Rook cannot move diagonally (at an angle). The Rook can move in only one direction at

Diagram 5

Diagram 6

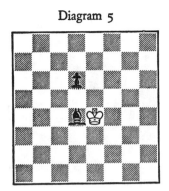

a time; and it can move any number of squares, unless it is blocked by its own or hostile men. In Diagram 7, the Rook can move to any square on the first rank, as indicated by the crosses along that rank; the Rook can also move to any square on the Queen Rook file, as indicated by the crosses on the file.

Diagram 7

Diagram 8

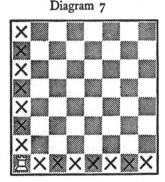

In Diagram 8, the Rook has moved to one of the 14 possible squares within its reach. The Rook moved to the first-rank square in the King file (check with Diagram 1). This square is known as K1; the move would thus be described as "Rook to King one," and written "R-K1."

The Rook cannot displace its own men, nor can it leap over any piece. Hence, in Diagram 9, if the Rook is to move vertically, it can make only one move. The White Pawn at QR3 prevents any further movement. If the Rook is to move horizontally, it can play only one square (to QN1), as the White Bishop on QB1 blocks further progress along the rank.

Diagram 9                    Diagram 10

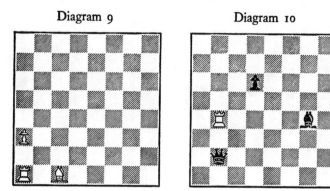

In Diagram 10, White can play RxB (horizontal move capturing the Bishop) or RxQ (vertical move capturing the Queen). But of course, the Rook cannot capture the Pawn, which is not within the range of the Rook's moving and capturing powers.

So we see that the Rook, like the King, captures the same way as it moves. In Diagram 11 we have the situation that results from RxB. In Diagram 12 we have the situation that results from RxQ.

Diagram 11                   Diagram 12

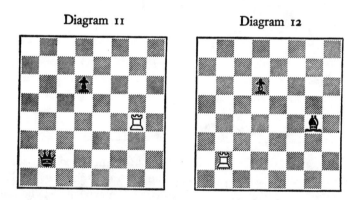

The Bishop, like the King, moves *diagonally* (on squares of the same color). The Bishop, unlike the King and the Rook, cannot move horizontally or vertically. On any given move, the Bishop has a choice of several possible directions (see Diagram 13) but he can move in only one direction at a time.

In Diagram 14, we see one of the Bishop moves that were possible in Diagram 13. (Written "B-R8.")

Diagram 13                          Diagram 14

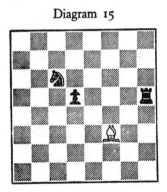                 

The Bishop's move in any direction is unlimited, except as he is impeded by the presence of a friendly or enemy chess force. He cannot leap over any pieces or displace his own pieces, but he can capture the same way he moves.

Thus, in Diagram 15, the Bishop can capture the Pawn (BxP) or the Rook (BxR). But the Bishop cannot capture the Knight, which is out of capturing range.

Diagram 15                          Diagram 16

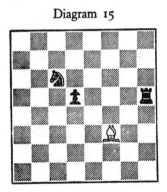                 

Assume that White plays BxR. The resulting position is shown in Diagram 16.

A Bishop always moves on squares of the same color; hence he cannot attack, threaten, or capture hostile pieces located on a square of the other color. That the Bishop commands only 32 squares might therefore be considered a serious weakness. But if you take another look at Diagram 1, you observe that each player has one Bishop on a white square, and another Bishop on a black square. Between them, the co-operating Bishops command every square on the board.

**The Queen** is by far the strongest piece on the chessboard. She moves like the King; but whereas the King can move only one square at a time, the Queen can move as far in any direction as is possible through the lack of impediments.

The power of the Queen is obvious from the fact that *she has the combined powers of the Rook and the Bishop.* In Diagram 17, for example, the Queen has no less than 27 possible moves, each indicated by a cross. (The maximum for a Rook is 14, for a Bishop 13.) The possible moves would be written as follows:

Horizontal: Q-KB5, Q-KN5,* Q-KR5, Q-Q5, Q-QB5, Q-QN5, Q-QR5.

Vertical: Q-K6, Q-K7, Q-K8, Q-K4, Q-K3, Q-K2, Q-K1.

Diagonal: Q-KB6, Q-KN7, Q-KR8, Q-Q6, Q-QB7, Q-QN8, Q-Q4, Q-QB3, Q-QN2, Q-QR1, Q-KB4, Q-KN3, Q-KR2.

Diagram 17                    Diagram 18

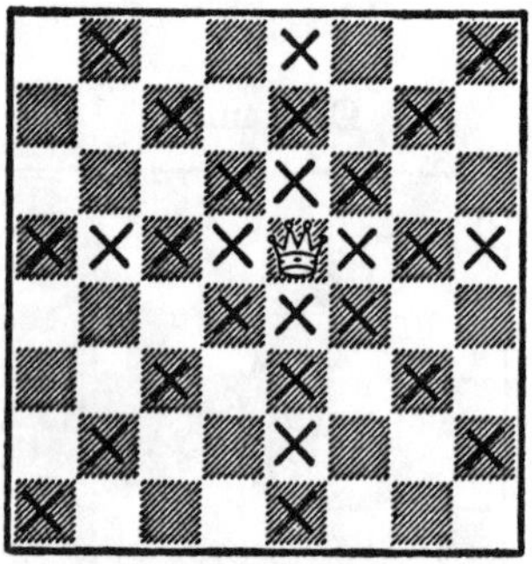

Diagram 18 shows one of the possible moves: Q-QR1.

The Queen, like all the other pieces, captures in the same way that she moves; and like all the other pieces, she captures by displacing the captured piece from its square. Like the King, Rook and Bishop, the Queen cannot leap over pieces and cannot displace any of her own pieces. On any given move, the Queen must not be moved in more than one direction.

* Note that the abbreviation for Knight is "N." Thus, "King Knight five" is written "KN5."

In Diagram 19, the Queen can capture the Rook or the Bishop or either Knight. One of the four possible captures is shown in Diagram 20.

Diagram 19                          Diagram 20

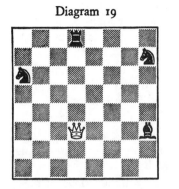

The **Knight** is the most picturesque piece of all.

His move is always of the same length. The method of moving the Knight is shown in Diagram 21; one of the possible moves is given in Diagram 22.

The Knight's move has been described as "L"-shaped. The long line of the "L" represents two squares; the short line of the "L" represents one square. Here is a good formula for describing the Knight's move: the Knight moves *one square vertically*, then *two squares horizontally*. Or, take it the other way around, the Knight moves *one square horizontally*, then *two squares vertically*.

Diagram 21                          Diagram 22

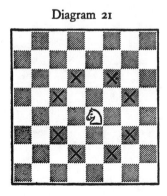
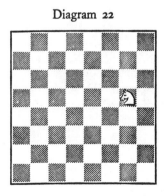

Let us apply the explanation of the Knight's move to the diagrams.

In Diagram 21, the Knight starts out at K4. If he moves up one square and two squares to the right, he lands at KN5. That is the situation we observe in Diagram 22. But the Knight could also have moved one square to the right, and then two squares up, landing at KB6. (Locate the cross for this on Diagram 21.) Or the Knight could have moved one square to the left, and two squares down, ending up at Q2. (Can you locate this square on Diagram 21?)

The Knight's move does require practice, and by making consecutive moves with a Knight on the empty board, you will soon acquire facility in moving this piece. See, for example, if you can make the following moves in chain sequence: starting from QR1 (the nearest left-hand corner at White's side), make the following moves—N-QB2, N-Q4, N-KB5, N-KR6, N-KB7, N-KR8. Thus we find that the Knight has ended up at the opposite corner of the board.

Here is an interesting property of the Knight's move: if the Knight is on a white square, his move will bring him to a black square. If he is on a black square, his move will bring him to a white square. This holds all the time; the color of the Knight's square changes with each move. (Thus, in Diagram 21, the Knight is on K4, a white square. All of his eight possible moves are to black squares.)

Another remarkable quality of the Knight: *he can leap over any forces,* his own or the enemy's. This is illustrated in Diagrams 23 and 24.

Diagram 23           Diagram 24

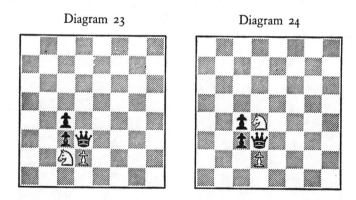

The Knight captures as he moves. Consequently, he can capture only on the end-square of his moves. (His leaping over an enemy piece does not figure as a capture.)

Note, therefore, in Diagrams 25 and 26, that the Knight can capture either Pawn, but cannot capture the Rook over which he leaps.

Diagram 25                          Diagram 26

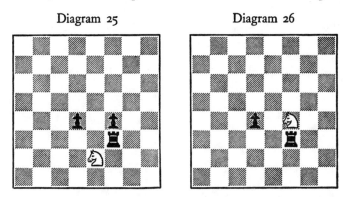

The Pawn can move *forward* only. In this respect it differs from all the other chess forces. How does this property of the Pawn apply in diagrams? Turn to Diagram 1. White Pawns *always* move up the page. Black Pawns *always* move down the page. This merely portrays the fact that over the board, the White Pawns move toward Black's side; Black's Pawns move toward White's side. "No retreat" is evidently the password for the Pawns!

A Pawn can move only one square at a time. Thus, in Diagram 27, White has a Pawn on King five (K5). To move, it advances one square (to K6). The resulting position is seen in Diagram 28. (That move is written "P-K6.")

Diagram 27                          Diagram 28

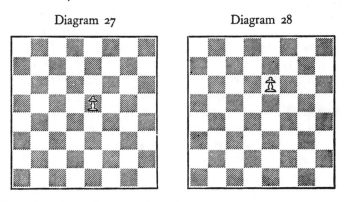

The White Pawn has moved up the page.

Now, look at Diagram 29, in which a Black Pawn is stationed at QR4 (in the case of Black forces, we calculate their location from the Black side). The Black Pawn advances (down the page, of course) to QR5, leading to the position pictured in Diagram 30. (That move is written "... P-QR5.")

Diagram 29                    Diagram 30

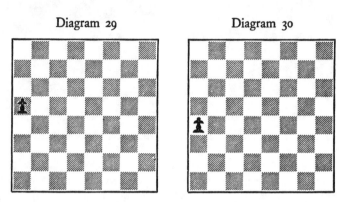

There is one important exception to the rule that the Pawn advances one square at each move. Turning back to Diagram 1, you will note that originally all of White's Pawns are on White's second rank, and that all of Black's Pawns are on Black's second rank. As long as any Pawn has remained unmoved, it has the option—*the first time that Pawn moves*—to advance one square or two.

This applies to any stage of the game—not merely the first move of the game. Once a Pawn has moved, it must abide by the one-square-at-a-time rule. In Diagrams 27 and 29, the Pawns in each case were already beyond the second rank—they had already moved, in other words—and they therefore had no option to advance one or two squares.

Let us see how this works. In Diagram 31 we have a position from the Scotch Game (p. 168). White wants to move his Queen Pawn (the Pawn on the same file with the Queen). This Pawn is still on the second rank; it is still unmoved. White therefore has the option of advancing it one square (P-Q3) or two squares (P-Q4). He decides to play it up two squares, and Diagram 32 shows the resulting position.

The Pawn is also unlike the other pieces in this respect: it moves in one way, *captures in another!* In capturing, it moves ahead, to be sure; but instead of capturing straight ahead, it captures one square to the left or right! In other words, *it captures ahead diagonally.*

Diagram 31                    Diagram 32

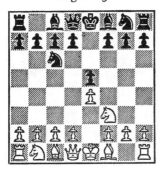          

Thus, in Diagram 33, if it is White's move, he can capture either Black Pawn. The resulting position is shown in Diagram 34. But White cannot capture the Knight, which is directly in front of the White Pawn.

Diagram 33                    Diagram 34

In capturing, the White Pawns move diagonally, but still up the page. The reverse is true of captures by Black Pawns. Thus, in Diagram 35, either Black Pawn can capture the White Pawn, moving down the page. Diagram 36 shows the situation after one of the Black Pawns has captured. Naturally, neither Pawn could have captured the Bishop or Rook.

There is more to learn about Pawns, but for the moment we shall conclude our discussion by observing that the Pawn does not leap over pieces, does not displace any of its own pieces, and cannot advance if a piece (its own or the enemy's) stands directly in front of it. This is the case in Diagram 31, where White's King Pawn and Black's King Pawn block each other's progress, each being unable to capture the other. On

Diagram 35                    Diagram 36

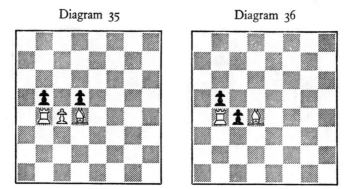

the other hand, in Diagram 32, Black can, if he wishes, capture White's Queen Pawn with his King Pawn ( ... PxP).

## HOW TO WIN

Now that you have learned the moving and capturing powers of the chessmen, you are ready to learn the rules for winning.

**Check.** You were told earlier that the King is the most important piece in chess. Whenever a hostile piece attacks the King, *that attack must be removed at once.* Such an attack is called a *check.* When the King is attacked, he is said to be *in check.* When the King is in check and cannot get out of check, he is said to be *checkmated;* the game is lost.

**Replies to Check.** It is therefore of paramount importance to get the King out of check whenever he is attacked. How is this to be done? There are three possible methods, and all of them are available in Diagram 37.

Here Black's King is being checked by the White Rook along the file. The most obvious reply is to move the attacked King out of the line of attack. In this case, if Black plays ... K-N2 (counting from Black's side), we get the position of Diagram 38. Now Black's King is out of check.

But another way to get out of check is to interpose one of your pieces between the attacking force and your attacked King. Thus, in Diagram 37, Black can play ... R-R3 (still counting from Black's side). This is the method of interposition. The result is shown in Diagram 39. Again Black's King is out of check.

Diagram 37                          Diagram 38

There is still one more way to get out of check: to capture the attacking piece. Returning to Diagram 37, we observe that Black can put the attacking Rook out of commission with ... NxR. The result is shown in Diagram 40.

Diagram 39                          Diagram 40

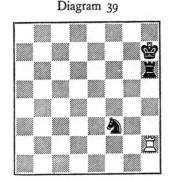

Since the King must be immediately removed from check, it follows that *you can never expose your King to check.* You can never move your King to a square which is controlled by enemy forces—a square which is within the capturing range of any enemy piece. A corollary of this is that *neither King can move to a square adjacent to the other King.*

Before learning more about these two propositions, we need to study some special kinds of checks.

**Discovered Check.** The word "discover" is used here in the sense of "uncover." A piece which is not attacking the King can suddenly draw a bead on him without moving! The attack crops up when another piece which has blocked the line of attack, moves out of the way. Take Diagram 41 as an instance. Black's King is not under attack. Yet White, by moving his Bishop, "discovers" a check by his Rook. After the Bishop makes one of his possible moves, we get Diagram 42, in which Black's King is in check.

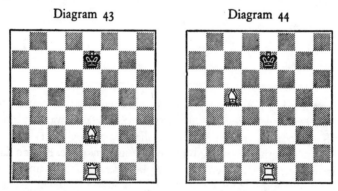

Diagram 41                     Diagram 42

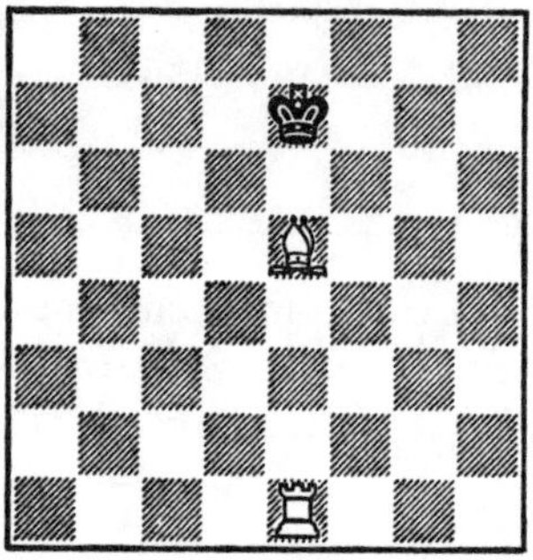

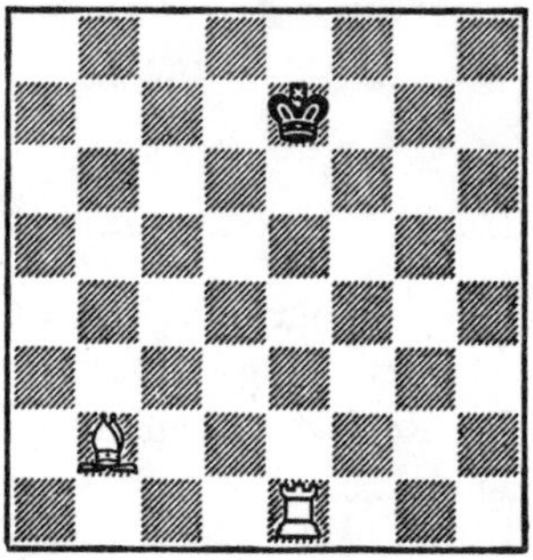

A **Double Check** is a variety of discovered check. The piece which moves out of the way to uncover check also attacks the King on its own; thus the King is doubly attacked. In Diagram 43, the Bishop will move, creating a discovered check; but, as you see in Diagram 44, the Bishop *also* gives check.

Diagram 43                     Diagram 44

The thing to remember about a double check is that interposition will not do by way of reply; the only way to get out of a double check is to move the attacked King.

**Forking Checks.** This term reminds us of something caught on several prongs of a fork; and it is painful indeed to be caught in a forking check. This is a *double attack* in which one of the objects of attack is the King. As the King must get out of check, the other piece under attack—often of great value—is lost. A very painful experience! The term "fork" is usually applied to the Knight, but the Queen, Rook, Bishop and Pawn also have this power. In Diagram 45 we have a typical Knight fork; in Diagram 46 it is a Rook which forks the King and another piece.

Diagram 45                            Diagram 46

The power of the fork illustrates something else which you must always keep in mind: *the priority of check*. The King must be extricated from check, whatever the cost.

Checkmate—or, as it is often called, simply mate—is the end of the game. The player whose King is checkmated is the loser. The player who engineers the checkmate is of course the winner.

Checkmate is the term used for a position in which a King is in check—under attack—and cannot escape from check, no matter what measures are undertaken.

The King is not actually captured; as long as he cannot escape, the game is over. ("Checkmate" is derived from a Persian word meaning "the king is dead.")

In Diagram 47 we have an example of a basic checkmate. Black's King is in check—attacked by the Queen. Black's King cannot capture the Queen, for that would put the Black King within capturing range of White's King. (We know that a King cannot voluntarily expose himself to attack.) Finally, Black's King can move only to squares which are within the capturing range of White's King and Queen. Thus, the Black King is in check; he cannot interpose; he cannot move out of attack; he cannot capture the attacking piece. This is checkmate.

Diagram 47

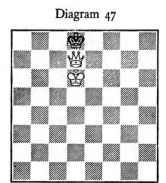

Diagram 48

In Diagram 48 we see another checkmate. The Black King is attacked by the Rook. He cannot capture the Rook; he cannot interpose a piece to ward off the attack; he cannot move along the rank, as these squares are within the Rook's capturing range. He cannot move to squares on the second rank, as these squares are within the White King's capturing range. Again we have a case of checkmate.

It would be a mistake to think that checkmate arises only after a great many moves have been played, and at a highly simplified stage. Checkmate may occur as early as the second move! This is of course an extraordinary situation, but checkmates within the first 20 moves are by no means rare. Their potential occurrence highlights the need for being solicitous at all times for the King's welfare.

In Diagrams 49 and 50 we have examples of checkmates arising while quite a few pieces are still on the board. In Diagram 49, Black's Knight is giving check. There is of course no interposition to a Knight check;

Diagram 49

Diagram 50

nor can the Knight, in this instance, be captured. However, a King move is not feasible, as both K-N2 and K-R1 are impossible because the Black Bishop covers those squares. *White is checkmated.*

In Diagram 50, it is the Black King who is being checkmated. He is attacked by the White Queen. The Queen cannot be captured, as she is protected by the Bishop at KN2. (As the King cannot expose himself to check, he cannot capture a piece which is guarded by one of its own men.) Black has no possibility of interposition, as his King is being checked on an adjacent square. Finally, the Black King cannot move to Q2, QB2, QN1 as all these squares are within the capturing range of White's Queen; nor can the Black King play to Q1, as this square is within the capturing range of White's far-advanced Pawn at K7. Again, *this is checkmate.*

## OTHER RULES

Now that we have learned the fundamental rules of chess, we can turn our attention to three refinements which have added a great deal to the colorful nature of the game. One of these rules concerns the King; the other two apply to the Pawn.

**Castling.** You have seen that the King is exposed to danger at all times, even the very earliest stages of the game. Chess has a great many interesting facets, a large number of them connected with direct attacks on the King. But since this piece is all-important, some measure had to be devised to make the King's existence less precarious. That is how *castling* came to be invented.

The most remarkable thing about castling is that it is the only move in chess in which *two pieces are allowed to execute a single move!* The two pieces involved are the King and one of his Rooks. In *King-side castling*—executed with the King Rook—the King is moved over to the King Knight file; in *Queen-side castling*—executed with the Queen Rook—the King is moved over to the Queen Bishop file. In either case the main object is achieved—that of removing the King from the cross fire of the enemy pieces in the center. The same reasoning applies to the Rook, but in reverse: castling takes the Rook out of the corner, where it is relatively inactive, and brings it near the center, where it can play a much more useful role.

Diagram 51 shows the position of King and Rook prior to castling. In King-side castling, White moves his King two squares to the *right* (next to the King Rook); then he places the King Rook immediately to the left of the King. In Queen-side castling, White moves his King two squares to the *left* (one square away from the Queen Rook) and then places the Queen Rook immediately to the right of the King.

Diagram 51                    Diagram 52

In Diagram 52 we see the positions which result from castling. (Black moves King and Rook in analogous fashion.)

Note that in King-side castling, the Rook moves *two* squares; in Queen-side castling, the Rook moves *three* squares. In terms of chess notation, the King plays to KN1 and the King Rook to KB1 in King-side castling. When castling on the Queen-side, the King goes to QB1 and the Queen Rook to Q1. (Check this on Diagram 52.)

Without going into considerable detail about the rather refined reasons, it should be stated that King-side castling is common in ninety-nine games out of a hundred. The inexperienced player does well to castle early as a matter of course—say before the tenth move—on the King-side.

Diagram 53                    Diagram 54

A player may castle only once during the course of a game. There are a number of cases where castling is *impossible for the time being.*

One of these applies to positions where the King is in check. This is illustrated in the position of Diagram 53, as White's King is in check. (If White avoids moving his King at this point, he can castle later on.)

In Diagram 54 White cannot castle because castling would place the King on a square (KN1) commanded by Black's King Bishop. You cannot castle into attack: this is an application again of the prohibition against voluntarily exposing one's King to attack.

However, if at some later point Black's Bishop moves away, or is driven from the diagonal, or the diagonal becomes blocked, White will then be able to castle.

Castling is also impossible if the King has to move over a square commanded by an enemy force. This is shown in Diagram 55, where White's Bishop at R3 controls KB8. However, if at some later stage the enemy no longer controls this square, then castling will become feasible.

| Diagram 55 | Diagram 56 |
|:---:|:---:|
|  |  |

Castling is temporarily impossible when any of the squares between the King and the castling Rook are occupied. Thus, in Diagram 56, Black can castle King-side because the squares between the King and King Rook are empty. But Queen-side castling is impossible—at least for the time being—because the squares between the King and the Queen Rook are not all empty.

But there are also instances when castling becomes permanently impossible. The most frequent case occurs when the King has already moved. Thus, in Diagram 57, White has played K-B1 and castling is no longer permitted.

Diagram 57                     Diagram 58

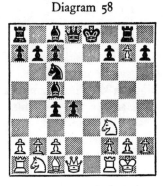

Castling becomes permanently impossible when a Rook has already moved from its original square. In Diagram 58, Black is temporarily prevented from castling King-side by the fact that a hostile Pawn at KN7 commands the square that the Black needs to cross. But in addition to this, castling is permanently impossible on the King-side because Black's King Rook has moved from its original square. But Queen-side castling is theoretically feasible here—once the intervening pieces have been removed.

One final point about castling: although the King cannot cross a square commanded by a hostile piece, the Rook does not have this disability, and can freely cross such squares during the castling process.

**Pawn Promotion.** The most important fact about the Pawn has yet to be stated: a Pawn, on reaching the eighth rank, *can be promoted to a Queen, Rook, Knight or Bishop.* Promotion is actually compulsory, though of course it is highly advantageous, and enormously increases the value of the Pawn.

Contrary to a widespread—and erroneous!—belief, there is no rule against having two or more Queens at the same time. The new piece generally chosen is in fact a Queen, as it is the strongest of the pieces. Queening a Pawn, as promotion is termed, is one of the most important events in a game—often the decisive one. This is explained later on (p. 41). At this point, we are interested only in the mechanics of queening. Thus, in Diagram 59, White's Pawn is on the seventh rank and is ready to queen.

White advances the Pawn to the eighth rank (Black's first rank). He picks up a White Queen, removes the Pawn, and replaces it with the Queen. The Pawn has been promoted to a Queen!

Diagram 59          Diagram 60

In Diagram 60 we see the new situation in which the White Pawn has been replaced by a Queen.

Just to clarify matters, Black's queening procedure is the same. But Black, of course, queens his Pawns on his eighth rank, which is White's first rank. The process is pictured in Diagrams 61 and 62.

Diagram 61          Diagram 62

In Diagram 61, Black's Pawn is about to advance and be promoted. In Diagram 62, Black has acquired his new Queen.

**Pawn Captures en Passant.** The Pawn captures forward one square to the left or right, as described on page 12. There is one exception to this rule. This exception is known as capturing *en passant* (in passing).

Note the following features of capturing in passing.

Only a Pawn can capture another Pawn in passing.

Capturing in passing is an option which must be exercised *at the first and only opportunity*. If the opportunity is not exploited, the option lapses.

Diagram 63 shows the typical introductory position. The Pawn which is to make the capture must be on its *fifth rank;* the White Pawn is placed on KN5. The Pawn which is to be captured must be on its original (second) rank on an adjacent file; the Black Pawn is at KB2. So far, so good.

The Black Pawn advances two squares. This is permissible, as we know, for a Pawn's initial move. This produces the position of Diagram 64.

Diagram 63                    Diagram 64

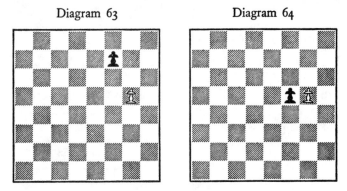

In the position of Diagram 64, White has the option—on his next move, and only on his next move—of capturing the Pawn *as if it had moved only one square.* White takes up his option and captures the Black Pawn (PxP e.p.) producing the position of Diagram 65.

Diagram 65                    Diagram 66

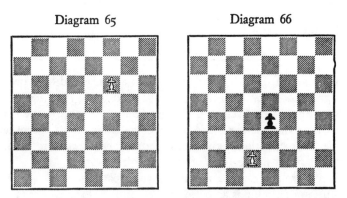

In Diagram 66, it is Black who has a Pawn on the fifth rank, which will be able to capture *en passant* in the event that the White Pawn on the adjacent file, now on its original square, should advance two squares to its fourth rank.

In Diagram 63, by the way, if we started out with the Black Pawn on the third rank and advanced it one square to the fourth rank, there would be no possibility of *en passant* capture.

There is one type of position in which capturing *en passant* is prohibited, namely when such capture would expose your King to check. This is logical enough, being merely another instance of the rule against voluntarily exposing your King to check.

Examples of capturing *en passant* will be found on pages 181 and 238.

## CHESS NOTATION

Only by learning how to record moves and how to read chess notation can we get the maximum amount of instruction in chess and obtain the maximum amount of pleasure from the game. A person who is unfamiliar with chess notation puts himself pretty much in the position of an unfortunate illiterate who cannot write a letter, keep records, read a book or newspaper, or decipher a dollar bill!

Chess notation presents some initial difficulties, and there is no gloss-

| QR8 | QKt8 | QB8 | Q8 | K8 | KB8 | KKt8 | KR8 |
| QR7 | QKt7 | QB7 | Q7 | K7 | KB7 | KKt7 | KR7 |
| QR6 | QKt6 | QB6 | Q6 | K6 | KB6 | KKt6 | KR6 |
| QR5 | QKt5 | QB5 | Q5 | K5 | KB5 | KKt5 | KR5 |
| QR4 | QKt4 | QB4 | Q4 | K4 | KB4 | KKt4 | KR4 |
| QR3 | QKt3 | QB3 | Q3 | K3 | KB3 | KKt3 | KR3 |
| QR2 | QKt2 | QB2 | Q2 | K2 | KB2 | KKt2 | KR2 |
| QR1 | QKt1 | QB1 | Q1 | K1 | KB1 | KKt1 | KR1 |

ing over the fact that these difficulties require application on the reader's part. But this application is a worthwhile investment for the acquisition of a skill which will afford a lifetime of pleasurable activity.

**Naming the Squares.** The following chart shows the names of all the squares. The chart can be mastered far more easily than its somewhat forbidding appearance might indicate.

Every square has two names, one being calculated from White's side of the board, the other name from Black's side of the board. Each square is named after the rank and file on which it is located. The ranks, you will recall, are horizontal rows numbered from 1 to 8. White's first rank is Black's eighth rank; White's second rank is Black's seventh rank, etc.

The files, unlike the ranks, have names which White and Black share in common. The files, as we know, derive their names from the pieces which are placed on them at the beginning of the game. For the sake of convenience, we repeat the diagram of the opening position:

Diagram 68

Both Queens are on the Queen file; the Pawns on that file are the White Queen Pawn and the Black Queen Pawn. Each Pawn is similarly named for the piece stationed in back of it in the opening position. (When a Pawn captures and thereby changes its file, it acquires the name of the new file on which it is located.) Reading from left to right in Diagram 68, we have the Queen Rook file, the Queen Knight file, the Queen Bishop file, the Queen file, the King file, the King Bishop file, the King Knight file, and the King Rook file. (The picture as seen from Black's point of view is of course the same, except that his reading would be from right to left. Try it!)

**Abbreviations.** It would be a cumbersome thing to have to write out every little detail. The square on which the King stands is King One; but it is so much more convenient to abbreviate to K1. Then the square on which the King Knight is placed at the beginning of the game— King Knight One. How much easier it is to write KN1!

And these abbreviations are easy enough to follow. (Check them on Diagram 67.) After all, KN1 is merely the square on the first rank and on the King Knight file. Consider the King Pawn—now on K2. Play it up two squares—to K4. The move is written: P-K4. If the Pawn advances again: P-K5. If the Pawn captures a Rook: PxR. What could be easier?

**Other Notation Details.** When we record the score of a game, we usually list the moves in two columns. The first column contains White's moves, because White always moves first. The second column contains Black's moves. Here's a sample:

| White | Black |
|---|---|
| 1 P-KB3? | P-K4 |
| 2 P-KN4??? | Q-R5 mate |

Mate? So it is! White must have played abominably to get mated in two moves. So he did. (This is the famous "Fool's Mate.") Hence the question marks, which indicate a bad move. Good moves are indicated by an exclamation mark.

We already know that PxP means "Pawn takes Pawn." So x is the symbol indicating "takes" or "captures."

Moves that give check are followed by "ch." Example: B-N5ch means "Bishop plays to Knight Five giving check." "Discovered check" is represented by "dis ch," and "double check" by "dbl ch." Capturing *en passant,* or in passing, is indicated by "e.p." Castling on the King-side is written "Castles KR"; castling Queen-side is "Castles QR." Moves are sometimes run on instead of being arranged in columnar fashion; for an instance of this, see page 60. In that case, White's moves are followed by a comma, Black's moves by a semicolon, thus: 1 P-K4, P-K4; etc. When Black's moves are given independently, they are always preceded by three periods, thus: 1 ... P-K4.

## DRAWN GAMES

There are a number of reasons why games occasionally end without victory for either side. Such tie games are called "draws." One cause of an indecisive result is the ultimate lack of adequate checkmating force. The types of insufficient mating force are listed on page 42.

Games may also be abandoned as drawn by agreement of the players. This applies unconditionally to friendly contests; in the case of tournament chess, there are usually strict rules forbidding an agreed draw before the thirtieth move.

The so-called "50-move rule" specifies that either player may claim a draw if no capture has been made, and no Pawn has moved, in the past 50 moves. Such claims are of rare occurrence, the chief purpose of the rule being to penalize bunglers or those who insist on playing on in positions which can only be won by a gross blunder on the part of their adversary.

As a practical proposition, this rule cannot be invoked unless the players have kept an accurate score of the game as it was being played. This proviso applies with even greater force to drawn games which end by threefold repetition. Here the rule states that where a position has already turned up twice in a game, with the same player on the move in each case, he may claim a draw *before* making the move which will produce the position a third time. This rule causes a lot of difficulty, because in the heat of the battle it is not always easy to keep track of the fine points that are involved.

**Perpetual Check.** This term is used to describe positions in which a player can compel his opponent to submit to an endless series of checks.

Diagram 69          Diagram 70

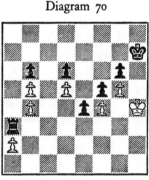

In Diagram 69, we see such a position: Black, though a Rook down, can escape disaster by means of a perpetual check. He plays 1 ... Q-R6ch. White must reply 2 B-R2. Then comes 2 ... Q-B8ch, when 3 B-N1 is forced. Now 3 ... Q-R6ch and after 4 B-R2, Black repeats with 4 ... Q-B8ch. This is obviously a drawn position.

**Stalemate.** We know that the King cannot expose himself to check. We know also that if the King is in check and has only moves that would still leave him in check, he is *checkmated*.

But if he is *not in check,* and has only moves that would put him in check, then he is stalemated, and the game is drawn! Such positions arise almost invariably toward the end of the game, where only a few pieces are left on the board. It is in fact the *scarcity of pieces* that leads to a *scarcity of moves* for the defender. Take Diagram 70 as a case in point, *with White to move.* White is a Rook down, and yet the game is drawn! Why?! Because none of White's Pawns can move, and the same is true of his King. The King cannot play to KR5 or KN4, as these squares are commanded by Black Pawns. But neither can the King play to KR3 or KN3, these squares being commanded by the Black Rook.

This is a perfect example of stalemate: *White's King is not in check, yet he is left only with moves that would put his King in check.* Result: draw!

# 2

# SIMPLE WINNING METHODS

You have now read all you *have* to read to be able to play chess. But the ground covered so far includes only the bare rudiments; the most interesting aspects of chess have yet to be touched on. And it is indicative of the fascinating character of this wonderful game that learning goes hand in hand with enjoyment.

## FUNDAMENTAL CHECKMATES

These basic procedures are worth knowing because from them we learn how to *force* a winning conclusion, given certain material advantages gained during the early part of the game. At the same time, the elementary checkmates offer the best kind of practice for acquiring skill in the handling of the chess pieces. Trying to work out these checkmates by yourself or with a friend is an ideal way to discover and exploit the potentialities of these pieces.

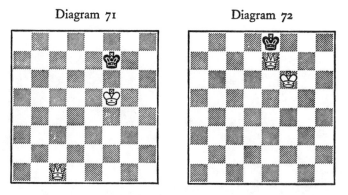

Diagram 71    Diagram 72

**Checkmate with the Queen.** The checkmate with the Queen is the easiest because of its enormous power. Remember that it has the com-

bined moves of the Bishop and Rook, which gives it fantastic mobility
and range. In Diagram 71, play proceeds as follows:

| 1 Q-B7ch | K-B1 |
| 2 K-B6 | K-K1 |
| 3 Q-K7 mate | |

Diagram 72 shows the mating position. Black's King is in check and
cannot move to a square which is not controlled by an enemy piece.

Note, by the way, that after Black's second move White can also play
3 Q-B8 mate. Here, too, Black's King is in check and has no legal move
available.

**Checkmate with the Rook.** The Rook is the next strongest piece
after the Queen, so that Rook checkmates are also fairly easy. As in the
case of the Queen checkmate, the procedure called for is to drive the
hostile King to the edge of the board. Only when the Kings face each
other on rank or file, with the weaker King at the side of the board, can
checkmate be forced.

The example of the Rook checkmate given in Diagram 73 is quite
simple. The play is:

| 1 R-K5 | K-N1 |
| 2 R-QR5 | K-B1 |
| 3 R-R8 mate | |

Diagram 73

Diagram 74

You will note, in Diagram 74, that all the requirements for the Rook
checkmate are present: the weaker King is on the last rank; the King
of the stronger side faces him on the file; the Rook mates along the
rank. After 1 R-K5, by the way, Black can also play 1 ... K-Q1. Then,

after a suitable move of the Rook on the King file, such as 2 R-K1, there follows 2 ... K-B1; 3 R-K8 mate.

When you practice these checkmates, you will get the most out of such practice by giving the weaker side plenty of scope. You might start with a position like this one: White King at KR1, White Rook at QR1, Black King at K5. The procedure then is to begin with a Rook move which cuts off the weaker King from a large segment of the board (1 R-R5, for example), continuing with the approach of the stronger side's King to the scene of action.

**Checkmate with the Bishops.** As one Bishop commands only squares of the same color, you need *two* Bishops to force checkmate. Not only must you get the weaker side's King to the last rank; you must get him into a corner. So you see that checkmate with the two Bishops is not child's play; it requires really harmonious co-operation on the part of the two Bishops and their King.

In Diagram 75, the lone King has been forced back to the edge of the board, and the problem is to drive him to the nearest corner. This is nicely accomplished in the following manner:

| | |
|---|---|
| 1 B-Q6 | K-R3 |
| 2 B-N4! | K-R2 |
| 3 K-B7 | K-R3 |
| 4 B-Q3ch | K-R2 |
| 5 B-B5ch | K-R1 |
| 6 B-K4 mate | |

Diagram 75             Diagram 76

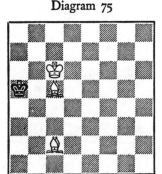 

Diagram 76 shows the finished job. The harmonious play with the Bishops, and the skill displayed in cutting off the lone King's escape, are really enchanting. You will derive endless pleasure from practicing this somewhat intricate checkmating procedure.

Diagram 77                         Diagram 78

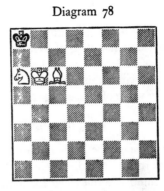

**Checkmate with the Bishop and Knight.** This type of checkmate is really difficult and calls for considerable patience and methodical maneuvering. Not only must the lone King be driven into a corner; he must be hounded into a corner which is of the same color as those of the squares on which the Bishop moves. In Diagram 77, for example, checkmate can only be forced when the lone King is forced into one of the white corners. Here is how it is done:

|   |         |         |
|---|---------|---------|
| 1 | B-Q3    | K-B3    |
| 2 | B-K2    | K-B2    |
| 3 | B-B3    | K-Q1    |

Black's King tries to edge away from the mating square, but he will be driven back.

|    |          |       |
|----|----------|-------|
| 4  | K-Q6     | K-K1  |
| 5  | B-R5ch   | K-Q1  |
| 6  | N-B5     | K-B1  |
| 7  | B-B7!    | K-Q1  |
| 8  | N-N7ch   | K-B1  |
| 9  | K-B6     | K-N1  |
| 10 | K-N6     | K-B1  |
| 11 | B-K6ch!  | K-N1  |

White has made considerable progress and is now ready for the kill.

|    |       |      |
|----|-------|------|
| 12 | N-B5  | K-R1 |

13 B-Q7!                    K-N1
14 N-R6ch                   K-R1
15 B-B6 mate

The picturesque mating position shown in Diagram 78 is a tribute to the clever handling of White's pieces which was needed to force this position.

We conclude this section on the basic checkmates by again emphasizing the value of practicing these checkmating processes repeatedly.

## ELEMENTARY MATING PATTERNS

At the start, the game of chess presents a bewildering variety of possible formations and combinations. It is true of most chessplayers that they cannot see the wood for the trees. What they need is a reduction of all these possibilities to a relatively small number of patterns that repeat themselves endlessly. The motifs illustrated here are not exhaustive. But they are practical guides to actual play; they do happen again and again; they are basic because they embody the potentialities which are inherent in the pieces. If these patterns did not exist, they would surely be invented!

The most prominent piece in these combinations is necessarily the Queen, because of her enormous power.

**The Queen and Knight.** These pieces complement each other admirably. However, as the Knight is a short-stepping piece, he must be well advanced to support the Queen in any aggressive activities. In Diagram 79, we see one of the most characteristic mating patterns of the game: mate at KR7 by the Queen, supported by a Knight at KN5.

Diagram 79                    Diagram 80

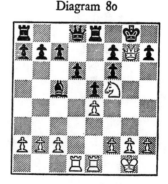

Diagram 80 shows the co-operation of Queen and Knight in a no less effective manner. This time the attack is aimed at KN7, and Black is helpless against the threat of Q-N7 mate. Note the breach in Black's castled position caused by the doubling of his King Bishop Pawn, which gives White's pieces access to the mating area. This weakness in the Pawn position will be stressed frequently later on.

**The Queen and Bishop.** These pieces can, if anything, cause even more havoc than Queen and Knight. What is insidious about the Bishop is that he can co-operate in an attack from a considerable distance. (Note, for example, the fine support given White's Queen by a Bishop in Diagrams 81 and 82.) What matters in the Bishop's case, then, is not so much *nearness* to the object of attack, as a *clear diagonal*. It is the open line that enables the Bishop to do damage. The Knight may be compared to the cut-and-thrust of hand-to-hand fighting; the Bishop is more like a long-range gun. The Bishop is good at infighting too—in fact, more versatile than the Knight.

Diagram 81                           Diagram 82

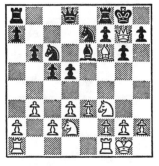        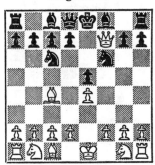

**The Queen and Rook.** The combined action of these two powerful pieces is often seen to good effect on open lines—vertically along open files, horizontally on the seventh rank. Attacks on this rank are particularly deadly, for in order to carry them out the invading forces must have penetrated into the heart of enemy territory. (The position of Diagram 83 is an impressive example.) To get on this rank, a Rook will almost invariably have to invade via an open file. This gives an immensely valuable hint for practical play: *if you have open files, place your Rooks on them!* If you don't have the files, create them! The question of open files will be treated later on, but the pattern shown in Diagram 84 indicates how to exploit open files.

Diagram 83

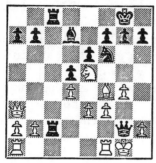

Diagram 84

**The Queen and Pawn.** To be of use in a mating attack, the Pawn, like the Knight, must be far advanced. Particularly suggestive in this respect is the Pawn wedge at KB6 in Diagram 85. This is a motif that is repeated endlessly, and familiarity with it will form the basis of many a threat and many an attack. Diagram 86 makes the same point.

Diagram 85

Diagram 86

**The Rook and Bishop.** A Rook on the open King Rook file, acting in combination with a Bishop on the long diagonal (from corner to corner), can often carry out a devastating raking attack against the hostile King. This is illustrated in Diagram 87. (The combination which led to this position is shown under Diagram 140.)

**The Rook and Knight.** The Rook on the seventh rank is particularly powerful when no hostile Pawns intervene to mitigate its pressure against the hostile King. When the rank is commanded in this way, the Rook is said to control "the absolute seventh." When supported by a Knight, as in Diagram 88, the Rook can actually conjure up mating

Diagram 87     Diagram 88

possibilities. The mating pattern which involves the cornering of the King by these two pieces is seen fairly frequently.

**Back-rank Mate with the Rook.** One of the most feared powers of the Rook is its ability to give mate on the last rank when the opposing King is imprisoned by his own Pawns. This characteristic stratagem is illustrated in Diagram 89. Some of the most amazing "sacrifices" of material have been made with a view to winding up with a back-rank mate.

Diagram 89     Diagram 90

**Mating Attack with Two Rooks.** Two Rooks operating on the seventh rank can create havoc in the enemy's ranks. But there are also times when, with one Rook controlling "the seventh rank absolute," a mating attack becomes possible on the last rank. Diagram 90 is an example of such a position.

## RELATIVE VALUE OF THE PIECES

Now that you are ready for the finer points of attack and defense, strategy and tactics, captures, threats, exchanges and other fascinating details, it is absolutely essential to have a clear idea of the value of the pieces.

You have been told that a game of chess is won by checkmate, and you have been shown how checkmate can be achieved by the Queen or Rook or two Bishops or Bishop and Knight. But you must bear in mind that the loser does not have to wait to be checkmated. Faced with overwhelming material superiority, he can concede defeat and "resign." That brings us to the obvious question: "What is material superiority?"

It is at this point that we see the relationship between material advantage and checkmate. We know that a Queen can force checkmate. If a player is a Queen ahead, what point is there in his opponent's continuing to play on? Most likely he will resign. The same reasoning applies in large measure to the Rook, which can also force checkmate.

Even if the weaker side insists on continuing to play, a large material advantage will yield dividends where checkmate cannot be immediately enforced. For the weight of extra material means a weight of excess force: the stronger side can apply more force to a given threat or a given target than the defender can muster. In chess we truly see that "to him that hath shall be given more." *Material advantage breeds greater material advantage.*

And material advantage has still one more power—not always realized or exploited by weaker players. Say you are a Queen ahead, and your opponent refuses to resign. Then your simplest course is to threaten exchanges of material which will eventually swap down to King and Queen against King. Since this simple ending is absolutely without hope for the weaker side, the player with a material minus will often permit more material loss in order to avoid exchanges.

So, for all these reasons, we must know the relative value of the pieces.

**Table of Relative Values.** For a great many years the following values have been accepted as conventional:

| | |
|---|---|
| Queen | 9 points |
| Rook | 5 points |
| Bishop | 3 points |
| Knight | 3 points |
| Pawn | 1 point |

Most of these values are fairly obvious. We know that the Queen is by far the strongest piece, so it is not surprising to see her at the head of the list. We know now, even though we had an inkling before, that it would be absurd to exchange the Queen for an enemy Bishop, say, unless ... checkmate could be forced directly, or we could win our opponent's Queen in some advantageous manner.

But, barring unusual and remarkable situations, the above table will be useful in ninety-nine out of a hundred situations. Here are some of the conclusions we derive from the table:

Two Rooks (10 points) are worth somewhat more than the Queen (9 points), especially in the endgame, when the Rooks have had time to get into the thick of the battle. At the beginning of the game, the Queen may be worth just as much as, or more than, the Rooks. This is explained by the fact that the Queen can become active fairly early in the game, whereas the Rooks are bottled up in the corners for some time.

A Rook (5 points) is definitely more valuable than a "minor piece" (Bishop or Knight, worth 3 points). Winning a Rook in return for a minor piece is "winning the Exchange." According to our scale of values, a Rook has roughly the same value as a minor piece plus two Pawns. We have to watch out for special circumstances, which may alter our calculations. Thus, if the Rook is very effectively posted (for example, on the seventh rank), it might be worth more than a minor piece and two Pawns. On the other hand, if the Pawns are very near to their queening squares and have no hostile Pawns on adjacent files to capture them in their progress, then the Rook is clearly at a disadvantage. Such Pawns, by the way, that are no longer subject to capture by hostile Pawns, are known as "passed Pawns."

The Queen (9 points) is definitely superior to Rook plus a minor piece (8 points); even when they are aided by a Pawn, they may be no match for the Queen, unless the Pawn is passed.

Bishop and Knight are approximately of equal value. Among good players there is a definite preference for the Bishop, but considerable knowledge and experience are required to make this rather subtle distinction. The inexperienced player is better off to assess these pieces as of roughly equal strength. You are on safe ground, however, in assuming that two Bishops are more effective than a Bishop and Knight. The difference in mobility here can be appreciated even by players who are not too experienced.

A minor piece is roughly equivalent to three Pawns, but here again the nature of the position is important. In the opening stage, when the Pawns are still on or near their original squares, the piece is likely to be of more value, especially if it is playing an active role. The more simplified the position gets, however, especially if the Pawns are good queening material, the more important the Pawns become.

A final point about what constitutes material superiority. The advantage of an extra Pawn does not mean too much in the opening stage, where there is a delightful variety of complicated possibilities. As the game reaches the ending, however, the extra Pawn takes on major importance because of its queening potentialities.

## CAPTURES AND EXCHANGES

Knowing the relative values of the pieces, it is now possible to study threats, captures and exchanges.

**Value for Value.** The great principle about exchanges is that you ought to win material where you can; avoid loss of material in any event; exchange value for value.

In Diagram 91 (from the Scotch Game, p. 168), Black plays:

| | |
|---|---|
| I .... | PxP |
| 2 NxP | .... |

Each side has captured a Pawn: value for value.

| | |
|---|---|
| 2 .... | B-B4 |

Now he attacks White's Knight on Q4, and threatens to win it, as it is protected only once.

| | |
|---|---|
| 3 B-K3 | .... |

This protects the Knight a second time, so that if 3 ... NxN; 4 BxN, BxB; 5 QxB and the players are still even in material.

| | |
|---|---|
| 3 .... | Q-B3 |

Instead of exchanging, Black attacks the Knight on Q4 a third time (with Bishop, Knight and Queen). Again the Knight requires additional defense—or White can play the Knight away from Q4, if he is so inclined.

| | |
|---|---|
| 4 P-QB3 | .... |

Now the Knight is protected three times, and thus adequately guarded.

Diagram 91          Diagram 92

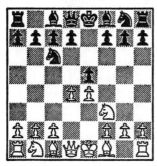 

In Diagram 92, we have a fascinating example of how to win material. It is the kind of position which can arise from the Queen's Gambit Declined (see page 197). White to play:

    1 B-K4               KR-B1

The Queen Bishop Pawn required protection.

    2 Q-B2               Q-Q3

Again the weak Pawn needed protection. Note that this Pawn is "pinned"; it cannot advance, for then the Black Bishop is lost.

    3 KR-B1              N-N1

Again the Pawn was menaced, and again Black defended it. Four times attacked, four times defended! But . . .

    4 N-K5!              . . . .

The fifth attack. Black can no longer defend the Pawn successfully. White will continue 5 BxP, BxB; 6 NxB and should win with his extra Pawn.

## PAWN PROMOTION

This subject has been touched on several times, but we are now in a particularly good position to appreciate its importance. Many games are never played out to checkmate because a player gains an overwhelming advantage in material as the result of promoting a Pawn, or as the result of winning material through threatening to promote a Pawn.

**Examples of Promotion.** Checkmate cannot be enforced with: (a) King and Bishop against King; (b) King and Knight against King; (c) King and two Knights against King! Yet, give the stronger side a "measly" Pawn and the game is an effortless win!

Diagram 93 illustrates the point nicely. Without White's Pawn, the position would be hopelessly dead drawn. With the Pawn on hand, the win is child's play, one of the most likely procedures being:

| | | |
|---|---|---|
| 1 | B-R3 | K-Q1 |
| 2 | K-B7 | K-Q2 |
| 3 | P-K6ch | K-Q1 |
| 4 | P-K7ch | K-Q2 |
| 5 | P-K8(Q)ch | .... |

Now that he has a Queen, in addition to his Bishop, White will of course bring about a quick mate.

Diagram 93                    Diagram 94

In Diagram 94, Black's passed Pawn, only one square away from queening, wreaks havoc. Black plays:

1 ....                    **R-R8!**

An impressive feature of the position is that although the players are quite even in material (count it up for both sides!), White is utterly lost!

Black's threat is simply 2 ... RxRch; 3 QxR, P-N8(Q) leaving him a whole Queen to the good!

If White tries 2 RxR, then 2 ... PxR(Q)ch again leaves Black a whole Queen to the good.

2 R-N1 ....

Blockading the queening square—but not for long.

2 .... RxRch
3 QxR N-B6

White must resign: his Queen is attacked by the Knight, yet she cannot move out of attack, for then the passed Pawn will queen.

**Passed Pawns.** A passed Pawn is one which is not impeded by hostile Pawns on neighboring files. In Diagram 96, both Pawns are passed. As we shall see in Chapters 4 and 5, most endgame play really centers around passed Pawns and their attempt to reach the eighth rank for promotion. At this point it will be useful to study an example of the strength of the passed Pawn.

Diagram 95 is instructive in this respect. Black is hopelessly lost, as he is a clear Rook down. However, remove the two White Pawns, when the Black Pawns are passed. This gives us Diagram 96—and remember that Black Pawns move down the page!

| Diagram 95 | Diagram 96 |
|:---:|:---:|

In Diagram 96, Black, to move, wins easily:

1 .... P-R7
2 R-QR7 P-N6

Followed by 3 ... P-N7 and one of the Pawns must queen. Black can also win, of course, by 1 ... P-N6, etc.

Nor would 2 R-QB1 be any better for White. Two mutually support-ing Pawns, when advanced this far, are irresistible.

In well-contested games, it is not uncommon for a passed Pawn, established as such about the 15th move, to win the game thirty or forty moves later! The passed Pawn is a powerful force, and should be recognized as such.

## SUMMARY

**Rules to Remember.** The fundamental checkmates may not often turn up in actual play, but they are the basic winning methods, and you should be familiar with their mechanism. Aside from this, constant practice with these mates—with the Queen, the Rook, the two Bishops, and with Bishop and Knight, will greatly enhance your skill in han-dling the pieces.

In addition to the fundamental checkmating positions, it is useful to know some of the frequently-recurring attacking patterns. Those which utilize the Queen are particularly important; since the Queen is the strongest piece, methods of using this piece in co-operation with the other forces will enormously increase your playing strength.

The relative value of the pieces comes only second to their moving and capturing powers as something you must know thoroughly—with-out having to think about it. As you become a better player, you will learn to modify academic values according to the nature of individual positions. At the start, however, it is better to accept these values without question.

In all cases of capturing, exchanging, or threatening the adversary's forces, you must apply the rule of *value for value*. Don't give away greater value in return for less—the only exception being, of course, the attainment of an advantage which outweighs material considerations by far. But this compensation must not be the result of a pipe dream or a brain storm—it has to be genuine, concrete compensation: an immi-nent checkmate, or something equally clear.

Pawn promotion, we now see, is one of the most frequent ways of deciding a game. The presence of a single Pawn often makes possible a victory that would otherwise be unattainable (Diagram 93). And far-advanced passed Pawns often cost the enemy fatal expenditure of mate-rial in the course of being promoted. Passed Pawns are therefore a very important asset, and must be watched carefully from their very birth.

Neglecting your own passed Pawn may deprive you of well-deserved victory; failing to guard against your opponent's passed Pawn may condemn you to a defeat which might have been prevented if proper precautionary measures had been taken.

# 3

# TACTICS

Tactics are the means whereby we enforce our will on the enemy. The goal of tactics is to bring more force to bear on some objective than your opponent can muster for defense. Sometimes tactics takes the form of "gitting thar fustest with the mostest," and sometimes it is a question of "hitting 'em where they ain't." Tactics, in short, is a matter of hitting fast and hitting hard.

## THREATS

Threats are ... well, threats. This is one of those self-evident concepts that are difficult to define. Suppose we put it this way: *a threat is a contemplated winning move.* You put your forces in position to execute something desirable: checkmate, the queening of a Pawn, the capture of valuable material. Your opponent has to do something about it: he defends against the threat, parries it, puts it out of existence, ignores it because he thinks it is worthless. One of his possible reactions to a threat may be to overlook it completely!

**Capturing Threats.** These are the most common of all threats, and you must be on guard against them at every single move. Sometimes moves are played for the purpose of threatening a capture; sometimes the threat is incidental to a larger purpose. In that case, the player achieves his purpose with gain of time. This is most noticeable when a piece attacks a hostile piece of greater value. A perfect example of this occurs in the Center Game (page 163) after the moves 1 P-K4, P-K4; 2 P-Q4, PxP; 3 QxP, N-QB3.

Black's Knight attacks White's Queen. As the disparity in value between the Queen and Knight is enormous, Black's attack on the Queen is a very serious threat, and the Queen must retreat, with no questions asked. We say of such situations that Black has gained time, White has lost time. Why? Because both players should bring out their forces fairly rapidly in the opening stages—we term this "developing" the pieces. With 3 ... N-QB3 Black develops his Queen Knight with gain of time. On the other hand, White's development of the Queen is of little value, as he has to move the Queen on the following move, instead of developing *another* piece.

Of course, not all capturing threats are equally valid. Sometimes a player sets up a threat the execution of which would be disastrous—for him, not for his opponent! A useful example of this arises in the King's Gambit Declined (page 165) after the moves 1 P-K4, P-K4; 2 P-KB4. White now threatens—we should say "threatens"—to capture Black's King Pawn. Black calmly disregards the "threat" and plays 2 ... B-B4.

Is Black's last move an oversight? No, indeed. For if 3 PxP??, the reply 3 ... Q-R5ch is deadly. The sequel is 4 K-K2, QxKP mate!—or 4 P-KN3, QxKPch; winning White's King Rook because of the *double attack*.

**Defending Against Threats.** Not all threats are of the simple hit-and-run variety. Sometimes they involve complex patterns of attack, defense, renewed attack, and renewed defense. This makes for delightful complications. In Diagram 97, which illustrates a position from the Scotch Game (page 168), it is White's turn to move. Black threatens to win a piece, as he attacks White's Knight on Q4 twice. White can play 1 NxN —one way to meet the threat—or he can retreat his attacked Knight, which is another way to meet the threat. He decides on *1 B-K3*, supporting the Knight with a developing move. Black replies *1 ... Q-B3*, attacking the Knight for the third time and again threatening to win a piece. This time White replies *2 P-QB3*, thereby defending the Knight for the third time and avoiding any loss of material. (The same position has been treated from a somewhat different point of view on page 40.)

Diagram 97                          Diagram 98

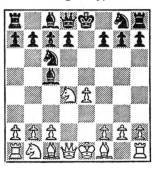 

The situation in Diagram 98 is extraordinarily interesting. It arises in the Vienna Game (p. 164); Black has captured a Pawn at White's K4 square. White, it would seem, can win a piece with the obvious reply 1 NxN. Not so, however, as Black counters with the *Pawn fork* 1 ... P-Q4—really a form of *double attack*. However, White is not interested in dallying with the acceptance of Black's sham sacrifice of material.

Instead White plays (in the position of Diagram 98) *1 Q-R5*. This move seems crushing; it threatens mate on Black's KB2 square, and it also threatens to win Black's advanced Knight by 2 QxKPch. Yet Black has a neat reply: *1 ... N-Q3*. This prevents the mate at Black's KB2 square, and it also saves the Knight from confiscation. Both threat and parry here are of a high order.

## ATTACKING TECHNIQUES

As we have seen, threats are not automatically successful. If one's opponent is alert and reasonably efficient, the threat is parried, and the defender is none the worse off. It follows, then, that we must familiarize ourselves with effective attacking methods. In that way we may hope to devise attacks which cannot be warded off easily.

**Pinning Attacks.** The *pin* is an attack on a piece which cannot move away because an even more important piece is being screened from attack. If the King is the secondary piece that happens to be screened from attack, then it is even illegal for the pinned piece to move out of the way, for this would mean exposing the King to check—which is strictly forbidden. Diagram 99 illustrates this point. White, to move, plays *1 BxB,* winning a piece. Clearly Black cannot play 1 ... PxB,

Diagram 99          Diagram 100

exposing his King to attack by White's Rook on the King Bishop file. Black's King Bishop Pawn is *pinned*.

Winning the piece in the position of Diagram 99 is very easy. But actually this is a simplified version of Diagram 100, in which White leads off with *1 BxN*. Black must play *1 ... QxB*, as his Queen is attacked by White's Rook at KB1. Then *2 QxQ, PxQ* produces the position of Diagram 99.

In Diagram 101, White prepares the *pin* very neatly with *1 RxN!* Then, after *1 ... PxR;* the King Knight file is opened, and *2 R-N1* wins Black's Queen because of the pin. This leaves White with Queen and Knight (12 points) against two Rooks (10 points), an overwhelming material superiority.

Black, by the way, helped to bring on this catastrophe by placing his King and Queen *on the same file*. This was a broad hint to White that his Rooks might find useful employment on the open file.

Diagram 101                                  Diagram 102

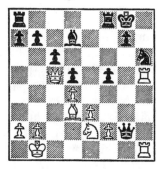                          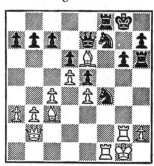

Diagram 102 reveals the power of two united Bishops shooting at the King-side. Note, to begin with, that the White Bishop at K6 pins the Black Knight at Black's KB2 square. This is an important factor in White's coming "combination." Note also that White wants to open the long diagonal (from QR1 to KR8) so that his other Bishop can function on it. He therefore decides to lose the Exchange—to "sacrifice" the Exchange. *1 RxN!, PxR.* Now the long diagonal is open for action. *2 B-R8!!* This astounding move threatens *3 Q-N7* mate, and Black must resign, as there is nothing he can do about the threat. He cannot play *2 ... NxB*, as the Knight is *pinned* and must not expose the King to attack. That *2 ... KxB* is impossible goes without saying, as the Bishop is guarded by the Queen.

We have just used two terms that require further explanation. A "combination" is a series of interrelated moves to achieve an advantage. What are the items to be related to each other? They are: the goal to be achieved, and the method to be used for the purpose. As a rule, the method involves a "sacrifice," that is, giving up a unit of larger value for one of smaller value. Of course, there is nothing noble about a chess "sacrifice." It may be, and often is, fascinating, profound, ingenious, astounding, very pleasing. It gives chess a delightful surprise element. It is the stroke of genius that often lights up what may seem dull plodding to the uninitiated. But the chess "sacrifice" is definitely a matter of self-seeking, a means toward an end. In Diagram 102, for example, White's first move is a sacrifice, made for the purpose of smashing open the long diagonal to set up a fatal mating position. It often happens that a startling sacrifice, ravishing in its neat solution of a difficult problem, is the only way to win in a given position. But the sacrifice is not pure genius; the elements that make sacrificing possible are practice, routine, and—naturally—creative imagination.

**Forking Attacks.** The *fork* is a simultaneous attack on two or more pieces. All the pieces, theoretically, can engage in *forking* activities; but this power is traditionally associated with the Knight, possibly because of the fear which the *Knight fork* arouses in the minds of inexperienced players. Unprotected pieces, or pieces which can ultimately be deprived of protection, are ideal targets of the *Knight fork*. In Diagram 103, a simple and effective example, Black's Knight is guarded by his Queen. Who would dream that this protection by the strongest piece of all, is utterly flimsy? White simply plays *1 QxN!* This sacrifice is naturally answered by *1 ... QxQ.* Now comes the *Knight fork 2 NxBch,* simultaneously attacking Black's King and Queen. And, since checks can

Diagram 103          Diagram 104

never be disregarded, Black must move his King out of check, leaving his Queen in the lurch. The sequel is *2 ... K-R1; 3 NxQ* and White has won two pieces!

In positions like the one shown in Diagram 104, we are impressed with the thought that the preparation for a *Knight fork* is often even more fascinating than the *fork* itself. Here is the procedure, in which the *Knight fork* N-B7ch looks like a tyro's oversight:

| 1 QxQ | BxQ |
|-------|-----|
| 2 RxR | RxR |
| 3 N-B7ch | .... |

And White wins a whole Rook.

*Forks* often work hand in hand with *pins*. This is less complicated than it sounds, and the combination of both attacking motifs packs a terrific wallop. The effects achieved are very pleasing. In Diagram 105, for example, White plays *1 N-N6!* *forking* Queen and Rook and thus winning the Exchange. The really delightful feature of this maneuver is that the intrusive Knight is immune from capture because Black's Pawn at his KB2 square is *pinned* by the White Bishop at QB4.

Diagram 105                          Diagram 106

The blending of the *pin* and *fork* motifs in Diagram 106 is really exquisite. Black's first move comes as a stunning surprise: *1 ... B-KN5!* As this *pins* the Queen, White has no choice: he must play *2 QxB*. But now comes the delightful reply *2 ... N-K6ch forking* King and Queen. The beauty of White's combination is that the Queen Pawn is *pinned;* consequently White cannot play *3 PxN*. He must move his King, allowing *3 ... NxQ*.

As has been pointed out, the *Knight fork* is merely a striking form of *double attack*. We proceed now to examine some of the other kinds of *double attacks,* which lead to many pretty effects and are of the greatest practical value.

**Double Attacks.** The most basic—and most dangerous!—form of *double attack* is the *double check,* explained on page 16. In Diagram 107, the winning process takes on a delightful quality because the winning side's Queen is under attack—*en prise.* Merely to give any old *discovered check* would not do; for example, if 1 N-B4ch?? (attacking Black's Queen), there follows 1 ... QxQch and White can resign. The right check is a *double check* which also attacks Black's Queen: *1 N-B8 dbl ch!* Now Black can resign. He cannot play 1 ... QxQch because White's Knight is giving check; he cannot capture the Knight at QB8 because White's Queen is giving check! So Black's King must move, and his Queen is lost.

Diagram 107        Diagram 108

In Diagram 108, the strength of the *double check* allows White to start with a truly stunning move: *1 Q-B8 ch!!* After *1 ... KxQ* there follows *2 N-N6 dbl ch.* It is now mate next move, as Black is forced to move his King to Q1 or N1, allowing *3 R-B8 mate.*

But double attacks, even where checks are not involved, often present insuperable problems to the defender. A typical instance is seen in Diagram 109, in which White plays *1 Q-B3,* attacking Black's loose Knight and loose Rook at Black's QN7 square. Something must give: Black cannot defend both menaced pieces. The best he can do is to come off with the loss of the Knight. The word "loose" is applied advisedly to the position of Black's pieces. If the Knight had been guarded by a Pawn on Black's KN2 square, the *double attack* would not have been feasible. Pawn protection often provides a secure anchorage for pieces that would otherwise be "loose."

Diagram 109          Diagram 110

 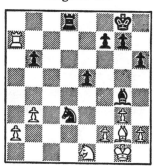

An amusing, as well as wonderfully instructive, example of *double attack* is seen in Diagram 110. The play here is *1 NxN, RxN; 2 R-R8ch, K-R2; 3 B-K4ch*. With his last move White attacks King and Rook simultaneously. Black must take care of his King, losing a whole Rook in the process. This form of *double attack* turns up in many games.

The Queen's power is admirably shown in Diagram 111: White plays *1 Q-N4!*, simultaneously attacking Black's Bishop at Black's KR5 square and the Knight at Black's Q2 square. Black must lose a piece.

Diagram 111          Diagram 112

In Diagram 112, Black loses only a Pawn, but this happens as the result of two *double attacks*! First White plays *1 NxP!* attacking Black's Queen and Bishop. The reply is of course *1 ... PxN*. But now White plays his second trump card: *2 Q-R4ch* attacking the King and Bishop. Black must take care of his King, leaving his Bishop in the lurch.

**Attacks on Overburdened Pieces.** This type of attack is often deadly, because it is directed against a piece which has an important defensive function. The menaced piece is thus at a tremendous disadvantage in trying to defend itself against a sneak attack. To fight back against such a thrust is like trying to fend off a footpad with one arm tied behind your back.

In Diagram 113, for example, White's Queen has the weighty problem of guarding the White King against a mating attack via the Queen Knight file. Black takes pitiless advantage of this set-up with *1 ... B-N4!* This *pin* is unanswerable, for if *2 QxB, QxNP mate!* So White despairingly tries *2 P-B4*, but after *2 ... BxP!*, he still cannot take the terrible Bishop, and must therefore lose his *overburdened* Queen.

Diagram 113          Diagram 114

Diagram 114 offers a very similar situation. It is White's move, and he seeks a move that exploits the Black Queen's defensive position at Black's KN3 square. The move is *1 R-KN4!*—a brutal *pin*. If Black picks off the Rook with his Queen, then follows *2 QxPch, K-R1; 3 QxRP mate*. The alternative is for Black to lose his Queen for a mere Rook—a fatal loss of material.

In Diagram 115, the situation is more complex, but lends itself to an interesting logical analysis. White threatens mate at KN7, pinning Black's King Knight Pawn. Black's Knight at K1 guards this mating threat. But White has a secondary threat: N-B6ch (fork plus pin), winning Black's Queen. If this threat were guarded only by the Knight at Black's K1 square, Black would be lost. (Imagine *1 N-B6ch, NxN; 2 QxNP mate!*) But, luckily for Black, his Bishop at K2 relieves his Knight of the double defensive function. If White plays *1 N-B6ch*, Black replies *1 ... BxN* and White has failed miserably.

But White's plan is much deeper—and really quite simple: he removes the guardian Bishop! Thus: *1 RxB!* This sacrifice of the Exchange is murderous, for after *1 ... NxR* there now follows *2 N-B6ch!* Now Black is crushed, as his Knight at K1 is an *overburdened piece*. (Remember that his King Knight Pawn is *pinned!*) If Black captures the Knight, he allows the mate at his KN2 square. If he moves away his King instead, then he loses his Queen to the intruder. All this has been beautifully reasoned out by White, but a practiced master sees all this in a flash.

Diagram 115                     Diagram 116

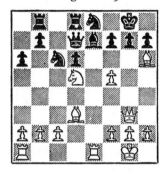     

The situation in Diagram 116 has a solution which is fairly obvious. The immediate *1 RxRch* gets White nowhere, as Black replies *1 ... QxR*. But this is suggestive: if the Black Queen were somehow deprived of its defensive function, then *RxRch* would be mate! Hence Black's Queen must be diverted from its defensive function. The solution: *1 Q-B4ch!* or *1 Q-N3ch!* Any price is cheap for attaining checkmate; even a Queen sacrifice is well worth while. Black has no good alternative to *1 ... QxQ; 2 RxR mate*. Why? If *1 ... K-B1; 2 Q-B7 mate*. Most interesting of all is *1 ... K-R1*. Now there follows *2 N-B7ch, K-N1; 3 N-R6 dbl ch*—neither checking piece can be captured!!—, *K-R1; 4 Q-N8ch!!, RxQ* and now White has the luxurious choice between *5 RxR mate (back-rank mate!)* or *5 N-B7 mate (smothered mate!)*.

**Attacks on Inadequately Guarded Pieces.** Closely related to the deadly if unchivalrous attack on *overburdened pieces* is the attack on *inadequately guarded pieces*. The necessary condition for successful operations here is that the guard can be driven off, captured, or rendered helpless to perform its proper function.

Diagram 117 is a very simple example. Black's Knight protects his

Rook, so 1 RxR, NxR cannot be the most forceful line. This consists in
*1 BxN!* knocking the props out from under the Black Rook. Black is
helpless, for if he captures the Bishop, he loses his Rook; and if he plays
*1 ... RxR,* then *2 BxR* likewise saves White's piece. A roguish touch!

Diagram 117

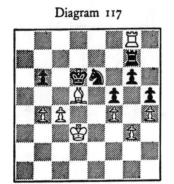

Diagram 118

In Diagram 118, we see a jumbled-looking position which has one
outstanding feature: White's Queen guards his Rook at QN6 and his
Knight at KB3. Both of these pieces are attacked. Black adds one and
one together and comes up with the right answer: *1 ... RxN!* White
loses a piece after *2 QxR, QxR.*

Black is already behind in material in the position of Diagram 119;
he has a Pawn as inadequate compensation for the loss of the Exchange.
But now comes *1 B-R3!* and Black's Queen has no refuge from which
to continue guarding the Black Rook against the depredations of

Diagram 119

Diagram 120

White's Queen. Black tries to bluster his way out with counterattack: *1 ... P-B3*. But after *2 BxQ, PxQ;* he loses another piece: *3 BxN/R4*.

There is always an element of sardonic humor in passive-looking moves which really fulfil an aggressive function. In Diagram 120, Black would be able to play ... RxP mate if White's Queen were not standing guard. What more natural than to *remove this valuable guard?* But how? *1 ... Q-KB1!* This move is astounding because it is virtually unheard of for a player to offer the exchange of Queens in the midst of a violent attack. Yet this apparently colorless move deprives White of any defensive resource: *2 QxQch, KxQ* and there is nothing to be done against the coming mate. Similarly, *2 Q-K2* allows an immediate mate. Only *2 Q-N2* staves off the mate, but at the ruinous material cost of giving up Queen for Rook.

**Discovered Attacks.** This is also a type of *double attack,* and for the victim, a very painful one. The mechanism works this way: a piece moves, attacking an enemy unit, and at the same time opening up a line of attack which has been screened. Diagram 121 shows a familiar example from Petroff's Defense: if Black retreats his menaced Knight, say to his KB3 square, there follows *N-B6 dis ch!* giving check and at the same time attacking the Queen. Salvation by ... Q-K2 is impossible, as the Black Queen can still be captured by White's advanced Knight. This is the most painful type of *discovered check* (see page 15).

Diagram 121                          Diagram 122

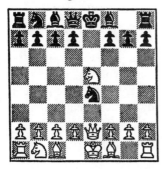     

In the position of Diagram 122, Black plays *1 ... N-K4!* In this way he attacks White's Queen and at the same time *discovers an attack* against White's foolishly exposed Knight. After White's Queen retreats, Black plays *2 ... QxN;* with a clear piece to the good.

In Diagram 123, we have a neat and effective example of the *double attack*: *1 NxQBP* wins a piece in broad daylight. The Knight, in moving, attacks the Black Bishop at QN7; but the Knight move also uncovers, or *discovers*, an *attack* by the White Rook on the other Black Bishop at Q2. The only choice now left to Black is to decide which Bishop he prefers to lose.

Diagram 123                                  Diagram 124

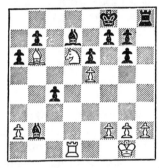     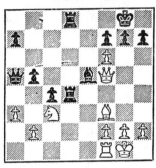

The *discovered attack* can sometimes be extremely refined. Thus, when Black plays *1 ... P-N5*, in Diagram 124, Black's threat to win the Knight is obvious. By no means so obvious is Black's threat of 2 ... BxPch; winning the Queen. In view of this latter threat, White's Knight must stand still and allow himself to be immolated while White saves his Queen.

With this example, we conclude our study of *double attacks*.

## COMBINATIONS ON THE LAST RANK

These usually involve a *Pawn promotion* or a *back-rank mate*. Sometimes the two motifs appear in the same combination, when the promoted Pawn has mating possibilities. Much rarer than these is the motif of *smothered mate*, which we have already encountered in connection with Diagram 116.

**Back-rank Mates.** A vulnerable back-rank has proved the downfall of many an inexperienced player. Unless one is guided by routine and precept in this sphere, it is very easy to forget that one's King may come to grief if he is hemmed in by his own Pawns in the castled position. Only prior and sad experience can give a player the instinctive realization that he must be solicitous of the King's welfare in situations where the last rank may become vulnerable.

Diagram 125 is a good example of the dangers which lurk in such harmless-looking positions. White's Rook guards the first rank, and White's Queen guards his Rook. But with the sensational Queen sacrifice *1 ... Q-R6!!,* Black upsets the whole defensive plan. For if White captures the Queen, there follows *2 ... RxR* mate. Or if *2 Q-N3, QxQ* and the guard disappears. Finally, if *2 RxR, QxRch* and mate next move. A drastic example!

Diagram 125             Diagram 126

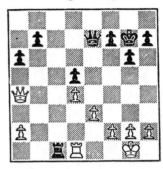    

Black's downfall in Diagram 126 is as sudden as a slap in the face. Instead of withdrawing his attacked Queen, White plays: *1 N-K7ch!* This has all the earmarks of a blunder, for after *1 ... QxN; 2 RxQ, RxQ;* Black has won a piece. His pleasure is very brief indeed: *3 R-K8 mate!!* The fact that Black's Knight is *pinned,* makes his first rank vulnerable! Note, by the way, that if Black tries *1 ... K-B1,* he loses the Exchange—and more.

As the game nears the ending stage, it is good practice to create a "loophole" for your King by advancing the King Rook Pawn or King Knight Pawn—or even King Bishop Pawn—one square. These moves are generally best avoided in the middle game, as they create targets which invite exploitation by the enemy. But in the endgame stage, such moves are much less likely to be weakening, and their value in freeing the first rank from sudden disaster is considerable. Once such a precaution has been taken, your Rooks are free for action, and need no longer be on guard for a sudden *back-rank mate.*

**Queening Combinations.** Obtaining a new Queen confers such an enormous advantage that it makes possible an endless variety of stratagems and sacrifices. The important thing here is not so much to classify every conceivable theme. What *is* important is to be thoroughly imbued with a recognition of the power of the far-advanced Pawn. Once your attention is concentrated on the terrific potentialities of such a Pawn, its exploitation will come as a matter of course.

In Diagram 127, White's continuation is as obvious as it is powerful: *1 Q-Q7.* This attacks Black's Rook, which cannot be guarded by 1 ... Q-K1, for then Black's Queen no longer prevents the mate on Black's KN2. On the other hand, if Black's Rook moves away from the White Queen's attack, then White queens his Pawn, necessitating ... RxQ. White in turn recaptures, and is then a piece ahead with an easy win.

Diagram 127          Diagram 128

In Diagram 128, White's passed Queen Pawn is poised at the queening square, but first White must dispose of the check at his KB1 square. There is a right way and a wrong way of doing this. As so often happens in chess, the wrong way looks quite plausible; the right way looks idiotic! The wrong way is 1 RxR?, QxRch; 2 Q-N1, Q-Q6 and Black draws, for if 3 Q-R7, Q-Q8ch; 4 Q-N1, QxP etc.

The right way is *1 Q-N1!* Then, after *1 ... RxQch; 2 KxR,* there is no way to stop the passed Pawn from queening, which leaves White a whole Rook ahead. This is a good moment at which to pause and reflect on the profound changes which are wrought by the *queening of a Pawn.* Before queening, White has only a Rook for the Queen; after queening, White will be a Rook ahead. It is the promotion power of the Pawn that makes such sacrifices possible.

This is made very clear in the combination worked out by White from Diagram 129:

| | |
|---|---|
| 1 RxB! | RxR |
| 2 QxQPch | R-K3 |

Or 2 ... Q-K3; 3 QxQch, RxQ; 4 P-B8(Q)ch winning. Another way, and even stronger, in reply to 2 ... Q-K3, is 3 P-B8(Q)ch!

    3 Q-Q8ch                R-K1

If 3 ... QxQ; 4 PxQ(Q)ch with crushing material superiority.

    4 QxQ                 ....

Another way to win is 4 QxRch, QxQ; 5 R-Q8 with a devastating *pin*.

    4 ....                 RxQ
    5 R-Q8ch                Resigns

For the Pawn queens whether or not Black exchanges Rooks. In any case, Black is left with a fatal material deficit. What is interesting about the winning method is that despite its simplicity, White has many ways of queening the Pawn. Obviously this greatly strengthens the power of the Pawn and enhances the effect of its queening power.

Diagram 129                    Diagram 130

There is a neat amalgam of *promotion* and *back-rank mating* motifs in Diagram 130:

    1 R-B8!!               ....

The beauty of this move is that it looks utterly nonsensical.

    1 ....                 RxR

If now 2 PxR(Q)ch?, Black simply replies 2 ... QxQ and wins. But White has a far more subtle continuation:

2 Q-K7!!                    Resigns!

What a position! If 2 ... QxQ; 3 PxR(Q)ch and mate next move on the back rank.

If 2 ... R-R1; 3 P-Q8(Q)ch leads to a back-rank mate.

Finally, if 2 ... R-KN1; 3 P-Q8(Q) and White remains with a Queen for a Rook, and consequently an easy win.

Again and again these examples of Pawn promotion drive home the theme that *queening a Pawn* completely upsets the existing material relationship. Very often, a player who was only a Pawn down, finds himself, one move later, a Queen down!

## DEFENSIVE PLAY

You cannot always attack; either the combinations are not available, or your position is simply not geared to attack. In that case, you must choose one of two courses. If your position is basically passive, you must meet threats as best you can, concentrating on exchanging as much as possible. For every time you exchange one of your passive pieces for an active piece of your opponent's, you lighten your defensive task and take some of the sting out of the attack.

It often happens, however, that a hard-pressed player will find that his position has tactical resources. These resources may not be enough to seize the attack, but they are often ample to divert its force or to establish equal prospects.

**Counterattack.** As has just been explained, counterattack is your best weapon whenever your position has the proper tactical possibilities for it. This is particularly true when your opponent has undertaken an

Diagram 131                    Diagram 132

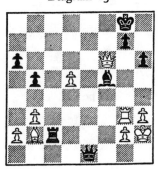 

attack with insufficient means. In such cases, where the counterattack is adequately grounded, it will have a crushing effect on the original attacker.

Thus, in Diagram 131, White seems to have his opponent on the ropes, threatening 1 QxP mate and also 1 QxB. Apparently Black is quite lost, yet he forces the game with *1 ... QxRch!!*, breaking the *pin;* after *2 KxQ, PxQ;* White is a Rook down, and his immediate resignation is in order.

The situation in Diagram 132 is equally critical, but the defender's counterplay has to be calculated to a hair. The *pin* on Black's Knight is extremely troublesome, and seems to condemn him to lasting passivity after 1 ... R-Q3. Instead, Black finds an extraordinary finesse:

|  |  |
|---|---|
| 1 .... | **RxB!!** |

Getting rid of the obnoxious *pin.*

|  |  |
|---|---|
| 2 RxR | **Q-QN2!** |

Setting up his own *pin!*

|  |  |
|---|---|
| 3 **Q-KN2** | .... |

The only defense. It gives Black the seductive opportunity of going horribly wrong with the Knight *fork* 3 ... N-B5??; which allows the brutal *discovered attack* 4 R-Q8ch winning Black's Queen!

|  |  |
|---|---|
| 3 .... | **Q-N8ch!** |
| 4 **Q-N1** | **Q-K5ch!** |

*Double attack!*

|  |  |
|---|---|
| 5 **Q-N2** | **QxQch** |
| 6 **KxQ** | **N-B5ch** |

Now the Knight *fork* wins the Rook, so that Black comes out a clear piece ahead. A lovely combination!

The conflict is not quite so sharp in Diagram 133, yet the clash of ideas is refreshing. White attacks Black's Rook and threatens to capture it. Instead of moving the menaced Rook, Black parries with:

|  |  |
|---|---|
| 1 .... | **Q-K3ch** |

*Double attack:* he gives check and attacks White's attacking Bishop. White has to think twice about how to answer this counterattack. The

reply 2 B-K5 looks plausible, but then the *pinned* Bishop goes lost after
2 ... P-KB3.

But how else can the Bishop be saved?

    **2 Q-K2!**                 ....

*Pinning* Black's Queen, so that ... QxB is impossible. Thus the threat
of BxR is renewed.

Diagram 133               Diagram 134

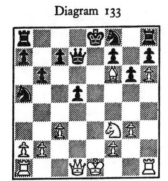 

As for Diagram 134, Black finds himself purely on the defensive,
being menaced with the loss of his Bishop in addition to a two-move
mate beginning with 1 QxBPch. Apparently Black is quite lost; yet
even a desperate position like this one is not devoid of hope. Black slips
out with:

    1 ....                         **Q-KN3!**

This parries the mating threat, and meanwhile the Bishop is immune
from capture, because Black threatens a *back-rank mate!* While White
takes steps against the threat of ... Q-N8ch, Black gets the necessary
time for saving his Bishop.

We see here a highly instructive example of the way in which even
desperate positions offer scope for the application of standard attacking
motifs. Without a knowledge of these motifs, many a position goes lost
which could have been saved by resourceful play.

## DIRECT ATTACK AGAINST THE KING

We have seen that many games are decided by resignation after one player has achieved a great advantage in material, as for example after queening a Pawn. But checkmate still remains the basic way to decide a game, and direct attack against the King is the basic way to achieve checkmate. Hence a knowledge of some of the techniques of attacking will be found useful.

**Attacks Against the Uncastled King.** To leave the King in the center condemns him to exposure to a powerful attack. It is true that in close positions—those in which the Pawn formations are more or less barricaded—the King is reasonably safe in the center, though his presence there is likely to hamper the harmonious development of the other pieces. And even a "close" position is only relatively close: a file can be opened through a Pawn capture, with a resulting increase in mobility and access to the hostile King.

The situation in Diagram 135 is an open position with a vengeance. The two center files are open, and White's Bishops look ominous on their powerful diagonals. Add to this the fact that White's King Rook stands on an open file, and it is clear that the position is ripe for explosive action: *1 QxPch!!* Black resigns, for if 1 ... NxQ; 2 BxP mate! This is a good example of the dangers to which a harried King may be exposed in an open file.

Diagram 135                    Diagram 136

The dangerous situation of Black's King and Queen on the open King file, in Diagram 136, has explosive possibilities. White's immediate threat is 1 R-K3 (*pinning!*) and if 1 ... B-K5; 2 Q-Q4 with a fearsome *double attack* against Bishop and Rook.

Black has no good defense. If he tries to get out of the pin with 1 ...
K-Q2; then 2 R-K3, Q-B1; 3 B-N4ch, B-B4; 4 Q-Q4! (attacking the
Queen Rook), R-R1; 5 BxBch, QxB; 6 QxPch, N-B2 (else the other
Rook falls); 7 R-B3 and Black's position caves in. Despite its length,
this variation is easy to follow; each move made by White involves a
crushing threat.

Now back to Diagram 136. Black has another futile try in 1 ... N-B2.
Then, after 2 R-K3, N-K4; 3 Q-Q4! (*double attack!*) and White menaces the Rook in addition to the threat of 4 NxN, PxN; 5 RxP and it
is all over for Black.

Back once more to Diagram 136. Suppose Black tries 1 ... N-KB3;
2 R-K3, N-K5; 3 B-B3. Again White threatens a fearsome *double
attack*: 4 BxN, BxB; 5 Q-Q4. What is to be done? Black might try
3 ... P-B4. This is beautifully refuted by 4 BxN, BxB; 5 RxB!, QxR;
6 NxPch *forking* Black's King and Queen!

The reader should play over these variations until he has their import
firmly fixed in his mind. In this way he will learn a great deal about the
attack on the King in the center and the kinds of threats that arise in
the course of such an attack.

The actual play (from Diagram 136) was:

1 ....                          Q-R5

A desperate effort to get the Queen off the fatal file. But White has
still other resources.

2 Q-R4ch!                       ....

To this there can be only one reply, as White threatens a grisly *discovered attack* with 3 NxPch!, winning Black's Queen!

2 ....                          K-K2
3 R-K3ch                        K-B1

If 3 ... B-K5; there are innumerable ways to win the *pinned* Bishop,
for example 4 N-Q2, etc.

4 Q-Q7                          Resigns

Black is hopelessly tied up. The sequel might be: 4 ... N-R3; 5 N-B3,
Q-B3; 6 R-KB1, K-N1; 7 N-Q4, etc. There are many other ways to win.

These examples give us a good idea of what happens in "open" positions where attacking lines are wide open. But letting the King roost

in close positions on his home square or in its vicinity, is rarely safe. In Diagram 137, for example, White can give up quite a bit of material in the course of a furious King-hunt:

    1 N-N5!            ....

This is a characteristic early-stage sacrifice in situations where a player has weakened the approaches to his King by a premature advance of his King Bishop Pawn.

White threatens NxKP and—more important—he makes Q-R5ch possible. Thus we see that four White pieces are actively engaged in badgering Black's King. It is bad enough that Black has weakened himself seriously; worse yet is the fact that his pieces are not properly posted for defense.

    1 ....            PxN
    2 Q-R5ch            ....

Contemplating a second sacrifice: if now 2 ... P-KN3; 3 BxNPch!, PxB; 4 QxPch!, K-K2; 5 BxPch and White wins the Queen, "to begin with."

    2 ....            K-K2
    3 BxNPch            N-B3

Hoping to save the Queen.

    4 PxNch            ....

This leaves Black with little choice, for if 4 ... K-Q2; 5 BPxP threatening PxR(Q) and with a discovered attack on Black's Queen at the same time.

    4 ....            PxP
    5 BxBPch!            ....

And this neat sacrifice is the whole point of White's combination.

    5 ....            KxB

Black must take the Bishop; but this exposes him to the *"skewer,"* which is really the opposite of the *pin*.

    6 Q-R4ch            Resigns

The Queen is lost.

Diagram 137                    Diagram 138

 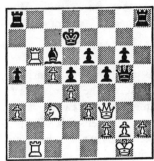

Diagram 138 leads to play which is really astonishing in view of one's first impression that Black's game is quite solid. True, White has no dynamic possibilities in the way of Pawn advances or Pawn captures. But, gifted with creative imagination, he does find a way to smash through:

> 1 RxB!                    ....

This removes Black's most useful defensive piece.

> 1 ....                    KxR
> 2 NxP!!                   ....

Having sacrificed the exchange, White now offers a piece. In the event of 2 ... PxN; 3 R-N6ch, K-B2; 4 QxQP leaves Black's King helpless against the concentrated attack of White's Queen and Rook. Prove this to your own satisfaction.

> 2 ....                    QR-QN1
> 3 N-B4 dis ch             K-Q2

Forced, as 3 ... K-B2? allows the merciless Knight *fork* 4 NxKPch winning the Queen. If then 4 ... K-Q2; 5 Q-Q5 ch! wins.

> 4 R-N7ch!                 RxR

Again forced, as 4 ... K-B1? allows 5 Q-B6ch and mate next move. 4 ... K-Q1? again allows the Knight fork 5 NxKPch, etc. (not to mention 5 RxRch, etc.).

> 5 QxRch                   K-K1

Note again if 5 ... K-Q1?; 6 NxKPch *forks* King and Queen (an "echo" theme!).

6 P-B6                                    Resigns

There are so many winning lines for White that further play is useless for Black. The threat is 7 Q-Q7ch, K-B1; 8 NxKPch, K-N1; 9 Q-N7 mate. Another threat is simply 7 P-B7, followed by queening the Pawn.

If Black tries 6 ... Q-K2; then 7 P-B7 followed by 8 P-B8(Q) wins at least a Rook for White. Or, more simply, 7 QxQch, KxQ; 8 NxNPch *forking* King and Rook! A versatile Knight.

**Attacks on the Castled King: Open Files.** The advice to castle the King early (page 20) is sound enough. If proof were needed of the risks run by a King who remains in the center of the board, the play in Diagrams 135-138 would furnish all the evidence that might be required. But it would be silly to imagine that castling automatically confers immunity. Frequently the opponent can muster overwhelming force on an open file which leads straight to the castled King's address.

A typical instance is seen in Diagram 139: *1 QxRPch!, KxQ; 2 R-R1ch* and mate next move. The open file, in conjunction with the powerful Pawn wedge at KB6, traps Black's King into submission.

Diagram 139                          Diagram 140

In Diagram 140 the denouement is, if anything, more startling: *1 Q-R8ch!!, BxQ; 2 RxB mate!* Here the combined action of the open King Rook file and the long diagonal is a portent of things to come. It is "landmarks" of this sort that tell the experienced player what to aim for without the need for conscious calculation.

The King Knight file, when open, is an equally potent weapon of attack. Take Diagram 141, in which White sets up the right position for a crushing attack with:

>    1 BxN!                    ....

This important move diverts the Black Queen from the defense, with sensational consequences.

>    1 ....                    QxB
>    2 B-K6!                   R-K2

The Rook must continue to guard the King Knight Pawn.

>    3 Q-R6!!                  Resigns

White's threat is 4 QxRPch!!, KxQ; 5 R-R3 mate!

Of course, if 3 ... PxQ; 4 R-N8ch, RxR; 5 RxR mate! All very beautiful, simple, and ... deadly.

Diagram 141                    Diagram 142

In the case of Diagram 140, the combination of the long diagonal and the open King Rook file was brusquely effective. As a rule, the long diagonal functions even more notably in conjunction with the open King Knight file. This is brought out very impressively in Diagram 142:

>    1 QxNPch!!                NxQ
>    2 RxNch                   K-R1

Now if White's Rook moves away with a discovered check, Black can interpose ... P-B3, and White's sacrifice is love's labor lost. But more sacrificing is in order:

| 3 R-N8 dbl ch!! | KxR |
| 4 R-N1ch | Q-N4 |
| 5 RxQ mate | |

These four examples give a good idea of the magnificent opportunities for violent attack which arise from utilizing open lines.

**Attacks on the Castled King: Weaknesses in the Pawn Structure.** It seems fantastic that the Pawn, which is the least valuable of all the forces, plays a role of the greatest importance for the security of the castled King. So long as the Pawns in front of the King remain unmoved, it is relatively difficult to work up a convincing attack; but let one of these "lowly" Pawns advance a step, and very often the whole castled position totters on the brink of disaster.

Diagram 143 is a convincing case in point. White is in danger because of the threatening position of Black's Rook at his KN3 square. Yet the position might be defensible if White's King Rook Pawn were still on KR2. Does it make so much difference that the Pawn is on White's KR3 square? Indeed it does: for now Black plays 1 ... Q-N6! with absolutely decisive effect. Note these points:

1. Black threatens ... QxNP mate.

2. His Queen cannot be captured, as White's King Bishop Pawn is *pinned* by Black's Bishop at his QB4 square.

3. White cannot guard against the mate by N-K1 because the Knight is *pinned* (N-K1 loses White's Queen).

4. If White's King Rook Pawn were at KR2, ... Q-N6 would have been impossible.

As matters stand, ... Q-N6 forces mate or ruinous loss of material.

Diagram 143          Diagram 144

In Diagram 144, the advance of Black's King Bishop Pawn turns out to have a fatally weakening effect. This advance has opened the diagonal of White's Bishop, leaving Black's King without a refuge in case of need. There follows: *1 QxPch!!, KxQ; 2 R-R4 mate.*

Diagram 145          Diagram 146

It is useful to know how a breach can be created in the Pawn bulwark which shields the castled King. In Diagram 145, for example, White's King-side is opened up with:

| 1 .... | NxNch |
| 2 PxN | B-KR6 |

A moment ago White's King was secure. Now there is a gaping hole in front of the King. Black's pieces have easy access to the King's vicinity, while—by a cruel paradox!—White's pieces are cut off from the defense by the Pawn at White's KB3 square. At the moment, Black threatens ... BxR, winning the exchange.

| 3 R-K1 | B-N4! |

An important link in Black's plans. He plans to occupy his KB5 square, a very aggressive station. The occupying piece can never be driven away, as White's King Knight Pawn has disappeared. This maneuver has the additional value of making room for the Queen.

| 4 K-R1 | B-B5! |
| 5 BxB | NxB |
| 6 R-N1 | Q-R5 |
| 7 Q-Q2 | QR-Q1! |

This is quite logical: Black will switch the Rook to his KR3 square, with venomous mating threats.

|        |        |
|--------|--------|
| 8 N-B3 | R-Q3   |
| 9 N-Q1 | B-Q2!! |

Threatening murder along the King Rook file. There isn't much that White can do about it, for if 10 R-N3, R-R3; 11 P-KR3, BxP; 12 K-N1, B-N7! and wins.

|         |      |
|---------|------|
| 10 N-K3 | .... |

There was no good defense. (See Diagram 146.) The breaking-up of White's rampart of Pawns in front of the castled position has given Black's pieces easy access to the critical squares.

|         |           |
|---------|-----------|
| 10 .... | QxRPch!!  |
| 11 KxQ  | R-R3ch    |
| 12 K-N3 | R-R6 mate |

Even the checkmate is a product of the broken-up Pawn position.

Sometimes a player weakens his castled position through sheer carelessness or ignorance of the consequences. But there are times when one of the King-side Pawns is advanced to clear up a situation which has become intolerable. In Diagram 147, for example, one of Black's Knights is pinned, his Queen Pawn is likewise pinned, freedom seems unattainable. To advance the King Rook Pawn for the purpose of kicking away one of the irritating Bishops seems as natural as it is logical. Yet the move is faulty because it gives White an opportunity to tear up Black's King-side position. (Proceed from Diagram 147.)

|         |      |
|---------|------|
| 1 BxRP! | PxB  |
| 2 QxP   | .... |

For the sacrificed piece, White has obtained two Pawns—not quite enough in the material sense. But the yawning breach in front of Black's King is the best possible compensation that White can have. His immediate threat is 3 N-N5 followed by 4 Q-R7ch and 5 QxP mate. We do not need to analyze the position in detail to see that Black cannot possibly hope to solve his problem.

Thus, if Black tries 2 ... N-K3; White proceeds victoriously with 3 B-Q3, and if then 3 ... N-B1; 4 N-N5 with an overpowering attack. Note, by the way, that after 3 B-Q3 there threatens the following char-

acteristic mate: 4 B-R7ch, K-R1; 5 B-N6 dis ch, K-N1; 6 Q-R7ch, K-B1;
7 QxP mate. This type of mate occurs frequently in positions where the
Pawn phalanx has been shattered.

Nor is 2 ... N-B4 a good enough defense. In that case we get 3 Q-B4,
N-N2; 4 N-N5, Q-K2; 5 Q-KR4 threatening 6 Q-R7ch and 7 Q-R8
mate. Again we see the same theme illustrated: Black's denuded King-
side presents too wide a front for adequate protection by Black's poorly
posted pieces.

|         |          |
|---------|----------|
| 2 ....  | N-N3     |
| 3 N-N5  | ....     |

The threat is 4 Q-R7ch, K-B1; 5 QxP mate.

|         |          |
|---------|----------|
| 3 ....  | N-B1     |
| 4 R-K1  | ....     |

Threatening simply to play 5 R-K3 with a view to 6 R-N3 or 6 R-R3.
The denuded state of Black's King-side continues to be the basic factor
of the position.

|         |          |
|---------|----------|
| 4 ....  | P-Q4     |

If he tries 4 ... N-K3 (to prevent White's R-K3); then 5 N-K4!—
intending 6 N-B6ch—ends it all. Note the important role played by
White's Pawn wedge at K5. The stationing of the Pawn here exerts a
powerfully constricting pressure on Black's game.

|         |          |
|---------|----------|
| 5 BxR   | QxB      |

See Diagram 148. Black seems to have freed himself, but actually he

Diagram 147              Diagram 148

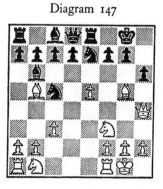

is quite lost: White's Rook now takes a hand in the attack against the exposed King.

| 6 R-K3! | B-K3 |
| 7 N-R7! | Resigns |

Thus the opening up of Black's King-side has proved fatal for him. If 7 ... NxN; 8 R-N3ch forces mate. If 7 ... N-N3; 8 N-B6 mate. The way in which cumulative pressure has been brought to bear on Black's vulnerable castled position is most interesting—in fact a model for this type of attack.

## SUMMARY

**Rules to Remember.** We began with the statement that tactics are the means by which we enforce our will on the enemy. This involves a knowledge of threats, how they are set up and how they are parried; specific attacking methods have been explained in detail. The general mechanism of attacking technique was seen to be the *double attack*. Simultaneous attack on two hostile units or on two points is almost certain to yield profitable results.

Of the specific attacking techniques, the *pin* is bound to be among the most effective. For the *pin* ties down at least one hostile piece, and sometimes more. This immobility is very favorable to the attacker, as the defense is seriously handicapped when aggressive pressure is applied. This also explains why the pin turns up so frequently as a subsidiary motif in a great many combinations.

As we went through this survey of attacking motifs, we had occasion again and again to notice that one of the great causes, or occasions, of successful attack is the fact that a hostile piece is "loose"—unguarded, isolated from support. In other cases—and this really amounts to the same thing—where a defender was on hand, it turned out that the defender could be neutralized, driven away, given too many or conflicting tasks.

In almost every instance, a Pawn is the best defender—because he is the *cheapest* defender! Why use a valuable piece for defense when a far less important unit will do the job just as efficiently and release a Bishop or Rook for more pressing tasks? Bear in mind that a *pinned* unit's defensive function is purely imaginary: refer again to Diagram 105, in which White wins the exchange because Black's King Bishop Pawn is pinned.

*Double attacks* in effect impose immobility on the defender. How can he hope to defend everything? Something must give. When two units are attacked simultaneously, it rarely happens that both can be defended simultaneously. The more important unit is saved, at the expense of the less important one. In the case of particularly nasty *double attacks,* such as the *forking check* and the *double check,* salvation may be very expensive.

Beware of giving a unit more than one defensive task. Such a piece may find itself *overburdened*—unable to defend all its charges. Here again, the more important the protective unit, the more wasteful its function. Inadequate guardianship is often seen in the case of the Queen. This sounds like a paradox when applied to so powerful a piece. The point is that the Queen is so powerful—and hence so valuable!— that she can easily be driven off by the unwelcome attentions of units of minor value. The Pawn, being of relatively slight value, does not suffer from such disabilities.

Loose pieces are particularly vulnerable to menace by *discovered attack.* Examine Diagrams 121-124, and in each case you will observe that the menaced piece is not guarded by a Pawn—that cheap, automatic form of protection.

Susceptibility to a *back-rank mate* is really a form of immobility: the potential mate immobilizes at least one protective piece. This possibility is banished easily enough by creating a loophole, as explained on page 59.

The imminent possibility of queening is one of the worst Damocles' swords to hold over an opponent's head. For the possibility of queening can reduce any number of enemy pieces to virtual immobility in the feverish effort to prevent the Pawn's promotion. To capture a newly promoted Queen is, as we have seen in Diagrams 127-130, usually very costly; so that, in effect, the fate of any given queening operation is vital to the outcome of that game.

In appraising the likely success or failure of any tactical device, the examination of the position for possible counterattacking resources is of the first importance. Where such resources are totally lacking, great risks may be taken, and rules of thumb will be found reliable. Diagram 147 is a good example of a sacrifice which is justified on general principles because it is ventured in a position virtually devoid of counterplay. On the other hand, we see in Diagrams 131-134 how a player, making the most of what his position offers, can worm himself out of a precarious situation. You must have faith in the defensive resources of even desperate-looking situations.

Direct attacks on the King are of course of the greatest interest and importance—the state of the King's health is basic to the result of the game. The examples given in Diagrams 135-138 reinforce the point that the King cannot be left in the center, and that his welfare demands an early removal to the side of the board, where he will be less exposed to attack.

But even after castling, there are ways and means of getting at the King. Often this is accomplished by making use of open lines (Diagrams 139-142); sometimes by exploiting a weakness in the Pawns which shield the King (Diagrams 143-148). In either case, whether by open lines or a breach in the defense, the attacker gets that initiative which is half the battle in chess tactics.

In general, tactics, to be successfully practiced, must offer "landmarks" —a loose piece, an open line, an overburdened unit, a far-advanced Pawn, an exposed King. These are the signposts which give us our bearings and our directions. Without these hints, we are in a strange country, uncertain and disoriented. But when these guides are available, and when we recognize them, they give our play an immense lift and upsurge. They tell us what to think about and how to plan. Sometimes their prodding is so insistent that they even serve as substitutes for thought. For the first-rate player, to take an instance, the sight of a loose piece suggests a *double attack* in a flash, without thought. Such is the value of good examples, pondered well and applied well.

# 4

# BASIC ENDGAMES

The endgame is the concluding stage of a game of chess. The meaning of the term "endgame" varies with the context. As far as we are concerned here, the "endgame" is the concluding stage of the game in which relatively few units are left on the board. Practically all the endgames which we shall study deal with the question of turning a material advantage to account.

In this chapter we are considering not merely endgames as such, but basic endgames. These are standard positions, akin to the theorems of geometry. Once these standard positions are arrived at, we are in the realm of general propositions and all-embracing theory. Instead of being on your own, you can follow procedures that are centuries old. Thus you see that the endgame is the most technical department of chess, and one in which memory plays a valuable role.

## MATERIAL ADVANTAGE

To know some of the standard positions in which a material advantage can be transformed into victory is of the greatest value. The goal of endgame procedures is generally *the promotion of a passed Pawn.* In turn, once we know the standard position in which a Pawn can become a Queen, we know what to aim for before reaching the standard-position stage.

Before proceeding to analyze some of the standard techniques for exploiting passed Pawns, we note this: *if you have no Pawns left, you* cannot force mate with less than a Rook. Thus, in Diagram 93, White has no chance of forcing checkmate without the Pawn; whereas with the Pawn, checkmate is child's play.

**King and Pawn Endings.** These are the most basic of all the endgames. You are to imagine that White has won material during the earlier part of the game. By steady exchanges he has finally reduced the game to a simple ending of King and King, with the extra Pawns still remaining to his credit. Thus we get the situation of Diagram 149, in which White is two Pawns ahead. These Pawns are connected, which means they can protect each other, both directly and indirectly. White moves first:

Diagram 149                           Diagram 150

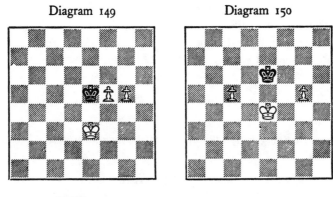

1 P-N6                       . . . .

After 1 P-B6, the Bishop Pawn would be protected directly.

      1 . . . .                    K-B3

Black dare not play 1 ... KxBP?, for then 2 P-N7 and his King can no longer prevent White from getting a Queen. Thus, after White's first move *his Bishop Pawn is protected indirectly*.

| | |
|---|---|
| 2 K-B4 | K-N2 |
| 3 K-N5 | K-B1 |
| 4 P-B6 | K-N1 |
| 5 K-R6 | K-B1 |
| 6 K-R7 | . . . . |

Another way to win is 6 P-N7ch, K-N1; 7 P-B7ch!, KxBP; 8 K-R7 followed by 9 P-N8(Q)—now that White's King commands the queening square.

But it would be a serious blunder to play 6 P-N7ch, K-N1; 7 K-N6?? —for then Black is stalemated, and the game is a draw! (See Diagram 70.)

| | |
|---|---|
| 6 . . . . | K-K1 |
| 7 P-N7 | Resigns |

Obviously Black cannot prevent White from queening the Pawn, with a quick mate in prospect.

White has many other winning procedures in Diagram 149, but the general idea is the same: the Pawns advance; White's King moves up to support them; the queening process is consummated, due regard being observed to avoid stalemate.

In Diagram 150, White's task is even easier, as he need not use his King in order to force the queening of a Pawn. There are several ways to work this out. If you are shown one method, you can reconstruct the others yourself:

|   |        |       |
|---|--------|-------|
| 1 | P-N6   | K-B3  |
| 2 | P-B6   | K-K3  |

If 2 ... KxP; 3 P-B7 and the Pawn, being out of reach, becomes a Queen.

|   |        |         |
|---|--------|---------|
| 3 | P-N7   | K-B2    |
| 4 | P-B7   | Resigns |

A Pawn must queen. Observe the stupendous increase in the powers of the Pawn! The manner in which the all-powerful Pawns reduce Black's King to helplessness suggests an important basic principle: the power of *the outside passed Pawn.*

Thus, in Diagram 151, White need only play *1 P-R4* and Black can resign: his King can never catch up to the White Pawn as it advances to the queening square. For example: *1 ... K-B2; 2 P-R5, K-K2; 3 P-R6, K-Q2; 4 P-R7, K-B2.* Too late! *5 P-R8(Q)* and wins. What makes this example all the more impressive is that it is all one whether Black has the King Rook Pawn or not. The outside passed Pawn (White's Queen Rook Pawn) is the only one that matters. This Pawn queens unaided, while the White King merely looks on. It is sometimes useful to know whether such a Pawn can queen unaided. About such cases we inquire whether the Black King is in the White Pawn's "quadrate." We construct a square, that is to say, one side of which is made up of six squares on the Pawn's path to queening. Here this is made up of QR3, QR4, QR5, QR6, QR7 and QR8. Another side of the square is made up of Black's first rank. If it is White's turn to move, Black's King must be inside the quadrate in order to stop the Pawn. If Black moves first, his King can be one square away from the quadrate and still be in time to stop the Pawn. Thus, with White moving first, we get:

| 1 P-R4 | K-B1 |
| 2 P-R5 | K-K1 |
| 3 P-R6 | K-Q1 |
| 4 P-R7 | .... |

... And the Pawn queens. Black's King was outside the quadrate. On the other hand, with Black moving first, play proceeds:

| 1 .... | K-B1 |
| 2 P-R4 | K-K1 |
| 3 P-R5 | K-Q1 |
| 4 P-R6 | K-B1 |
| 5 P-R7 | K-N2 |

Just in the nick of time to stop the Pawn! Here, Black's first move put his King into the quadrate.

Diagram 151                    Diagram 152

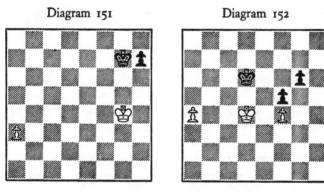

In Diagram 152, we have an admirable illustration of the power of a remote passed Pawn. In this case, Black's King is inside the quadrate, but he is lost all the same. The point is that White's single Pawn on the King-side *holds back both Black Pawns*. Once Black's King is forced to dash off to the Queen-side, his own Pawns will be left in the lurch, falling an easy prey to the White King's invasion. White wins regardless of who moves first.

| 1 P-R5 | K-B3 |
| 2 P-R6 | K-N3 |
| 3 K-K5 | KxP |
| 4 K-B6 | K-N3 |
| 5 KxNP | K-B3 |

| 6 KxP | K-Q2 |
| 7 K-B6 | K-K1 |
| 8 K-N7 and wins | |

White's Pawn queens by force. This is one of the many typical instances in which a remote passed Pawn makes victory possible.

We are now ready to consider the most basic of all endgame positions: King and Pawn on the sixth rank against King. This is shown in Diagram 153. When the Kings face each other in this manner, with an odd number of squares between them, the Kings are said to be "in opposition." If it is Black's turn to move, he is lost: White "has the opposition." Here is what happens:

| 1 .... | K-B1 |
| 2 P-Q7 and wins | |

The Pawn cannot be stopped from queening. The other possibility—and the more typical one—is:

| 1 .... | K-Q1 |
| 2 P-Q7 | K-B2 |
| 3 K-K7 and wins | |

White protects the queening square, leaving Black helpless against 4 P-Q8(Q), etc.

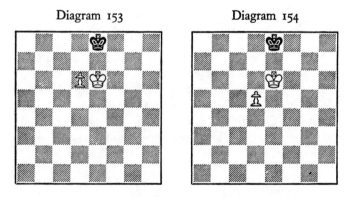

Diagram 153              Diagram 154

From the play following Diagram 153 we derive two basic rules:

If the player with the Pawn has the opposition *after advancing his Pawn to the sixth rank*, he wins.

If the Pawn advances to the seventh rank *without giving check when the Kings face each other*, the Pawn will queen.

To understand the significance of these rules, imagine that in Diagram 153 it is *White's* turn to play. In that case, *Black has the opposition*, and the position is drawn. For example:

    1 P-Q7ch           . . . .

This violates the second rule: the Pawn gives check as it advances to the seventh rank.

    1 . . . .              **K-Q1**

Now White has only one move to retain the Pawn:

    2 K-Q6            **Drawn!**

Black is stalemated! He is not in check, and he has no legal move. (See the discussion following Diagram 70.)

Going back to Diagram 153, there is no way in which White can gain the opposition, if Black plays correctly. Try this:

    1 K-K5           **K-Q2**
    2 K-Q5           **K-Q1!**

Black loses after 2 ... K-B1??; 3 K-B6—or 2 ... K-K1??; 3 K-K6. In either case *Black has lost the opposition.*

    3 K-B6           **K-B1!**

Black still has the opposition, and White is not making any headway.

In Diagram 154, White has a win no matter who moves first. This is due to the fact that his Pawn has not yet moved to the sixth rank, giving him the opportunity *to gain or lose a move for the opposition* as circumstances may require.

If White moves first, he follows our first rule:

    1 P-Q6            . . . .

White has the opposition after advancing the Pawn to the sixth rank. Therefore he wins.

Suppose that Black moves first in Diagram 154:

    1 . . . .              **K-Q1**

Now if 2 P-Q6?, K-K1! when Black has the opposition and draws!

|                    |         |
|--------------------|---------|
| 2 K-Q6!            | K-K1    |

If 2 ... K-B1; 3 K-K7 controlling the queening square and thus forcing the promotion of the Pawn.

|                    |         |
|--------------------|---------|
| 3 K-B7             | K-K2    |
| 4 P-Q6ch           | K-K1    |
| 5 P-Q7ch           | K-K2    |
| 6 P-Q8(Q)ch and wins |       |

In Diagram 155, where the forces are all far away from the queening square, the draw is already foreshadowed, because Black can always keep the opposition with accurate play. (This always holds good in such positions where the King of the materially stronger side is in back of the Pawn or at its left or right.) Suppose Black moves first (from Diagram 155):

|                    |         |
|--------------------|---------|
| 1 ....             | K-Q4    |
| 2 P-Q4             | K-Q3!   |

A serious blunder here is 2 ... K-B5??; for after 3 K-K4 Black's King can never regain his frontal opposition against the White forces. Hence 2 ... K-B5?? loses.

|                    |         |
|--------------------|---------|
| 3 K-K4             | K-K3    |
| 4 P-Q5ch           | K-Q3    |
| 5 K-Q4             | K-Q2    |
| 6 K-K5             | K-K2!   |

And here 6 ... K-B2?? loses because of 7 K-K6, K-Q1; 8 K-Q6 and White has the opposition. Thus, if 8 ... K-K1; 9 K-B7 wins, or if 8 ... K-B1; 9 K-K7 wins—in either case, through White's control of the queening square Q8.

|                    |         |
|--------------------|---------|
| 7 P-Q6ch           | K-Q2    |
| 8 K-Q5             | ....    |

And now, if 8 ... K-B1??; 9 K-B6, etc. Or 8 ... K-K1??; 9 K-K6, etc. In either case, White has the opposition and must win.

|                    |         |
|--------------------|---------|
| 8 ....             | K-Q1!   |
| 9 K-K6             | K-K1    |

Now Black has the opposition and the Pawn must give check on the seventh rank. The draw is unavoidable.

|          |          |
|----------|----------|
| 10 P-Q7ch | K-Q1   |
| 11 K-Q6   | Drawn  |

This stalemate finish is already familiar to us from page 83.

Diagram 155                          Diagram 156

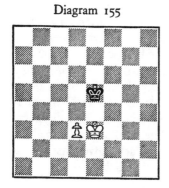  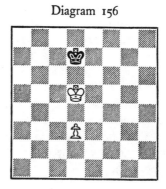

In Diagram 156, White's King is placed in the most favorable manner. If Black moves first, he loses the opposition right off. But if White moves first, Black still loses the opposition:

    1 P-Q4!              . . . .

The point. By interpolating the Pawn advance, he compels Black's King to give way.

|          |          |
|----------|----------|
| 1 . . . . | K-K2    |
| 2 K-B6    | K-Q1    |
| 3 K-Q6    | . . . . |

Black does not have the opposition, therefore his King must give way. If 3 ... K-B1; 4 K-K7 and White can advance the Pawn right to the queening square.

|          |          |
|----------|----------|
| 3 . . . . | K-K1    |
| 4 K-B7    | K-K2    |
| 5 P-Q5    | K-K1    |

Black is helpless: he cannot prevent the Pawn from queening.

|          |          |
|----------|----------|
| 6 P-Q6   | K-B1     |
| 7 P-Q7 and wins |    |

The Pawn queens.

The moral to be derived from the endings arising from Diagrams

155-156 is that when the Pawn is still on the second, third, fourth and fifth rank, White can win if his King is *in front of the Pawn,* and only draws if his King is *in back of the Pawn or at its side.* This presupposes that the enemy King is in opposition, so that the stronger side's King cannot advance directly.

In Diagram 155, White's King was at the side of the Pawn, and frontally opposed by Black's King; White could make no progress. In Diagram 156, White's King is also frontally opposed by Black's King; but the important feature is that White's King is *in front of his Pawn* and thus has ample maneuvering space for obtaining the opposition.

A very easy example of the opposition appears in Diagram 157. If White moves first, then Black has the opposition, and the game is a draw. (Thus, if 1 K-Q4, K-Q3 and White can make no inroad into the hostile position.) On the other hand, if Black moves first, White has the opposition, and White wins with little trouble:

|       |       |
|-------|-------|
| 1 .... | K-Q3 |

Or 1 ... K-B3; 2 K-Q5, K-K2; 3 K-B5, K-K3; 4 KxP, K-K4; 5 K-B4, and White queens long before Black. (Play the ending out and prove this to your own satisfaction.)

Having lost the opposition, Black's King has had to give way. White's King makes the first capture, and his Pawn will be the first to queen.

|         |       |
|---------|-------|
| 2 K-B5  | K-Q4  |
| 3 KxP   | K-B5  |
| 4 K-B4  | KxP   |

White will queen his Pawn in four moves. In this time Black will move his King out of the way, and advance his Pawn to the seventh rank.

|           |        |
|-----------|--------|
| 5 P-N5    | K-R6   |
| 6 P-N6    | P-N5   |
| 7 P-N7    | P-N6   |
| 8 P-N8(Q) | P-N7   |

With a Queen for a Pawn, White has an easy win.

**Queen vs. Pawn Endings.** We have just said that Queen vs. Pawn is an easy win. This stands to reason, given the tremendous disparity in power (and value) between the Queen and the Pawn.

Diagram 157                    Diagram 158

But positions like that of Diagram 158 make one wonder. Black's Pawn is just on the point of being promoted. Obviously, if the Pawn promotes successfully, Black draws even in material and there is no reason in the world for him to lose.

However, there is a clear (and very logical) winning process at White's disposal in Diagram 158. White's first aim is to force Black's King to stand in front of the Pawn (that is, on the queening square).

| 1 Q-N1 | K-R7 |
|---|---|

Threatening to queen the Pawn.

| 2 Q-R7ch | K-N6 |
|---|---|

He makes it hard for White. After 2 ... K-N8 (just what White wants) the Pawn is not threatening the queen, so that White has time to bring his King to the Queen-side.

| 3 Q-N6ch | K-R7 |
|---|---|

Again threatening to queen.

| 4 Q-R5ch | K-N6 |
|---|---|
| 5 Q-N5ch | K-R7 |
| 6 Q-R4ch | .... |

This *forces* Black's King to the desired square. Note how White's Queen has steadily narrowed down the number of squares available to Black's King.

| 6 .... | K-N8 |
|---|---|
| 7 K-K3 | .... |

Now that Black does not threaten to queen, White can proceed with Part 2: bringing his King to the Queen-side. Eventually White will bring about a mating position in which Black's Pawn will have no significance whatever.

|       7  .... | K-B8 |

Black is stubborn. He again threatens to queen, so White repeats his zigzag checking maneuver.

|  8 Q-QB4ch | K-Q8 |
|  9 Q-N3ch | K-B8 |
| 10 Q-B3ch | .... |

Again forcing Black's King in front of the Pawn.

| 10 .... | K-N8 |
| 11 K-Q2 | .... |

The King approaches a step nearer.

| 11 .... | K-R7 |

Once more threatening to queen.

| 12 Q-B2 | .... |

This *pins* the Pawn.

| 12 .... | K-R8 |

If 12 ... K-R6; 13 Q-N1 winning very easily, as the Pawn will soon be lost.

| 13 Q-R4ch | K-N8 |

Now White has a chance to blunder badly: 14 K-Q1?? creating a stalemate! (see page 29) as Black's King would have no moves.

| 14 K-B3 | .... |

Generously allowing Black's King one move, which leads to mate!

| 14 .... | K-B8 |
| 15 Q-B2 mate | |

A very instructive ending which should be practiced repeatedly until you have mastered it thoroughly.

The general rule is that the Queen wins regularly against Knight Pawn, King Pawn, and Queen Pawn. You will see later on (page 95) why endings with Rook Pawn and Bishop Pawn are sometimes impossible to win.

**Endings with Minor Pieces.** As we have seen (Diagram 93) King, minor piece and Pawn against King is a win for the stronger side. This holds good despite the fact that the minor piece cannot force checkmate. What matters is that the Pawn, supported by the extra piece, can be promoted to a Queen, which will then enforce checkmate.

When the weaker side has other material in addition to the King, the win is generally easier. Take the case of minor piece plus one Pawn vs. two Pawns, as seen in Diagram 159. White, to move, has many possible winning procedures. Here is one:

| 1 B-B4 | P-Q4 |
|---|---|

It would be a grievous blunder to play 1 ... K-B2? because of 2 P-B5! (*pinning!*) and Black loses a Pawn right off.

| 2 P-B5! | .... |
|---|---|

White in turn would blunder grievously by playing 2 PxP?—for with the removal of his last Pawn the game becomes a draw!

| 2 .... | K-R3 |
|---|---|

Now it is time to reveal White's strategy. He must (1) preserve his Pawn; (2) play to win Black's weak Pawn—the Bishop Pawn.

| 3 K-Q4 | K-N4 |
|---|---|

White wants to play K-K5 and K-Q6, but he must stop to guard his Pawn. Hence the following move, which releases his King from protective duty:

| 4 B-K3! | K-N5 |
|---|---|
| 5 K-K5 | K-B5 |
| 6 K-Q6 | K-N4 |

Protecting his Bishop Pawn. But now comes an instructive moment.

| 7 B-B2! | .... |
|---|---|

Black is in *Zugzwang* (a German word meaning move-compulsion).

Everything is momentarily protected, but whatever move Black makes will lose material. For example:

7 ....                               K-R3
8 KxBP                               ....

This ensures the queening of the White Pawn, after which the mate will be achieved in a short time.

Diagram 159                          Diagram 160

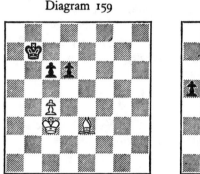 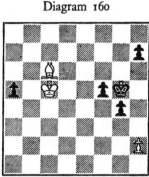

On the other hand, the situation in Diagram 160 is most instructive in illustrating the power of Pawns against a minor piece. White has Bishop and Pawn against four Pawns. Two of the Black Pawns (Queen Rook Pawn and Bishop Pawn) are passed, and therefore require special attention. The Queen Rook Pawn is an outside passed Pawn, and therefore creates difficulties for White: he has to guard against the advance of a Black Pawn on either wing. This splits White's forces, and reduces their effectiveness.

1 K-N5                               ....

He takes steps to remove the dangerous Pawn.

1 ....                               P-B5

The Pawns must be kept moving toward their queening squares. Time is of the essence!

2 KxP                                ....

Now Black has only two Pawns for the piece, which ordinarily is inadequate. But White's King, after gobbling up the Pawn, is far from the scene of action.

|   2 ....     | P-B6  |
|   3 K-N4     | ....  |

The King is to rush back to the threatened sector as rapidly as possible.

|   3 ....     | K-B5  |

Black's advancing Pawns have the active co-operation of their King.

|   4 K-B4     | K-K6  |

Very important: he blocks off the White King's approach by K-Q3, etc.

|   5 K-Q5     | P-R4  |
|   6 B-Q7     | P-B7  |

Threatening to queen the Pawn, and thus forcing White's reply.

|   7 B-N5     | K-B6  |
|   8 K-K5     | K-N7  |

Picking up White's last Pawn. The Black King is in the thick of the fight, while White's King is only a bystander.

|   9 K-B4     | KxP   |
|  10 K-K3     | P-N6  |
|     Resigns  |       |

White is helpless against 11 ... P-N7—after which one of the Black Pawns must queen.

Endings of King, minor piece and Pawn against King and minor piece revolve about the attempt to queen the Pawn—obviously the only winning possibility. The weaker side has very considerable drawing chances in the opportunity to give up the remaining minor piece for the hostile Pawn. The opponent will then be left with King and minor piece vs. King: a dead draw.

Whether the Pawn can be preserved or not, is therefore the burning issue in such endings. In Diagram 161, for example, White cannot naïvely advance 1 P-K7?, for then 1 ... BxP draws at once. But there *is* a win, and it makes an interesting study:

|   1 B-K7!    | B-B7  |

And not 1 .. BxB; 2 KxB with an easily won King and Pawn ending.

        2 B-B8                    ....

Threatening to advance the Pawn and then queen it.

        2 ....                    B-R5

So that if 3 P-K7?, BxP again drawing.

        3 B-N7! and wins

No matter how Black plays, he is helpless against 4 B-B6, which enforces the victorious advance of the all-important Pawn on its way to promotion.

Another winning method is 2 B-N4, B-R5; 3 B-B3 followed by 4 B-B6, etc.

Diagram 161                        Diagram 162

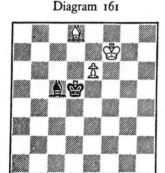              

In Diagram 162, we have an example of the Knight's most serious weakness. The Bishop is admirably *centralized,* controlling every possible square to which the Knight can move. The consequence is that Black's Knight has no move whatever—a danger that may arise when the Knight is placed at the side of the board.

The winning process is very simple but wonderfully instructive:

        1 K-Q7                    ....

Now Black is in *Zugzwang* (move-compulsion, see page 89). His Pawn is guarded for the moment, but whatever move he makes will cost something.

|       |        |
|-------|--------|
| 1 ... | K-R3   |
| 2 KxP | K-R2   |

Black's situation is hopeless: his Knight is immobilized, and the Pawn marches right down for promotion:

|          |        |
|----------|--------|
| 3 K-Q7   | K-N2   |
| 4 P-B6ch | K-N3   |
| 5 P-B7   | ....   |

And the Pawn queens.

**Rook and Pawn Endings.** In this type of ending we are ruled by different considerations from those that prevail in minor-piece endings. Remember that the Rook—unlike the Bishop or Knight—can enforce checkmate. Consequently, in the ending King, Rook and Pawn *vs.* King and Rook, the weaker side cannot seek a way out by giving up the Rook for the Pawn. However, there are many cases where the weaker side can draw such an ending, assuming that circumstances are favorable. Thus, if the weaker side's King has a good blockading position and the Rook has ample mobility, a drawn ending becomes a concrete possibility.

Diagram 163 shows the basic winning position for Rook and Pawn *vs.* Rook. It should be practiced thoroughly, until there is no doubt left in your mind that you can win this type of position.

White's problem is twofold: (1) he must drive away the Black King so that his own King can get out of the way of his Pawn; (2) he must play his Rook in such a way as to shield his King from endless checks by the Black Rook, once the White King leaves his present shelter. Here is how it is done:

|           |        |
|-----------|--------|
| 1 R-Q1ch  | K-B2   |

Now White's King can come out, but to no purpose at this stage: 2 K-K7, R-K7ch; 3 K-B6, R-KB7ch; 4 K-N6, R-KN6ch; 5 K-B5, R-KB6ch and obviously White is not getting anywhere: the only way to escape the checks is to head his King back to KB8!

|          |        |
|----------|--------|
| 2 R-Q4!  | ....   |

Thus he prepares to shield his King from the coming checks.

|          |        |
|----------|--------|
| 2 ...    | R-N8   |
| 3 K-K7   | R-K8ch |

    4 K-B6               R-KB8ch

    5 K-K6               ....

Now if 5 ... K-B1; 6 R-Q5 and the coming R-KB5 makes it possible to promote the Pawn.

Or 5 ... K-B3; 6 R-K4 followed by 7 K-K7 (protecting the queening of the Pawn), and wins.

    5 ....                R-K8ch

    6 K-B5               R-KB8ch

    7 R-KB4 and wins

The checks are blocked off, and the Pawn will queen.

Rook and Pawn endings are the most common type of endgames, and are therefore well worth mastering. In a good many of them, one player is a Pawn ahead, and the above winning procedure is one of the basic items in every player's repertoire of endgame techniques.

Diagram 163               Diagram 164

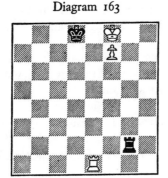 

Winning with the Rook Pawn is sometimes difficult, but Diagram 164 illustrates a very useful finesse:

    1 R-R8!               RxP

Black must capture, as the Pawn is threatening to queen.

    2 R-R7ch and wins

Black's Rook is lost. This type of stratagem is known as the *skewer* attack.

## DRAWING POSSIBILITIES

If you have followed the discussion of winning techniques carefully, you have noticed that drawing possibilities arise rather frequently. In the endgame stage, the difference between winning and drawing is often hair-thin. Hence a knowledge of some of the most common drawing possibilities is very useful.

In the discussion of King and Pawn endings (pages 78-86) we have seen that winning or losing *the opposition* is the most important aspect of many of these endings. In Diagram 165, we see a remarkable situation (Black to move). With two Pawns ahead, Black cannot win! He is in *Zugzwang* (see page 89): no matter where he plays his King, White picks up the more advanced of the two Pawns. The remaining Pawn is then inadequate for winning purposes, because, with Black's King starting out in back of the passed Pawn, he will never have the opposition— unless White blunders. The general ideas underlying such endings have been expounded following Diagram 155.

Diagram 165                     Diagram 166

     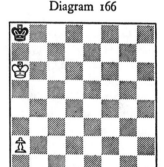

In many types of endings, the Rook Pawn gives trouble because of the inherent drawing possibilities. This is particularly true of King and Pawn endings. Take the position of Diagram 166, and shift all the forces to the Queen Knight file. In that case, White wins with childish ease, as the moves to be made by his Pawn assure him of taking and maintaining the opposition. (Diagram 156 serves as a model.)

As Diagram 166 stands, however, the position is drawn! For example:

| | 1 K-N6 | K-N1 |
|---|---|---|
| | 2 P-R4 | K-R1 |

| 3 P-R5  | K-N1    |
|---------|---------|
| 4 P-R6  | K-R1    |
| 5 P-R7  | Drawn!  |

Black is stalemated! The Rook file is the *only* file on which such a position is drawn.

There are other positions in which the Rook Pawn is afflicted with diabolical drawing weaknesses. Take Diagram 167 as an example. Despite White's enormous material advantage, he cannot win!

| 1 K-N6 | .... |
|--------|------|

Or 1 P-R7ch, K-R1; 2 K-N5, K-N2; 3 K-R5, K-R1 and White cannot make any progress toward winning, as he cannot budge the Black King out of the corner. (If 4 K-R6, Black is stalemated!)

| 1 .... | K-R1 |
|--------|------|

If now 2 B-K5, Black is stalemated.

| 2 B-B5   | K-N1 |
|----------|------|
| 3 P-R7ch | K-R1 |

And again Black will be stalemated unless White allows the King out of the corner (say by 3 K-N5). But then Black can simply play the King back and forth between QR1 and QN2. Again no progress can be made towards winning.

The reason why this ending cannot be won is that *the Bishop does not command the queening square*. If the Bishop were on white squares, the position would be a very simple win. For example, with the Bishop on QB4, the ending could proceed (Bishop on QB4, all the other forces

Diagram 167                              Diagram 168

as in Diagram 167): 1 K-N6, K-R1; 2 B-Q5ch (see the difference?!), K-N1; 3 P-R7ch, K-B1; 4 P-R8(Q)ch, etc.

Nor does this exhaust the Rook Pawn's bag of tricks. There are times when the Rook Pawn can draw against a Queen!

Thus, in Diagram 168, Black cannot be defeated in the manner adopted in the position of Diagram 158. After *1 Q-KN3ch,* Black plays *1 ... K-R8.* This blocks the passed Pawn, to be sure. But White derives no benefit from this and cannot bring his King to the scene of action, for after 1 ... *K-R8,* Black is in a stalemate position! If White moves his Queen to lift the stalemate, Black moves out his King and again threatens to queen his Pawn.

There are times when a draw can be achieved with a Bishop Pawn in somewhat similar fashion. Thus, in Diagram 169, White has no success with the standard maneuver *1 Q-N3ch.* Ordinarily Black would have to play 1 ... K-B8, blocking his passed Pawn and giving White's King time to approach. But here Black plays *1 ... K-R8!* Then, if the Pawn is captured, Black is stalemated! Thus we see that the Bishop Pawn and Rook Pawn can often achieve a draw against the mighty Queen!

Diagram 169                                    Diagram 170

Diagram 170 illustrates one of the rare cases where the Queen can win against the Bishop Pawn. What makes the win possible, is the proximity of the White King.

     1 Q-N2!                    . . . .

This *pin* forces Black's reply.

    1 . . . .                         **K-K8**

Now it would be a serious blunder to play 2 Q-K4ch?, K-B8 and Black draws, for example 3 K-B3, K-N8; 4 Q-KN4ch, K-R8; 5 Q-B3ch, K-N8; 6 Q-N3ch, K-R8!; 7 QxP, stalemate!

    2 K-B3!!                        P-B8(Q)
    3 Q-Q2 mate!

As has been pointed out, only the proximity of the White King makes this pretty mate possible.

Another frequent drawing resource is based on Bishops on opposite color: each player has a Bishop and some Pawns, and the Bishops move on different colors. There are favorable positions for the weaker side in which the advantage of a Pawn, or even of two Pawns, is meaningless.

Take the situation in Diagram 171, for example. White is two Pawns ahead, but his Pawns are blocked and the blockading Black King can never be driven away. The fact that White's Bishop does not control black squares, makes any winning attempt hopeless.

Diagram 171                     Diagram 172

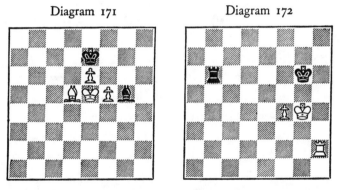

To know when it is possible to draw with a Rook against Rook and Pawn, is one of the most important details of endgame play. Many an apparently lost ending can be saved in this way. Diagram 172 gives us the general scheme. Black's procedure is to keep his Rook on the third rank until the Pawn reaches the sixth rank. *At that point,* the defending Rook goes to its eighth rank for checking purposes.

    1 R-Q2                          . . . .

As Black is to keep his Rook on the third rank, he can retreat with his King without having to fear that he will be forced into the position of Diagram 163.

| 1 ....      | K-N2   |
|-------------|--------|
| 2 K-N5      | R-QB3  |
| 3 P-B5      | R-QN3  |
| 4 R-QR2     | ....   |

As we shall see, Black need not fear the coming Rook check on the seventh rank.

| 4 ....      | R-Q3   |
|-------------|--------|
| 5 R-R7ch    | K-N1   |
| 6 P-B6      | ....   |

Now it would be fatal for Black to take a passive position with his Rook on the first rank, for example 6 ... R-Q1?; 7 K-N6! and Black is helpless against the threat of R-N7ch, K-B1; 8 R-KR7!, K-N1; 9 P-B7ch, K-B1; 10 R-R8ch, K-K2; 11 RxR, KxR; 12 P-B8(Q)ch and wins. This variation requires careful study!

| 6 ....      | R-Q8!  |
|-------------|--------|

Aggressive play.

| 7 K-N6      | R-N8ch |
|-------------|--------|
| 8 K-B5      | K-B1   |
| 9 K-K6      | R-K8ch |

Note how Black's Rook check breaks up White's winning plans.

| 10 K-B5     | K-N1   |
|-------------|--------|

White can make no progress; the ending is drawn. Black's Rook is in position to check the White King when he reaches the sixth rank.

## SUMMARY

These basic endgame positions are of great value, because they illustrate concrete, standard positions which have been reached at the conclusion of countless games. A knowledge of these positions will enable you to win many a game which you would otherwise only have drawn —or to draw a game which you would otherwise have lost.

A final important point about drawing possibilities. Most of them, you will have noted, arise in the case of *drastically reduced material.* It is a good idea, when you are ahead in material, to simplify to some extent; *but try to keep several Pawns on the board.* Your plus in material will often make it possible for you to win more material, and in any event you will be steering clear of the drawing possibilities which are inherent in considerably simplified positions.

When you are behind in material, the converse applies. *Simplify as much as you can,* in the hope of reaching some basic endgame position which is a draw.

From these examples, and from the general principles that govern them, we draw the grand general conclusion that *material advantage in the endgame can best be turned to account when a fair number of Pawns are still left on the board.* Our next chapter will be devoted to this theme.

# 5

# WINNING IDEAS
# IN ENDGAME PLAY

The endgame has certain attractive features for the average player. One of them is its quality of finality. If you have an advantage, its consequences soon become tangible: you force checkmate, or you queen a Pawn—which puts you well on the way to checkmate—or you win a piece as a result of a Pawn promotion, after which your victory should be quite clear.

Contrast this with the opening, where an advantage gained—unless it is of the most radical character—may require a lot of nursing before it can finally result in victory. In the endgame, the goals are pretty clear-cut.

Another aspect of endgame play which makes it attractive, is its simplicity. Instead of playing with sixteen men on each side—a very complicated affair—the material is reduced in the endgame to, say, about ten units all told on the board. In some cases, it may be as little as three units! (King and Pawn against King). This simplicity is very reassuring to inexperienced players. They are less likely to be overtaken by cruel tactical surprises; the game quiets down to a calmer tempo, and planning is freed from the hazard of brusque surprise.

A word of caution: simplicity does not necessarily mean "simpleness." Endgame play abounds in finesse: the difference of a single move may make all the difference between winning and losing. On the other hand, the possibility of exact calculation and far-reaching planning in the endgame offers the nearest approach which chess has to mathematical certitude. In no other stage of chess is simple counting as important as it is in the endgame!

## MATERIAL ADVANTAGE

In over-the-board play, the problem of turning an extra Pawn to account is one of the outstanding tasks which fall to a player's lot.

Repeatedly it will happen that he wins a Pawn in the opening or middle-game stage. This may come about through his own irresistible threats, or through his opponent's oversight—in any case, the material advantage is there, and what is to be done about it?

Generally speaking, the player with the material advantage wants to exchange Queens. *The player who is behind in material strives for complications, traps, diversions. The player who is ahead in material wants clarity, simplicity, calm waters;* in short, he wants an exchange of Queens, which will reduce the complications to a minimum.

Once the Queens have been exchanged, what then? The extra material does not win automatically. It has to be turned to account by planned, purposeful effort. The player who is ahead in material must post his pieces aggressively; he must bring his King into action; he must see to it that his extra Pawn is a good, healthy Pawn; he must plan to obtain a passed Pawn; if he *has* a passed Pawn, he must strive to advance it—with due protection; he must concentrate on hostile weaknesses; if they do not exist, he must create them.

All this is less complex than it sounds. It boils down to this: your forces must be aggressive, co-ordinated, and they must move in relation to some foreseen objective.

You want an endgame that is simple, but not too simple. Thus, Bishop and six Pawns against Bishop and five Pawns is generally an easy win. If, eventually, your opponent has to give up his Bishop for your extra Pawn when it becomes a Queen, you win very easily with Bishop and five Pawns against five Pawns. *But* Bishop and Pawn against Bishop offers the weaker side many drawing chances, for if your opponent gives up his Bishop for your lone Pawn, victory is impossible.

Another aid to the stronger side—and this applies with special force to Rook and Pawn endings—is to have the Pawns distributed over the King-side *and* Queen-side, or over one wing *and* the center. When *all* the Pawns are in one localized sector, the defense can adopt a compact formation which often makes a draw possible. When the Pawns are more dispersed, the stronger side can make better use of superior mobility, capturing threats, feinting attacks and the like.

Familiarity with actual examples will highlight these points.

**King and Pawn Endings.** The advantage of a Pawn in a King and Pawn ending is conclusive in something like ninety per cent of such endings. If the Pawns are distributed over the board, the defending King has an impossible task. Obviously he cannot stop a passed Pawn with his King in one sector, and parry a hostile attack on his Pawns in another sector. Generally speaking, this policy of *subjecting the weaker side to multiple threats* is a highly effective technique for breaking the back of the defense.

Sometimes, as has been mentioned, endings cannot be won because of Pawn weaknesses in the camp of the stronger side. Doubled, isolated Pawns, for example, are often useless for winning purposes. But sometimes a clever player will find an ingenious way. This was not the case with the position of Diagram 173. Black's doubled, isolated King Pawns seem to make any winning attempt futile. Black cannot advance a Pawn, and if he moves 1 ... K-B4; he is chased back by 2 K-K4. Black therefore gave up the position as a draw—only to have a master come along and demonstrate a clever win! Here is his method:

| 1 .... | P-K5ch! |
|---|---|

The Pawn *can* advance after all!

If, in reply, White tries 2 K-K3, PxP; 3 KxP, Black has made important progress: he has liquidated his weak, doubled, isolated King Pawn, and he can maneuver to win White's remaining Pawn. The play might proceed like this: 3 ... K-Q5; 4 K-N3, K-K6; 5 K-N2, K-B5; 6 K-R3, K-B6 and now White must lose his last Pawn. (*Zugzwang!*)

| 2 PxPch | K-B4 |
|---|---|
| 3 K-B3 | .... |

White has the opposition—the only way to prevent an invasion by Black's King.

| 3 .... | P-K4! |
|---|---|

Now *Black* has the opposition: White's King must give way, and the temporary equality of material will soon disappear.

| 4 K-Q3 | K-N5 |
|---|---|
| 5 K-K3 | K-B5 |
| 6 K-B2 | K-Q5 |
| 7 K-B3 | K-Q6 |

Again Black takes the opposition, and forces the White King to give up the protection of the King Pawn.

| 8 K-B2 | KxP |
|---|---|

And Black wins. In a few moves, he will pick up White's remaining Pawn.

The important lesson to be learned from this ending is that the materially stronger side profits from having a greater number of Pawns on the board. Change the position of Diagram 173 so as to remove both Knight Pawns, and the game is a draw.

Diagram 173                          Diagram 174

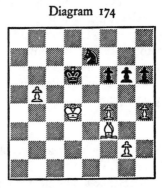

**Endings with Minor Pieces.** In minor-piece endings in which a player is a Pawn ahead, he must be on his guard lest excessive Pawn exchanges raise the possibility that the other side *can draw by giving up a piece for the remaining Pawn.*

The general technique is to strive for a passed Pawn which will keep the enemy occupied—and preoccupied. In Diagram 174 we see such a situation. White's Queen Knight Pawn is passed, and Black's King must keep an eye on it. At the same time, Black's King must not retreat to QB2, for then White gains further ground with K-B5. The Bishop for the time being supports the passed Pawn's advance, but this piece can be put to even better use.

    1 B-K4!                          . . . .

Very important: the Bishop is *centralized* and thereby attacks in *two* directions. It not only supports the passed Pawn; it also attacks Black's Knight Pawn. *This immobilizes Black's Knight.* We have seen that Black's King must not retreat. Hence all that is left for Black is a Pawn move. (If 1 ... K-K3; 2 K-B5, and White's King will support the passed Pawn to the promotion square.)

Which Pawn is Black to move? If he plays 1 ... P-B4; all his Pawns are placed on white squares and *consequently become vulnerable to the*

*attack of the Bishop.* Thus: 2 B-B3, N-B1; 3 B-Q5!, N-K2; 4 B-B7. Now
the Knight is tied down, and Black's King must give way. But after
4 ... K-Q2 comes 5 K-K5 followed by 6 K-B6 and Black's Pawns fall.
This is a characteristic variation: White's passed Pawn ties down
Black's forces, and yet the decision is forced on the King-side!

|  |  |
|---|---|
| 1 .... | **P-N4** |

Relatively best, as he gets the Pawn on a black square (out of the
Bishop's jurisdiction) and he exchanges Pawns—in the hope of a draw
by simplification.

|  |  |
|---|---|
| 2 **BPxP** | **BPxP** |

Note that 2 ... RPxP? is even worse; for then 3 P-R5! gives White
*an outside passed Pawn.* Black would then be helpless against two
widely separated passed Pawns.

|  |  |
|---|---|
| 3 **PxP** | **PxP** |
| 4 **P-N6!** | **P-N5** |
| 5 **P-N7** | **K-B2** |

With the Pawn on QN7 threatening to queen, Black's forces are
nailed to guard duty of the promotion square. *Now White's King is
free to invade on the King-side.*

|  |  |
|---|---|
| 6 **K-K5** | **P-N6** |
| 7 **K-B4** | **N-N1** |
| 8 **KxP** | **N-B3** |
| 9 **B-B3** | **N-Q2** |

Black cannot possibly contend against *two* passed Pawns.

|  |  |
|---|---|
| 10 **K-B4** | **K-Q3** |
| 11 **K-B5** | **K-K2** |
| 12 **B-B6!** | **N-N1** |

Forced.

|  |  |
|---|---|
| 13 **B-N5!** | **Resigns** |

Why? Black's Knight can no longer move, and only King moves are
available. But after 13 ... K-B2; 14 K-K5, K-K2; 15 P-N4, K-B2; 16
K-Q6, White wins the Knight and then obtains a Queen by promotion.
This ending shows perfect technique:

(1) The passed Pawn is used to tie down the defender's pieces.

(2) The *centralized King* advances against unprotected units once the blockade gives way.

(3) The defender finds that he cannot fight against two widely dispersed passed Pawns.

Note, by the way, the far-ranging activity of the Bishop in this ending.

**Rook vs. Minor Piece.** The advantage of the Exchange raises interesting problems of exploitation. A Rook is generally stronger than a minor piece and Pawn, and about equivalent to a minor piece and two Pawns. If the two Pawns are passed, connected and well advanced, the player with the Rook is likely to find himself at a disadvantage.

We saw early in this book (pages 38 and 39) that the Rook has more scope than a minor piece (Bishop or Knight). That is precisely why a Rook is stronger than a minor piece. To make the advantage of the Exchange tell, therefore, it is merely necessary to produce a position in which the Rook's superiority can be demonstrated.

Now here we have an advance in difficulty on the treatment of Diagram 174. There we started out with a passed Pawn. Here (Diagram 175) White does not have a passed Pawn. His task is to give the Rook mobility, and increase that mobility. What will be achieved thereby? The goal will be: *weakening Black's Pawns to the point where they can no longer be guarded adequately.* Once this happens, White will win one or more Pawns. It will then become possible for him to obtain passed Pawns.

Thus we see that the process is longer, but that the consequences are the same.

Here are the features of Diagram 175 that give us clues to future action:

(1) Black has three weak Pawns—his King Pawn and Knight Pawns. *They are weak because they cannot be guarded by Pawns.* They must be guarded by the Black King. This obligation imposes severe limits on the Black King's freedom of action.

(2) White's Rook has at present three open files. Nevertheless, he will strive to put even more open lines at the Rook's disposal.

(3) White's King must operate more aggressively and find some way of penetrating into Black's position.

This steady increase of one's mobility and command of terrain is standard procedure in any ending; but here it is more necessary than ever because White's King-side Pawns are worthless in every sense but the arithmetical one. His three Pawns to two on the King-side ought to crystallize into an eventual passed Pawn; but with his Pawns doubled and/or isolated, it is hopeless to try to evolve a passed Pawn exclusively from Pawn moves.

Hence White *must rely on the simultaneous increase of his own mobility and the cutting down of Black's command of the board.*

Now here is a fine example of economy of means: the Pawns are useless for fashioning a passed Pawn, but they can play an important role in creating new open lines for White: by playing P-QB4 and P-KB5 at the right moment, White will enormously increase his mobility.

Here is how the play continues from Diagram 175:

| | |
|---|---|
| 1 P-B4! | K-B3 |

Black is reluctant to capture, for after 1 ... PxPch; 2 KxP, White's King is aggressively poised for invasion at QN5.

| | |
|---|---|
| 2 R-N5 | B-K2 |
| 3 P-KB5! | .... |

Beautiful play. White gains considerable terrain for his forces.

| | |
|---|---|
| 3 .... | QPxPch |
| 4 KxP | PxP |
| 5 RxBP | B-B3 |

White's next task is to check on the sixth rank with his Rook. *This will drive Black's King back to the second rank.*

| | |
|---|---|
| 6 P-B4 | K-Q3 |
| 7 R-QN5 | K-B3 |
| 8 P-B5 | .... |

If now 8 ... B-R8; 9 R-N1, B-B3; 10 R-K1 followed by the invasion on the sixth rank: 11 R-K6ch, etc.

| | |
|---|---|
| 8 .... | B-N4 |
| 9 R-K5! | B-B3 |
| 10 R-K6ch | K-B2 |
| 11 K-N5 | B-Q5 |

The ideal position for Black, as his Bishop protects both Knight Pawns. But the superior mobility of the Rook must tell:

12 R-QB6ch!                    . . . .

A dagger pointed at Black's heart. Wherever he moves his King, he will have to lose a Pawn because *the Rook's attack is stronger than the Bishop's defense.*

For example: 12 ... K-N2; 13 R-B4, B-N7; 14 R-K4, B-B3; 15 R-K6, B-Q5; 16 R-Q6! Now Black cannot save his Bishop and also guard against 17 R-Q7ch or 17 RxNPch. (Thus, if 17 ... B-K6; 18 R-Q7ch wins the King Knight Pawn; or, if 17 ... B-N7; 18 RxNPch, etc.)

| 12 . . . . | K-Q2 |
|---|---|
| 13 R-B4! | B-B4 |

Moving the Bishop on another diagonal permits 14 KxNP.

14 R-KN4!                    . . . .

This wins the King Knight Pawn, as ... B-Q5 is impossible. A convincing demonstration of the Rook's superiority!

| 14 . . . . | K-K2 |
|---|---|
| 15 RxPch | K-B3 |
| 16 R-N6ch | KxP |
| 17 RxRP | Resigns |

For White can simply continue with 18 RxP, giving back the Exchange to reduce the game to a simple, winning King and Pawn ending.

In this endgame, handled with perfect technique by White, we see how the combined vertical-and-horizontal power of the Rook on open lines leaves the Bishop helpless.

Diagram 175                    Diagram 176

Diagram 176 shows another position in which a player (this time, Black) is the Exchange ahead in return for a Pawn. But this time, the player with the minor piece has the advantage. He has two connected passed Pawns, far advanced, and they are ably supported by his pieces. The Black Rooks are passive and have little scope. Actually, the imminence of queening and the superior activity of White's pieces leads to a much quicker win than the inexperienced player might anticipate:

1 B-B5! . . . .

This *pin* is troublesome to meet.

1 . . . . R-Q1

Releasing the *pin*, and protecting the threatened Knight.

2 R-Q1 . . . .

A new *pin*.

2 . . . . N-B2

Again the only plausible reply to get rid of the pin and save the Knight.

3 RxRch . . . .

Exchanges only heighten the power of the passed Pawns.

3 . . . . NxR<br>4 B-Q6 R-B2

Now the path is clear for one of the passed Pawns.

5 P-B7 RxQBP

The only move to stop the Pawn from queening.

6 BxR Resigns

With a piece ahead, *and* a passed Pawn still on hand, White must win easily.

The lesson taught by these four endings is that *promotion of passed Pawns is paramount*. If a Pawn is passed, it should be advanced. If there is no passed Pawn, it should be created from a Pawn preponderance. At the same time, the player with the material advantage must strive incessantly to increase his mobility and limit his opponent's freedom of action.

## POSITIONAL ADVANTAGE

To the uninitiated, the idea of winning the game from a position in which one does not enjoy an outright material advantage, seems to verge on the miraculous. That endings can be won in this fashion is, however, of the very essence of chess.

The formula is: *accumulate the positional advantages* until you force the win of material or otherwise exert coercion on your opponent. Transform this coercion into a definitive winning process. The best way to understand this advice is to see how it operates in actual play.

**King and Pawn Endings.** In Diagram 177, material is even. Yet any experienced player can see that White *must* win! Why?

White's King Bishop Pawn is passed and, unless it is constantly observed by Black's King, will advance to be promoted to a Queen. Thus we see that *Black's King is tied down to a specific defensive task*.

But, it will be objected, on the Queen-side Black has four Pawns to three. Can he not advance them and create a passed Pawn for himself? The answer: No! The fact that Black's Queen Bishop Pawn is *doubled* makes it impossible for him to obtain a passed Pawn. This sounds incredible, but there is a simple proof. Set up White's Queen-side Pawns at QR3, QN2 and QB3. Place Black's Queen-side Pawns at QR4, QN5, QB5 and QB4. It is quite out of the question for Black to make any use of his academically "extra" Pawn. He can play ... P-N6—blocking the position completely—or capture either Pawn, in which case White recaptures with his Knight Pawn. In the first case, three White Pawns blockade four Black Pawns. In the second case, two White Pawns blockade three Black Pawns.

To sum up: White has a passed Pawn which ties down Black's King to the defense; Black's Queen-side majority of Pawns is useless. Therefore White must win, and this despite the material equality. This is a perfect example of a *positional advantage*.

Play proceeds:

1 **P-B4**      ....

White sets up one of the formations in which Black's Queen-side majority is useless. Thus, if now 1 ... P-N4; 2 P-QB5 or 2 P-N3 and in either case Black's doubled Queen Bishop Pawn has the value of a single Pawn. *Black's positional disability (doubled Pawn) is so great that it is equivalent to being a Pawn down.*

As a matter of fact, after 1 ... P-N4; White has still another solution: 2 PxP, PxP; 3 P-N4! In that case, one White unit (the Knight Pawn) holds back two Black units (the Queen Rook Pawn and Queen Bishop Pawn). In other words, Black's positional disadvantage would persist but take a different form.

| 1 .... | P-B4 |
|--------|------|
| 2 P-N3 | P-R4 |
| 3 P-B5 | K-B2 |

Or 3 ... P-B3; 4 P-R4, P-N3; 5 K-B4, K-B2 (Black has no Pawn moves); 6 K-N5 winning the King Rook Pawn.

| 4 K-K5   | K-K2 |
|----------|------|
| 5 P-B6ch | K-B2 |
| 6 K-B5   | P-N3 |
| 7 K-N5   | P-B3 |
| 8 K-B5   | P-N4 |

Black struggles in vain. He will soon run out of Pawn moves. His last hope is that White will blunder: 9 PxP??, PxP and now Black's Pawns are *undoubled*. He threatens to obtain a passed Pawn with ... P-B5, with at least a draw and possibly a win!

**9 K-N5!**                            ....

White simply waits for the Pawn moves to be exhausted.

| 9 ....   | P-R5 |
|----------|------|
| 10 K-B5  | P-R6 |

A Pawn capture would not affect the outcome. Take this line: 10 ... RPxP; 11 RPxP, PxP; 12 PxP—Black is out of Pawn moves.

| 11 K-N5 | P-N5 |
|---------|------|
| 12 K-B5 | K-B1 |

Alas! Black has no choice, as the Pawn position is completely blocked: his King must give way.

| 13 K-N6 | Resigns |
|---------|---------|

Black must lose his King Rook Pawn, and his King will then be helpless against the two White passed Pawns. A classic example of a winning *positional advantage*.

Diagram 177                    Diagram 178

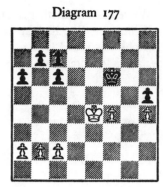

In Diagram 178, the situation is even more astounding. Here White is a Pawn ahead, and yet Black's *positional advantage* must win! Black, as we shall see, is in a position to get an outside passed Pawn which must win. Black proceeds in this manner:

    1 ....                         P-QN4!!

The reason for this move will become clear later on.

Now White's King cannot renounce the protection of his advanced King Pawn. Hence White must move one of the Queen-side Pawns.

    2 P-N3                       P-N4ch!!

The winning idea.

    3 PxP                        PxPch

Spurning this Pawn will do White no good. Thus, if 4 K-K3, KxP; 5 K-B3, P-N5ch!; 6 K-K3, P-N6; 7 K-B3, P-N7; 8 KxP, KxP. Now Black's King dashes across the board and wins the remaining White Pawns.

Here is the kernel of Black's winning idea: his King Knight Pawn is *an outside passed Pawn which entices White's King from the real scene of action:* the Queen-side.

    4 KxP                        KxP
    5 P-R4                       P-N5!

He foresees that he will win White's Knight Pawn, after which his own Knight Pawn must win the game.

    6 P-R5                       KxP

| 7 K-B6 | K-Q6 |
|---|---|
| 8 K-K6 | K-B6 |
| 9 K-Q6 | KxP |
| 10 K-B6 | K-B5 |
| 11 K-N6 | P-N6 |
| 12 KxP | P-N7 |
| 13 K-R7 | P-N8(Q) |

White hopes for the position of Diagram 168, but he is much too optimistic. Black's King is too near the scene of action.

| 14 P-R6 | K-B4 |
|---|---|
| 15 K-R8 | K-B3 |
| Resigns | |

If 16 P-R7, Q-N2 mate. Or 16 K-R7, Q-N6ch winning White's Pawn, followed by the standard checkmate with the Queen.

And now for the significance of 1 ... P-QN4!!: Black gained a whole move thereby for the queening of his Queen Knight Pawn, and also removed this Pawn from the range of the White King's later attack. Note that 1 ... P-QN4!! did not give White an opportunity to do anything of importance, as his King was chained to the defense of the King Pawn.

From these two endings, we can see the importance of *positional advantages.* Often they outweigh considerations of material gain. There are times when a player forgoes winning material, if that gain of material involves the renunciation of an existing positional advantage.

**Rook and Pawn Endings.** We have just seen that the nature of the Pawn position plays a vital role in King and Pawn endings. The fact is that the Pawn position plays a decisive role in *all* types of endings. A player whose Pawn position contains some weakness is halfway on the road to catastrophe: the enemy has a welcome object of pressure.

The soul of Rook play is mobility; and the mobility of the Rooks is in turn pretty much determined by the nature of the Pawn position. If you have weak Pawns, your Rook will be on the defensive; if your Pawns are safe and sound, your Rook is freed for aggression. If you can't indulge in outright attack, then you must seek counterattack. If counterattack is not available, then you are limited to passive defense. And if you are limited to passive defense, you are in a bad way.

This is convincingly exemplified in Diagram 179, where Black's Rook is strictly limited to defense of the weak Queen Rook Pawn. White's

Rook attacks, Black's Rook defends. Note also how aggressively White's King is posted. Black's King is on the defensive; a retreat will allow a further inroad by White's King, either K-K5 or K-B5 according to circumstances.

    1 **P-K4!**              ....

Forcing exchanges, whereupon White's Rook increases its mobility.

| | |
|---|---|
| 1 .... | **BPxP** |
| 2 **PxP** | **PxP** |
| 3 **KxP** | **R-R2** |

Black's Rook is so badly off that the pendulum maneuver .. R-R2-R1-R2-R1 is all that is available!

    4 **K-B4!**          **P-R3**

He cannot allow K-N5 and K-R6, which would create another weakness for him to defend.

| | |
|---|---|
| 5 **P-KR4!** | **K-K3** |
| 6 **K-N4** | **R-R1** |
| 7 **P-R5!** | **P-N4** |

If 7 ... PxPch?; 8 KxP and White wins a Pawn. (This is a good example of how *positional advantage* leads in due course to material advantage.)

With his last move, Black has avoided immediate disaster. Nevertheless, although material is even, he must be considered to have a lost game because of his three weak Pawns and his passive Rook position. Note also that in due course White will be in position to play **K-B5** intending a massacre by means of K-N6 and KxRP.

Against these positional factors, there is nothing that Black can do which will have any constructive value.

| | |
|---|---|
| 8 **P-N3** | **R-R2** |
| 9 **K-B3** | **R-R1** |
| 10 **K-K4** | **R-R2** |
| 11 **K-Q4** | **K-Q3** |
| 12 **K-K4** | **K-K3** |

As if drawn by a magnet, Black's King dodges back and forth to prevent an invasion by the White King.

13 **R-K5ch!**          . . . .

Despite the state of material equality, this move has the same decisive effect as 12 R-B6ch! on page 108. Black must give way now, leaving one wing or the other indefensible.

Thus, if 13 ... K-B3; 14 R-QB5, R-QB2; 15 P-R4!, K-K3; 16 P-N5! (a winning *pin!*), K-Q3; 17 RxBPch, RxR; 18 PxR, KxP; 19 K-B5 (the indicated invasion!) and the King and Pawn ending is dead lost for Black.

There follows, for example, 19 ... K-B4; 20 K-N6, K-N5; 21 KxRP, KxP; 22 KxP, P-R4; 23 P-R5 and White wins very easily. (Play out the remaining moves.)

| | |
|---|---|
| 13 . . . . | **K-Q3** |
| 14 **R-K8** | . . . . |

Again Black has a chance to reach a lost King and Pawn ending: 14 ... R-K2ch; 15 RxR, KxR; 16 K-K5! and the opposition wins for White; for if 16 ... K-Q2; 17 K-B6 leads to the confiscation of Black's King-side Pawns, and if 17 ... K-B2; 18 K-Q6 leads to a win on the Queen-side. Again and again you observe the inexorable power of *positional advantages*. All this time Black has retained material equality, and yet his resistance is approaching the crumbling stage.

| | |
|---|---|
| 14 . . . . | **P-B4** |
| 15 **R-Q8ch!** | . . . . |

Very neat: if Black's King goes to the second rank, 16 R-KR8! threatens 17 RxP in addition to the main menace of 17 R-R7ch. (Thus the motif of 13 R-K5ch! reappears!)

| | |
|---|---|
| 15 . . . . | **K-B3** |
| 16 **R-B8ch** | **K-N3** |
| 17 **RxP** | **R-R2** |
| 18 **R-K5** | **K-B3** |

Black cannot avoid further loss of material, as his Pawn position is as bad as ever.

| | |
|---|---|
| 19 **R-K6ch** | **K-N4** |
| 20 **K-B5** | **R-B2ch** |
| 21 **R-B6** | **Resigns** |

No matter how Black plays, he must lose at least another Pawn.

Black's downfall was caused by his faulty Pawn position, which *con-demned his own forces to passivity and offered objects for attack by the White pieces.*

Diagram 179                    Diagram 180

In Diagram 180, it is White who suffers from a Pawn weakness. Black has a King-side majority of Pawns (four to three) which in due course will result in a passed Pawn. White has a Queen-side Pawn majority (two to one); but, as his Queen Rook Pawn cannot advance, he can never obtain a passed Pawn.

Note, also, that Black's King is far advanced and (like the White King in Diagram 179) effectively *centralized*—poised for action on either wing. Black's positional advantages add up to a won game.

|       |        |       |
|-------|--------|-------|
| 1 ....  |        | P-R3  |
| 2 R-K3  |        | P-N4  |
| 3 PxP   |        | PxP   |
| 4 R-N3  |        | ....  |

White's Rook is passive.

|       |        |         |
|-------|--------|---------|
| 4 ....  |        | R-B1!   |
| 5 R-K3  |        | R-KR1!  |

Black's Rook will be more effective than ever on this *open file.*

|       |        |       |
|-------|--------|-------|
| 6 R-K2  |        | P-B5  |
| 7 PxP   |        | PxP   |
| 8 K-B2  |        | R-R7!  |

The aggressive Rook position, aided by Black's menacing Pawn mass, must win for him.

A plausible possibility is now 9 K-Q2, P-K6ch!; 10 PxPch, PxPch; 11 K-Q1, RxR; 12 KxR, K-K5 and the King and Pawn ending is quite lost for White. Even here the uselessness of his Queen Rook Pawn hounds him!

Thus, after 13 K-K1, K-Q6; 14 K-Q1, P-K7ch; 15 K-K1, K-K6; White *must* play 16 P-R4. Then, after 16 ... PxP; 17 P-N5, P-R6; 18 P-N6, P-R7; 19 P-N7 there follows 19 ... P-R8(Q) mate!

| 9 K-N3 | R-R6ch! |
|--------|---------|
| 10 K-N2 | R-Q6 |
| 11 R-B2 | P-B6 |
| 12 K-B1 | P-K6! |

At last he obtains the long-awaited passed Pawn.

| 13 PxPch | KxP |
|----------|-----|
| Resigns | |

White is quite helpless against ... P-B7 and the promotion of the advanced Pawn.

Both of these Rook and Pawn endings are enormously impressive because of their emphasis on the role of the Pawn position as *a determining factor for the outcome of the game.* In Diagram 179, Black's weak Pawn position foreshadows his defeat; in Diagram 180, the same comment applies to White's Pawn position.

**Endings with Minor Pieces.** In endings of Bishop against Knight, positional considerations again play a predominant role. The nature of the Pawn position, as in all endings, is our first big clue. If the Pawns are fairly well dispersed over the board, then the chances are that the Bishop will be preferable. The Bishop points in several directions at the same time; hence he controls more territory, travels faster, threatens more captures, than the Knight. *The Bishop is a long-range weapon, the Knight a short-stepping attacker.*

Another slight but noticeable advantage of the Bishop is that when favorably placed, he can deprive the Knight of possible moves. In Diagram 181, for example, White cannot play N-B5 or N-N5 because the squares in question are covered by the Bishop. This imposes a certain degree of passivity on the Knight which augurs ill for his future activities.

If the Bishop is theoretically preferable, his superiority is enhanced when he is supported by a King which is more aggressively posted than the opponent's King. This is the case in Diagram 181, where the Black King is poised for invasion in the event of a retreat on the part of the White King. This invasion may take the form of ... K-K4-B5-N5 attacking the King Rook Pawn, or ... K-B4-N5 attacking the Queen Knight Pawn.

This brings us to the last point to be noticed about Diagram 181. White's Queen Knight Pawn is weak *because it is not supported by a colleague—and must therefore be guarded, as the occasion arises, by White's King or Knight.* The need for such defense further emphasizes the passive character of White's formation—and passivity in the endgame is the first step towards defeat.

The weakness of the Queen Knight Pawn becomes even more glaring in view of the fact that it is on a white square, and hence a potential target for the Bishop.

Hence, despite the fact that material is even in Diagram 181, we conclude that White is probably lost. Black's Bishop is more mobile than White's Knight; Black's King is more aggressive than White's King; Black's Pawn position is sounder than that of White. (Bear in mind, by the way, that if White loses his Queen Knight Pawn, Black will have an outside passed Pawn—the Queen Rook Pawn—which will give him a sure win.)

Now back to Diagram 181. Black plays:

| 1 .... | **B-B1!** |
| 2 N-B3 | **B-R3ch!** |

This is the same kind of move as 12 R-B6ch! (page 108) and 13 R-K5ch! (page 115). White must renounce the protection of one wing or the other. He guards one wing, and the other wing is left in the lurch.

For example: after 3 K-K3, K-B4; 4 N-N5, K-N5; the Queen Knight Pawn is lost. There follows 5 NxBP, KxP; and White is defenseless against the irresistible advance of Black's passed Queen Rook Pawn.

3 **K-B3** ....

The alternative 3 K-K3, K-B4; 4 K-Q2 is instructive: 4 ... K-N5; 5 K-B2, B-N2!; 6 N-K1, B-Q4; 7 N-Q3ch, K-R6; 8 P-QN4, B-K5!; 9 P-N5, K-R5. Now Black continues with ... BxNch and picks up the Queen Knight Pawn. The advance of his passed Queen Rook Pawn is then decisive.

Thus we see that White's King *must* head for the Queen-side.

3   ...          **P-R3**

The immediate ... K-K5 is answered by N-N5ch.

4 **N-Q4**          **P-N3**

Preventing a future N-B5. Note the use of the Pawn moves *to take away squares from the Knight.*

| 5 N-B2 | K-K5 |
| 6 N-K3 | P-B4! |
| 7 K-Q2 | P-B5 |
| 8 N-N4 | P-R4 |
| 9 N-B6ch | K-B4 |

The Knight is taking a severe beating. If now 10 N-Q5?, B-N2! is decisive. Note the long-range effect of the Bishop's moves.

10 **N-Q7**          **B-B1!**

A new dilemma for White. On 11 N-B5, K-N5; 12 N-Q3, B-B4! wins at least a Pawn. Worse yet for White is 11 N-N8, B-N2!; 12 P-B3, K-K3! and Black wins the wretched Knight by .. K-Q3 and ... K-B2.

11 **N-B8**          **P-N4!**

And now, if 12 PxP, KxP; the Knight is trapped! There follows simply ... K-R3 and ... K-N2, with no escape for White.

| 12 P-N3 | NPxP |
| 13 PxRP | K-N5 |
| 14 N-N6 | B-B4 |
| 15 N-K7 | B-K3 |
| 16 P-N4 | .... |

Despair. If 16 N-N6, Black can try a different tack: 16 ... K-B6; 17 P-N4, B-B4; 18 N-K7, B-R2. Black will then pick up the Bishop Pawn and play to queen his own Bishop Pawn. Always the specter of Pawn promotion turns up after material gain by Black.

| 16 .... | KxP |
| 17 K-Q3 | K-N5 |

Now Black has a passed King Rook Pawn, the candidate for queening. The Pawn cannot be stopped, as White's forces are disorganized and far from the scene of action.

| 18 K-K4 | P-R5 |
| 19 N-B6 | B-B4ch! |

Driving off White's King.

| 20 K-Q5 | P-B6! |
| 21 P-N5 | P-R6 |
| 22 NxP | P-R7 |
| 23 P-N6 | P-R8(Q) |
| Resigns | |

This model ending illustrates to perfection the superiority of the Bishop on the open board. Black's *positional advantage* (greater mobility of the Bishop, better King position, and—above all—favorable Pawn position) enabled us to forecast a win while material was still even.

Diagram 181                 Diagram 182

Diagram 182 is an ideal example of the relatively infrequent cases where a Knight is definitely superior to a Bishop. This happens when the player with the Bishop has all or most of his Pawns placed on the same color as that of the squares on which his Bishop travels.

In Diagram 182, for instance, White's Bishop moves on white squares, and, as it happens, all his Pawns are on white squares. The consequences are (1) the Bishop's mobility is cut down very considerably, as *each Pawn occupies a square to which the Bishop cannot move;* (2) the Bishop is limited to the purely defensive function of guarding his Pawns; (3) *the black squares are not guarded by the White Pawns—*

and of course they cannot be guarded by the Bishop; (4) hence the black squares, as far as White is concerned, are great, gaping holes through which Black's forces can pour into the White camp; (5) the brunt of trying to stem this invasion falls to the lot of White's King—although the task of holding back the invaders is hopeless.

Note that this situation is ideal for the Black Knight. He changes the color of his square every time he moves, as we know. Hence, *by moving to one of the unguarded black squares, he is able to menace a White Pawn on a white square.*

The uninitiated may say, "True, White's formation is passive. But perhaps he can just manage to hold the line by dogged defense." To this the answer must be a brusque "No!" White's weakness on the black squares is one of those *positional disadvantages* which tell us that a player has a lost game even when material is still even.

One of the points in Black's favor here is the "change-of-front" policy. He can attack on either side, or both, at will. We have already observed in earlier endings that this change of front is a favorite policy with the attacker—one that, because of the attacker's superior mobility, is bound to reduce the defender to utter helplessness.

Black's procedure (from Diagram 182) is most instructive:

| 1 .... | P-R5! |

A profound idea. White cannot possibly reply 2 PxP, for then Black plays 2 ... KxBP and wins the Queen Pawn as well. The result is that White is left with a Queen Knight Pawn which lacks Pawn-protection.

| 2 B-Q1 | PxP |

If now 3 BxP, N-Q2 followed by 4 ... N-N3 and Black wins a Pawn.

| 3 PxP | .... |

Now that the Queen Knight Pawn has no Pawn-protection, the Bishop's defensive duties are increased. Note, by the way, the effect of *the Black King's aggressive position.* A move by White's King allows either ... K-K6 (demolishing White's King-side Pawns) or ... K-B6 (demolishing White's Queen-side Pawns).

| 3 .... | N-Q6 |
| 4 B-K2 | N-B5 |
| 5 B-B1 | .... |

Forced. White's passivity is a clear indication of his helplessness.

| 5 .... | N-R4! |
| 6 B-K2 | N-N6 |

Note how the Knight has a field day on the vulnerable black squares. The threat now is 7 ... NxB; 8 KxN, K-B6 and White can resign!

| 7 B-Q3 | P-R4 |
| 8 B-N1 | P-R5 |
| 9 B-Q3 | P-KB4 |
| 10 B-N1 | P-N4 |
| 11 B-Q3 | P-B5 |

White's Pawns are completely nailed down on both wings, and Black has completed all his preparations for the final phase.

| 12 B-N1 | N-B8ch! |
| 13 K-K2 | N-K6 |
| 14 K-B2 | K-B6 |
| Resigns | |

With his forces split and tied down, White cannot prevent the loss of his Queen Knight Pawn and the subsequent advance and queening of Black's Queen Knight Pawn.

Thus, Diagram 182 offers still another instance in which the Pawn position tells the story. White's weakness on the black squares, plus the helplessness of his Bishop and King—all these factors add up to a decisive *positional advantage* for Black. The moral of all these endgames is that the possibility of victory is apparent *before any material gain has been achieved*.

Endings in which each player has a Bishop in addition to some Pawns are of two types: (1) those in which both Bishops travel on the same-colored squares; (2) those in which the Bishops travel on opposite-colored squares. (If you find it difficult to visualize just what this means, you will find that Diagram 183 illustrates the first type of ending, while in Diagram 184 we have the second type.)

By this time, you will not be surprised to learn that the Pawn position is all-important in Bishop and Pawn endings. Material is even in Diagram 183, for example, but an experienced player can tell at a glance that Black is lost! Just what is the nature of White's *positional advantage* that makes this judgment so certain?

The clue to our appraisal lies, as usual, in the Pawn position. The mobility of Black's Bishop is reduced to almost nil by the Black Pawns on KB3, K4, QB4 and QR4. The first diagnosis of Black's position is therefore: *passivity*. But, in addition, Black has three isolated Pawns, two of them requiring protection by the Bishop. So Black is not only passive; he has Pawns which are direct targets of attack. Third, we notice that Black's Queen Bishop Pawns are isolated and doubled. This increases their weakness still more.

On the other hand, White's position is full of plus items. Most of his Pawns are on white squares, so that his Bishop's mobility is at a maximum. None of his Pawns are weak, so the Bishop is free to pursue an exclusively aggressive course. Another point in White's favor is that his Bishop can attack the hostile Black Pawns fixed on the squares QR5 and QB5. This alone assures White the initiative; and this is emphasized by the fact that his King will have a magnificent attacking square at QB4.

Thus we have the complete picture: *White attacks, Black defends.* But there will come a time when Black's defensive burden will be too great, and he will have to lose material. Play proceeds from Diagram 183:

| | | |
|---|---|---|
| 1 | K-B1 | K-B2 |
| 2 | K-K2 | K-K3 |
| 3 | K-Q3 | P-B4 |
| 4 | P-B3 | P-B5 |
| 5 | K-B4 | K-Q3 |

Both Kings have arrived at their indicated posts—White for attacking, Black for defending. White's next move foreshadows an intensified attack on the Pawn at QB5.

| | | |
|---|---|---|
| 6 | B-K1! | P-N4 |
| 7 | B-B2 | B-N3 |

The position is still in equilibrium; but now White prepares a new attack, for which Black does not have a corresponding defense.

| | | |
|---|---|---|
| 8 | P-B3! | P-R4 |
| 9 | P-N4! | . . . . |

The point: this *pin* forces the win of a Pawn.

| | | |
|---|---|---|
| 9 | . . . | RPxP |
| 10 | PxP | B-R2 |

11 **P-R5!**                    ....

Now Black's Bishop cannot return to N3. But since the Bishop must continue to guard the Queen Bishop Pawn, the Bishop is tied down to R2. The Black King cannot move, as this would likewise lose the Pawn. Hence Black is confined to nothing but Pawn moves. The noose is tightening around his neck.

11 ....                    **P-N5**

White can play 12 BxPch here, but after 12 ... BxB; 13 PxBch, K-B2 the position is a draw, as White's King cannot make progress. The same observation applies to 12 PxPch, etc. (Note that White turned down this possibility on the previous move as well. To maintain the pressure with material even is more important than to renounce the pressure for the sake of material gain.)

12 **P-R4**                    **P-N6**
13 **B-N1**                    ....

Now Black is in *Zugzwang*. He must move King or Bishop (his Pawn moves are exhausted), allowing the loss of a Pawn in a manner particularly unfavorable to him.

13 ....                    **B-N1**
14 **BxPch**                    **Resigns**

Quite right too, for after 14 ... K-B2; 15 P-R6, Black is helpless against the coming 16 P-R7, which wins a piece.

Note the incisive logic of White's play in this ending. He removed the weak Queen Rook Pawn and thereby obtained a passed Pawn; he concentrated on, and captured, the weak Queen Bishop Pawn; and he utilized this capture to make possible a decisive advance of his passed Pawn.

As has been remarked in the discussion of Diagram 171, endings with Bishops on opposite colors often lead to a draw. The inexperienced player dutifully accepts this maxim, not realizing that in a great many cases there are specific reasons why such endings can be won.

Take Diagram 184 as an example. Material is even, so we pass on to the Pawn position. This favors White very strongly. Black has a passed Pawn which is easily stopped, and the fact that his Queen Bishop Pawn is doubled and isolated practically leaves him a Pawn down.

Diagram 183                    Diagram 184

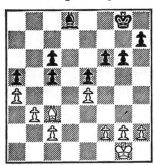    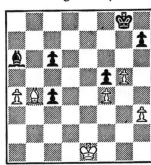

White, on the other hand, has an outside passed Pawn which really requires Black's attention. Furthermore, Black must watch out on the King-side for *the potential creation of a second White passed Pawn* by means of P-R4, P-R5 and P-N6. Thus the Black King and Bishop are reduced to that passivity which we know is likely to have ominous consequences.

Black has still one more weakness to guard: his King Bishop Pawn. This reminds us that White's King can come into action very rapidly by means of K-Q2-B3-Q4, etc.

Proceeding from the position of Diagram 184, White first sets up his threat to obtain a second passed Pawn.

|   |   |   |
|---|---|---|
| 1 P-R4! | K-B2 |
| 2 P-R5 | K-K1 |

Black keeps his King in the center, ready to go to either wing as required.

3 K-Q2                    ....

White's King threatens to march to QN6, winning Black's Bishop for the passed Queen Rook Pawn.

3 ....                    B-B1

Black decides to try to defend on the King-side with the Bishop, bringing the King to the Queen-side when necessary. Note what gymnastics Black must resort to, in order to guard his weaknesses.

|   |   |
|---|---|
| 4 K-B3 | B-K3 |
| 5 K-Q4 | B-B2 |

In order to provoke 6 P-R6?, after which Black can draw by playing his King to the Queen-side, and rendering the King-side secure with ... B-N3.

| 6 P-N6! | .... |
|---------|------|

This Pawn sacrifice leaves White a Pawn down, but it establishes his second passed Pawn. Black's defensive problem will be strained to the breaking point.

| 6 .... | PxP |
|--------|-----|
| 7 P-R6 | B-N1 |

The only move to prevent promotion of the passed King Rook Pawn.

| 8 K-K5 | .... |
|--------|------|

The familiar "change of front." The King attacks on the King-side, despite his previously foreshadowed support of the Queen Rook Pawn.

| 8 .... | B-R2 |
|--------|------|
| 9 K-B6 | .... |

With the fearsome threat of K-N7, enforcing the promotion of the King Rook Pawn.

| 9 .... | P-B4 |
|--------|------|

Desperation. White chooses the simplest reply.

| 10 B-Q2 | K-B1 |
|---------|------|

Black defends successfully on the King-side; but how about the deserted Queen-side?

| 11 P-R5! | Resigns |
|----------|---------|

For he cannot prevent the passed Queen Rook Pawn from queening.

Again we have seen an impressive example of the overriding importance of the Pawn position. At the very start of the ending, it is apparent that White must win because he has an outside passed Pawn on the Queen-side, and a potential passed Pawn on the King-side. This is a *positional advantage* which makes successful defense impossible.

**The Two Bishops.** If one Bishop is often superior to a Knight, it follows that two Bishops will be immensely powerful against two Knights. Two co-operating Bishops have a power which cannot be expressed in purely mathematical terms. You might think that two

Bishops are twice as strong as one Bishop; but there is more to it than that. Each Bishop, we know, commands only squares of one color; when both Bishops are available, they command *all* the squares.

And this combined action often leads to a dominant position which leaves the opponent with rather meager prospects. The Bishops command several lines at one time, they can switch quickly from one side of the board to the other, they can hound the enemy King, they can pounce on enemy weaknesses.

The superiority of the Bishop-pair is less marked when opposed by Bishop and Knight. Nevertheless, it is a rule of thumb, proved thousands of times in master play of the last eighty years, that the Bishop-pair is a mighty force. Few average players are acquainted with this power of the Bishops, and what they can accomplish. In 1880, few masters had a true understanding of the power of the Bishops. Today, most good club players are familiar with the concept. We are now reaching the point where even the learners can familiarize themselves with the power of the Bishops.

That power is clearly manifested in Diagram 185. White's Knight has no moves; N-N5? or N-B4? or N-N1? simply loses a piece. Nor will 1 N-B2 do, for then 1 ... BxN; 2 KxB, BxP wins a Pawn for Black, with a rather easy endgame win. (And this reminds us of one of the greatest strengths of the Bishop-pair: there often arise advantageous opportunities to exchange one Bishop to achieve a directly decisive advantage. Thus, here, White's trouble is that his Knight is as useless as a fifth foot, and yet the exchange of this useless piece loses the game anyway!)

But the Knight's helplessness is not the only significant point. We come back again to what we have recognized as the most important element in endgame play: the Pawn position. The weakness of White's Queen Pawn is immediately noticeable: Black's King attacks this Pawn, White's King defends it. Again, Black's Bishop at QR3 attacks the Queen Pawn, White's Bishop defends it. Again the usual picture: *the player with the weak Pawn has to defend in a cramped manner; the opponent attacks with superbly mobile forces.*

Now we can appreciate how Black's Bishops co-operate in Diagram 185: Black's Bishop at K6 stalemates the Knight; Black's Bishop at QR3 hammers away at the Queen Pawn. Again we have one of those positions which, because of the material equality, might be carelessly dismissed as fairly even. Actually, White totters on the brink of defeat.

Black begins (from Diagram 185):

|   1 ....  | B-QN4! |
|----|----|

We have already seen that White cannot move his King or Knight without losing material. However, if he tries 2 B-N1, there follows 2 ... B-R5! and now White's Bishop has no moves! And if 3 P-R3, B-B8!; whereupon Black wins the Rook Pawn and has an outside passed Pawn which wins quickly.

Another possibility is 2 B-N1, B-R5!; 3 K-K1, K-B6; 4 K-K2, P-Q5; and Black will win the Bishop with 5 ... K-N7. These variations give us some idea of the power of Black's game.

| 2 P-R4 | B-Q2 |
|----|----|

Now Black has a new target to aim at: White's Rook Pawn. Thus, if White tries 3 B-Q1, there can follow 3 ... B-R3; 4 N-B2, K-B6 followed by ... K-N5 and Black wins the Rook Pawn.

| 3 K-B3 | K-B6! |
|----|----|

White has little choice now: the Queen Rook Pawn must fall, however he plays.

| 4 KxB | P-Q5ch! |
|----|----|
| 5 K-K2 | .... |

On 5 K-K4, Black drives White's King away from the Queen Pawn with 5 ... B-B3ch! before playing ... KxB.

| 5 .... | KxB |
|----|----|
| 6 N-B4 | BxRP |

White is rid of the Bishops, his Knight is free—but at a price. He cannot hold back Black's Queen Rook Pawn.

| 7 N-K6 | B-N6! |
|----|----|
| 8 NxQPch | K-N7 |
| 9 N-N5 | P-R5 |
| 10 K-K3 | P-R6 |

Forcing White to part with his Knight.

| 11 NxP | KxN |
|----|----|
| 12 K-Q4 | K-N5 |
| Resigns | |

White sees no point in continuing, as the extra piece is bound to be too much for him. The continuation might be: 13 K-K4, K-B4; 14 P-Q4ch, K-Q3; 15 K-K3, K-Q4; 16 K-Q3, B-Q8 and in due course all of White's Pawns are lost, and Black queens a Pawn. The process can take another twenty moves, but the outcome is quite certain, so White resigns.

What happened here after 3 ... K-B6! was quite interesting. This was an example of the way in which one of the Bishops can be renounced for the purpose of gaining a decisive material advantage. It may seem inconsistent to give up one of the Bishops after their power has been stressed so emphatically. But the whole point of the gradual-constriction technique is to produce just such a position, where the opponent, at a loss for moves, finally reconciles himself to the loss of material.

Diagram 185                Diagram 186

Queen and Pawn endings are a severe test of anybody's patience. The Queen, having enormous range, is often capable of checking repeatedly, sometimes actually achieving a perpetual check, sometimes regaining lost material by a long-distance divergent check. A typical Queen and Pawn ending of forty moves may be made up of thirty checks and only ten moves which are to the point!

However, the example we are to study (Diagram 186) will stress the constructive aspects of the winning process in Queen and Pawn endings. It is Black's move. Although White has a passed Pawn, it is blockaded. Moreover, it is a weakness, because it is isolated. In fact, White's Queen-side Pawn formation is most unfavorable, as his Queen Knight Pawn is also weak. Black's Queen is effectively *centralized*, attacking both these weak Pawns—and the King Knight Pawn as well!

Once more the nature of the Pawn position determines the course of the game: *White's Pawn weaknesses condemn his Queen to passivity,* while Black's freedom from weakness allows his pieces to operate at their most effective level.

But the Pawn position tells us more: Black has a King-side Pawn majority of three to two which can be turned into a passed Pawn. And so we again have one of those positions in which material is even, and yet the downfall of the positionally weaker side is foreordained. The *positional advantage* is decisive.

Black proceeds from Diagram 186:

| | |
|---|---|
| 1 .... | P-B3 |
| 2 K-K3 | Q-B5 |
| 3 P-N3 | P-N4 |
| 4 PxP | PxP |

Black has been gaining ground steadily.

White does not care for 5 K-K4, Q-Q4ch; 6 K-K3, P-N5; 7 Q-K2, Q-N4ch; 8 K-B2 dis ch, K-Q4; when material loss will be inevitable. This inevitability of loss as the result of *positional disadvantage* conforms to the standard pattern we have observed repeatedly in these endings.

White's reaction is also standard. Instead of waiting for the ax to fall, he makes a stab at counterplay.

| | |
|---|---|
| 5 Q-KR2 | Q-N6ch |

Now 6 K-K2?? or 6 K-Q2?? would lose the Queen by a skewer check (how?); and if 6 K-B2, Q-N7ch; 7 K-N1, QxQch (the simplest); 8 KxQ, K-Q4; wins easily for Black; he picks up the Queen Pawn and Queen Knight Pawn as well.

| | |
|---|---|
| 6 K-K4 | P-N5! |

Threatens 7 ... Q-KB6 mate! White must lose a Pawn.

| | |
|---|---|
| 7 Q-K2 | QxKNP |
| 8 Q-B4ch | K-K2 |
| 9 Q-B8 | Q-KB6ch |
| 10 K-K5 | Q-KB3ch |
| 11 K-Q5 | Q-Q3ch |
| 12 K-K4 | Q-K3ch |
| 13 QxQch | KxQ |
| Resigns | |

The ending is quite hopeless for White, as his King must hold back the two connected passed Pawns. Black has many ways to win, for example: 14 K-B4, K-Q4; 15 K-K3, P-N6; 16 K-B3, P-R5; 17 K-K3, P-N7; 18 K-B2, P-R6; 19 K-N1, KxP; etc.

## SUMMARY

The great lesson that should remain with us after a study of these endings is that *the Pawn position is our best clue* as to what can happen, what should happen—if not what will actually happen. The Pawn position tells us who is vulnerable and why; it even dictates what procedures can and should be followed. Relying on the Pawn position makes planning easy. Without studying the Pawn position, we must necessarily play in haphazard style.

While the Pawn formation dictates the general plan of the game, it also tells us specifically what technique is to be used. In concentrating on weaknesses, the exploiting party must rely on *superior mobility*. The use of this weapon takes on an ever more coercive aspect until the opponent parts with material. A telling instance of the utilization of superior mobility is the "change-of-front" policy, whereby attacks are shifted from one part of the board to another, with a rapidity which the defender cannot possibly imitate.

With this emphasis on *positional advantage* in the endgame, goes the realization that the positional factor is just as potent in the middle game. This gives us our point of departure for the next chapter.

# 6

# STRATEGY IN THE MIDDLE GAME

Most players have no plan at the start of the game. They are attracted by simple one-move threats, or, worse yet, play by impulse or simply because it is their turn. To be able to plan is therefore of the greatest importance.

The possibility of planning is based on the presence of some landmark, some key, some clue, to the character of the position. To be able to recognize the presence of this guide is an enormous step forward, signifying a considerable increase in playing strength.

## PAWN FORMATIONS AND POSITIONAL ADVANTAGE

In Chapter 5 we came to recognize the value of studying Pawn formations for clues. We saw repeatedly that study of the Pawn formation indicates the presence of *positional advantages*. The simplified character of endgame positions, with just a few units on the board, makes it comparatively easy to perceive and appreciate the significance of the Pawn formation. In the middle game, where a great many more forces are involved, the processes of recognition and resultant planning are not so easy to work out. But, *precisely* because the middle-game positions are more complicated, the ability to plan—to bring order out of chaos—is all the more valuable.

The following concrete examples will best demonstrate how study of the Pawn formation aids us to plan our strategy in the middle game.

**The Overwhelming Pawn Center.** When a player is able to set up his two center Pawns abreast on the fourth rank, he assures himself of an excellent development for his pieces. Most players are aware of this. What is less well known is that this type of Pawn center has a very hampering effect on the opponent's development.

In Diagram 187, for example, White's overwhelming Pawn center makes it impossible for any Black pieces to move to KB4, Q4 or QB4. It is no coincidence that Black's pieces are huddled together on the last three ranks. The present lack of mobility is not quite conclusive; but what makes Black's cramped position catastrophic is that there is no prospect of *future* freedom.

White's position is free and comfortable. His Bishop on QN3 has a particularly effective diagonal pointing down to Black's vulnerable spot KB2. Nor can Black drive away the Bishop with ... N-QR4 (because of RxN); while ... B-K3 is equally impossible (because of P-Q5). White's freedom of action, as contrasted with Black's crabbed immobility, is based on the Pawn formation: White's Pawn center tells the story.

How is White to proceed; what is his plan? The process is pretty much the same as in the endgame phase: White increases his mobility, seeks new lines, tries to cut down Black's sphere of action more and more. The logical plan for White is to direct more pressure on the center, leading to the opening of a new line. The indicated move for this purpose is P-KB4. So White proceeds (from Diagram 187):

> 1 N-KN1                    ....

In order to make way for the King Bishop Pawn.

> 1 ....                     P-N4

With this desperate move he prevents P-KB4—but only for the time being. At the same time, ... P-N4 has weakened the Black King's position and deprived his Knight on KB3 of valuable Pawn support.

This is an instructive moment, very typical of such positions. The player with greater freedom threatens to seize even more terrain. The underdog tries to prevent him, *but only at the cost of creating an organic weakness in his position.*

> 2 P-N3!                    ....

White is stubborn. He will advance the King Bishop Pawn after all.

| | |
|---|---|
| 2 .... | B-B1 |
| 3 P-KB4! | NPxP |
| 4 NPxP | PxBP |
| 5 BxP/B4 | N-Q1 |

White's plans have worked out admirably. His position has become much freer, the opened King Bishop file beckons for occupation, and Black's King has forfeited much of his security with the departure of the King Knight Pawn.

|        |          |        |
|--------|----------|--------|
| 6      | R-KB1    | N-K3   |
| 7      | B-K3!    | ....   |

The simplest way.

|        |          |        |
|--------|----------|--------|
| 7      | ....     | B-N2   |
| 8      | R-B2     | N-R2   |
| 9      | QR-KB1   | ....   |

The relentless pressure accumulates on the King Bishop file. Black's pieces are still a jumbled mass.

|        |          |        |
|--------|----------|--------|
| 9      | ....     | R-K2   |
| 10     | Q-Q1     | Q-B1   |
| 11     | N/N1-B3  | B-K1   |
| 12     | N-R4!    | ....   |

Absolutely decisive, the threat being N-N6 (*fork* plus *pin!*), winning the exchange, or the Queen for a Rook and Knight.

Baffled by these troubles, Black commits a fearful blunder. This, by the way, is very common in bad positions. The difficulties, purely technical though they may be, seem to have a definite effect on a player's spirits, and this makes him prone to blunder.

|        |          |        |
|--------|----------|--------|
| 12     | ....     | N/K3-N4?? |

By further opening up the diagonal of White's Bishop on QN3, Black makes 13 ... PxN physically impossible in reply to White's next move.

|        |          |        |
|--------|----------|--------|
| 13     | N-N6!    | Resigns |

As Black's King Bishop Pawn is *pinned*, he must suffer ruinous loss of material. A very convincing example of the power of an overwhelming center.

In Diagram 188, White's overwhelming Pawn center is immediately seen to have a stifling effect on Black's game. His unfortunate Knights have no good squares, as ... N-K4 and ... N-B4 are impossible. Black has a bit of pressure on White's Queen Pawn, which, however, has more than ample protection. Black's Queen has no prospects. It is not clear what Black's Rooks can accomplish.

White, on the other hand, enjoys considerable freedom. He can now come to a radical decision by way of further utilizing his formidable Pawn center.

Diagram 187          Diagram 188

1 P-K5!          . . . .

This advance, made with gain of time, buries Black's King Bishop alive. It also prevents a future . . . N-KB3. Thus Black's mobility is still further reduced.

| 1 . . . . | Q-B2 |
| 2 N-N4 | Q-R4 |

He cannot very well allow his Queen-side Pawn position to be shattered after NxB.

3 Q-Q2!          . . . .

An interesting gain of time. The threat is 4 NxP!, QxQ; 5 NxPch followed by 6 NxQ, and White has won two Pawns.

3 . . . .          KR-K1

Now 4 NxP? loses a piece after 4 . . . QxQ; 5 NxPch, RxN; etc.

4 NxB          QxN

White has two Bishops against Bishop and Knight. His command of the board is more noticeable than ever.

5 B-B1!          . . . .

This harrying of the Queen is very painful for Black. He dare not play 5 . . . Q-N3; for then 6 P-Q5! (*double attack*) wins a piece: 6 . . . N/K3-B4; 7 P-QN4!, winning the *pinned* Knight.

6 . . . .          Q-R6

| 7 P-QN4! | N-B2 |
| 8 N-N5!! | N-N3 |

Black's pieces struggle vainly for good squares, and his Queen is out on a limb. Again, bear in mind that *the disorganized character of Black's position arises from White's Pawn monopoly of the center.*

| 9 N-K4! | Resigns! |

Now Black discovers to his horror that his Queen is trapped! The threat is 10 R-N3, Q-R5; 11 N-B5 winning the Queen.

The prettiest variation is 9 ... N-N4; 10 R-N3, Q-R3; 11 N-B5 and the Queen is trapped after all!

These two examples offer graphic evidence of the stifling pressure exerted on the enemy's game by an overwhelming Pawn center.

**Overwhelming Superiority in Development.** We usually think of superior development making itself felt in terms of quickly conclusive attack. The concept is easy enough to grasp: an attack *based on heavy local superiority* is bound to crush the defender. What happens more often, and is paradoxically less well known to the average player, is that a generally superior development will often create insoluble problems for the defender, without any specific danger to the defender's King.

In Diagram 189 we have such a position. (Although the Queens have been exchanged, this may legitimately be considered a middle-game position, as plenty of material is left on the board.) Pawn exchanges in the center have resulted in a situation which presents severe difficulties for Black. White controls the open Queen file and a beautiful long diagonal for his fianchettoed Bishop. (We "fianchetto" a Bishop when we develop it at KN2 or QN2.) *Black cannot mobilize his Queen-side forces;* and it is not apparent how this problem is to be solved.

White need make no violent threats. He merely goes about his business, developing more and more pieces. The burden of Black's lack of development becomes ever more crushing. Sooner or later—as in the previous endgame positions—something must give. Here is how the play proceeds from Diagram 189:

| 1 .... | P-QR4 |

Black sees a slim ray of hope for developing his Queen Rook.

| 2 B-B4 | R-R3 |
| 3 QR-B1 | .... |

Getting his last inactive piece into play with gain of time. Black cannot retreat his menaced Bishop; for example, if 3 ... B-K2; 4 RxB!, RxR; 5 BxP and White comes out a Pawn ahead!

|          |            |
|----------|------------|
| 3 ....   | P-QN3      |
| 4 N-Q3   | B-K2       |
| 5 R-B7   | ....       |

The Rook's occupation of the seventh rank has all its proverbial power. Now 5 ... B-Q1? loses a piece, while if 5 ... R-K1; 6 B-B6 wins at least the Exchange.

|          |       |
|----------|-------|
| 5 ....   | N-Q2  |
| 6 N-K5!  | ....  |

This well-calculated move forces some material gain. This is hardly surprising, in view of White's tremendous advantage in development and mobility.

|          |       |
|----------|-------|
| 6 ....   | NxN   |
| 7 RxB    | N-N3  |
| 8 R-B7   | ....  |

Now, if 8 ... NxB; 9 PxN and White threatens to win a whole piece by simply doubling Rooks on the Queen Bishop file!

|          |       |
|----------|-------|
| 8 ....   | P-K4  |
| 9 B-K3   | P-B4  |

If he tries 9 ... B-K3 (to get the Bishop out—at last!—) there follows 10 B-N7, R-R2; 11 BxP winning the Exchange! White's enormous advantage in mobility could not be demonstrated more dramatically!

|              |       |
|--------------|-------|
| 10 B-Q5ch    | ....  |

White's reason for driving the King into the corner will soon become clear.

|                  |       |
|------------------|-------|
| 10 ....          | K-R1  |
| 11 R/Q1-QB1      | ....  |

This wins a piece.

|          |       |
|----------|-------|
| 11 ....  | P-B5  |

Black's attacked Bishop cannot move!

| 12 RxB | PxB |
| 13 RxRch | NxR |
| 14 R-B8 | PxPch |
| 15 KxP | Resigns |

Black is unable to protect his *pinned* Knight. This example has shown in the most graphic fashion how a telling advantage in development can be exploited relentlessly.

Diagram 189                  Diagram 190

In Diagram 190, Black's plight is not so glaring; yet his position has the drawback of being without dynamic features. The position is deceptive: White's superiority does not seem too menacing, but the fact is that Black is constantly presented with a series of disagreeable "either-or" choices, resulting in spineless decisions that lead to an inevitable deterioration of his position.

| 1 N-Q5 | Q-Q3 |

White's Knight is powerfully established at Q5 and is therefore an unwelcome intruder. But if 1 ... NxN; 2 PxN, Black's King Pawn is exposed to attack and a fine diagonal is opened for White's Bishop at Q3.

| 2 B-KN5 | N-K1 |
| 3 Q-B2 | B-Q1 |

White naturally declines this invitation to exchange; he prefers to let Black's pieces stew in their own juice.

| 4 B-K3 | P-QN3 |
| 5 B-QN5! | .... |

Threatening to win a Pawn by 6 BxN and 7 NxKP and thus gaining time for the coming occupation of the Queen file.

| 5 .... | B-N2 |
|---|---|
| 6 QR-Q1! | .... |

With the immediate tactical threat of 7 NxNP (*discovered attack*) winning the exchange and a Pawn. More important, however, White seizes control of the only open line. Black cannot dispute this control because he has two pieces skulking on the back rank.

| 6 .... | Q-K3 |
|---|---|
| 7 R-Q2! | .... |

White prepares to occupy the open file in force. *This accumulation of power in an open file* is a characteristic maneuver with which the student should be familiar. The increment of force will automatically pay dividends later on.

| 7 .... | R-B1 |
|---|---|
| 8 Q-Q1 | .... |

Note throughout how careful White is to avoid P-B4. In that case Black could play ... N-Q5 and block White's pressure on the open Queen file. But the placement of White's Pawn on QB3 makes this impossible. This is an instance of the lasting importance of the Pawn formation in the appraisal of a given position.

| 8 .... | P-KR3 |
|---|---|
| 9 P-R3 | N-B3 |

Black wants to play ... B-K2 and ... KR-Q1 to dispute White's control of the file. Yet the move, plausible as it seems, loses a Pawn. This is typical of positions in which the defender tries to shake off unrelenting pressure.

| 10 NxNch | BxN |
|---|---|
| 11 BxRP! | .... |

This sham sacrifice wins a Pawn, for if 11 ... PxB; 12 R-Q6, Q-K2; 13 R-Q7 and White regains the piece, remaining a Pawn to the good.

| 11 .... | KR-Q1 |
|---|---|

Now at last Black is ready to fight for the file, but the damage is done: he is a Pawn down.

| | |
|---|---|
| 12 B-N5 | RxR |
| 13 QxR | R-Q1 |
| 14 Q-K2 | BxB |
| 15 NxB | Q-R3 |
| 16 Q-K3! | . . . . |

He protects the Knight because he wants to play B-B4, menacing Black's KB2 square. White is justified in carrying on an aggressive policy, because it will yield much quicker results than the necessarily slow process of exploiting his Pawn advantage.

| | |
|---|---|
| 16 . . . | N-R4 |

To prevent B-B4.

| | |
|---|---|
| 17 P-QN4! | PxP |
| 18 RPxP | B-B3 |
| 19 B-R6! | . . . . |

If now 19 . . . N-N2; 20 P-N5 wins a piece. So Black's reply is forced.

| | |
|---|---|
| 19 . . . . | B-N2 |
| 20 B-B1! | . . . . |

This temporary retreat is far stronger than the colorless 20 BxB, NxB.

| | |
|---|---|
| 20 . . . . | N-B3 |
| 21 B-B4 | . . . . |

White has had his way after all. The pressure on Black's KB2 square will decide the issue.

| | |
|---|---|
| 21 . . . . | R-Q2 |
| 22 NxP! | . . . . |

Beginning a very pretty combination. White relies on a *pin*.

| | |
|---|---|
| 22 . . . . | RxN |
| 23 QxQ | PxQ |
| 24 R-Q1! | Resigns |

So White triumphs on the open Queen file after all!

Black has no good move against the threatened 25 R-Q7. Thus, if 24 . . . K-B1; 25 BxR, KxB; 26 R-Q7ch (*double attack*), followed by 27 RxB. Or 24 . . . B-B1; 25 R-Q6, N-K2; 26 R-KB6, winning the *pinned* Rook.

These two examples will suffice to illustrate the intense power of superior development. The chief impression left by these examples is that an advantage in development, with the slightest encouragement, will generate new advantages, new pressures, new means of exploitation.

**Maneuvering Against Weak Pawns.** One of the most significant aspects of the Pawn formation, as we came to see when we were studying endgames, is the weak Pawn. Once a player is burdened with a weak Pawn, it is almost impossible for him to rid himself of the weakness. It is an *organic* weakness. It has the same relation to a player's position as a bad heart or an ulcer has to the human body. Because this weakness is usually fixed and immutable by its very nature, it makes an ideal target for exploitation by the opponent.

The most common type of Pawn weakness is the isolated Pawn. This, as the name indicates, is a Pawn which has no Pawn neighbors. Thus, in Diagram 191, Black's King Pawn and Queen Bishop Pawn have disappeared. Now Pawns are the best, because the cheapest, protectors. When the Pawn protectors have disappeared, an isolated Pawn is created, and such a Pawn must of necessity be guarded by pieces.

This is a very troublesome situation for the defender. His pieces are relegated to the menial task of guarding a "mere" Pawn, which implies a qualitative reduction in their efficiency. And, as we have seen in the endgame examples, the task of defending produces a state of passivity which can have dangerous consequences. For the attacker, on the other hand, the isolated Pawn is made to order. His pieces are active, menacing, exerting their utmost power as they aim at the isolated Pawn. Above all, they exercise constraint on the enemy, and there is a world of difference between the active, threatening attitude of the attacker, and the cramped, intimidated reaction of the defender.

All these ideas appear "in the flesh" in Diagram 191, where we see Black burdened with an isolated Queen Pawn.

Black's isolated Queen Pawn has to be protected by pieces. At the moment, Black's Rook, Knight and Bishop are devoted to its welfare. As for White, he has Queen, Rook, Knight and Bishop trained on the weak Pawn. With four units attacking the Pawn and three units defending it, one would take for granted that White can win the Pawn directly. However, Black has counterplay: if 1 NxP, NxN; 2 BxN, BxB; 3 RxB, RxR; 4 QxR, Q-B8ch and 5 ... QxNP.

White expects to win the Queen Pawn outright, and he naturally avoids parting with his healthy Queen Knight Pawn in exchange for the weakling.

1 K-N2                          ....

This prevents the Black Queen from coming to QB8 with a check. Black's Queen Pawn is now definitely menaced and must be defended directly.

1 ....                         Q-K4

Equally unavailing is 1 ... Q-B3 because of 2 B-Q1!, followed by 3 B-N3 and 4 P-B4!, with 5 P-B5! to come, driving off the defending Bishop.

2 P-N4!                         ....

Now Black's Rook can no longer defend the weak Pawn.

2 ....                          R-B5
3 NxP!                          ....

This has to be calculated very carefully, for if now 3 ... RxR; 4 PxR?, NxN!; 5 PxQ, N-B5ch (*forking* check) followed by 6 ... NxQ and Black has won a piece!

However, on 3 ... RxR; White interpolates 4 NxNch! Then, after 4 ... QxN; 5 PxR White is a Pawn to the good.

3 ....                          BxN
4 RxB                          R-B6

Or 4 ... NxR; 5 QxR, N-N3; 6 Q-K4!, and White wins a second Pawn.

5 RxQ                          RxQ
6 R-R5! and wins

White picks up a second Pawn, leaving him with an easy endgame win. This is a good example of the vulnerability of an isolated Pawn.

The backward Pawn is another type of weakness. This is a Pawn on an open file whose neighbors have advanced, so that it is left without Pawn protection. In Diagram 192, Black's Queen Bishop Pawn is a backward Pawn. White proceeds to put more pressure on it than Black can withstand. As a matter of fact, in the diagram position, with White to move, the Pawn is definitely lost; but the average player can hardly be expected to see that at a glance. However, the winning process is logical, instructive, and bound to be useful.

Diagram 191                    Diagram 192

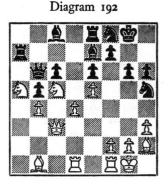

**1 B-K4!**                    . . . .

Now the weak Queen Bishop Pawn is attacked twice. Black naturally brings up his reserves.

    1 . . . .                    **R-B2**
    **2 Q-B3!**                    . . . .

A third attack on the weak Pawn, and now it must fall. To emphasize the weakness of a backward Pawn, let us imagine that Black's Queen Knight Pawn (now at QN4) were at QN2. In that case Black's Queen Bishop Pawn would not be backward, and would be perfectly secure. But, as matters stand, the weak Pawn is lost.

    2 . . . .                    **B-Q2**

A third defender, but he is immediately liquidated.

    **3 NxB**                    **NxN**

And now the Pawn falls.

    **4 NxP and wins**

Black has no compensation for the lost Pawn. White will win in due course.

In Diagram 193, we have another example of a backward Pawn. This time it is White's Queen Bishop Pawn that is backward, and Black has doubled his Rooks on the open Queen Bishop file for a crushing frontal assault on the backward Pawn.

However, Black has a problem: if White can play N-N2, and then

N-B4, he will be able to mask the weakness of the backward Pawn. It requires very fine play on Black's part to forestall this excursion of the White Knight.

|       1 ....       |       Q-B4!       |

This threatens to win a piece by ... QxQ (White's Queen Bishop Pawn is *pinned*).

Nor can White reply 2 N-N2, because of 2 ... RxP!; winning the weak Pawn right off.

The reply 2 QxQ is also inadequate because of the simple rejoinder 2 ... NxQ; and the weak Queen Bishop Pawn goes lost directly. White manages to find the best reply.

|   2 R-K4    |   N-Q4!   |
|   3 N-N2    |   ....     |

And now, if only White could play N-B4, he would be safe.

|       3 ....       |       N-B6!       |

Unfortunately for White, he must capture the Knight, for if 4 R/K4-K1?, QxQ; 5 NxQ, N-R7; and Black wins the weak Queen Bishop Pawn.

Worse yet for White is 4 R/K4-K1?, QxQ; 5 PxQ, N-K7ch! winning the Exchange by a *forking* check, unless White prefers 6 RxN, RxRch—which still costs him the Exchange.

|   4 BxN    |   RxB    |
|   5 Q-K2   |   B-R3!  |

Driving off the defender of the weak Queen Bishop Pawn. White is now reduced to desperation, and tries to complicate matters.

|   6 P-N4     |   Q-B3              |
|   7 R-K8ch   |   RxR              |
|   8 QxRch    |   K-N2             |
|   9 R-B1     |   RxBP and wins    |

White has no compensation for the lost Pawn, and Black must win in due course. This is a highly instructive example, for it shows that the weakness does not always fall of its own dead weight; there are times when really ingenious play is required to make the advantage tell.

A glance at Diagram 194 shows that White's Pawn structure is shaky.

Diagram 193                     Diagram 194

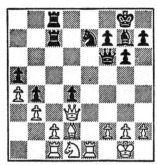    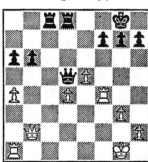

His advanced King Pawn is supported by the Queen Pawn—a frail reed, as it is a backward Pawn. In addition, White's Queen Rook Pawn is isolated. From previous study of weak Pawn positions, we can guess that White's defensive task will prove too much for him.

Black begins from the position of Diagram 194 with the most logical move:

1 ....                    **R-B5!**

This attacks the weak Queen Pawn and the weak Queen Rook Pawn as well. White's choice of a defensive move is a difficult one.

Thus, if White tries 2 R-Q1 (intending to answer 2 ... RxRP with 3 QxP), Black replies 2 ... Q-B3! guarding his own weak Queen Knight Pawn, putting further pressure on White's Queen Rook Pawn and, above all, threatening ... R-B7; attacking White's Queen and menacing mate at the same time.

|   |   |
|---|---|
| 2 QxP | RxQP |
| 3 RxR | QxRch |
| 4 QxQ | RxQ |

At first sight, the impression prevails that White has come off not too badly. But then we observe that White's King Pawn has become isolated and must be lost; for 5 R-K1 (to defend against Black's next move) is answered by 5 ... RxP.

|   |   |
|---|---|
| 5 K-B2 | R-K5 |

So White's weaknesses were too much for him after all!

|   |   |
|---|---|
| 6 K-B3 | RxKP |

Black has won a Pawn and should win the ending.

In these four examples of attack against weak Pawns, we have seen the same principles at work as in the previous endgame examples. *Weak Pawns are a burden to their defender, and condemn his pieces to passivity.* Even passive defense, laborious and necessary though it is, often proves to be love's labor lost. In short, weak Pawns are a welcome target. Their presence should be recognized, their meaning assimilated, and the attack formulated accordingly. Thus planning shapes itself in our minds almost without conscious effort. With practice and experience, there comes a time when observing the weakness is almost synonymous with plotting its subsequent downfall. That is the essence of good chess.

**Maneuvering Against Weak Squares.** That there can be such a thing as a weak Pawn is not too difficult to understand; but a "weak square" is rather mysterious. Do we mean that the wood, plastic or cardboard of which this or that square is made, is weak? Not at all. The concept of the weak square plays a definite role in chess strategy, as we saw in the endgame which evolved from Diagram 182.

When we turn to Diagram 195, we see that White's QB4 square is weak. (Before you read what follows, it will be a good idea to reread the discussion of Diagram 182.) This weakness of the QB4 square is based on the fact that (1) it cannot be commanded by a White Pawn and (2) it lacks protection by the White Bishop that moves on white squares. That Bishop has disappeared as the result of an earlier exchange.

Incidentally, White suffers from other disabilities: his Queen Bishop Pawn is backward on an open file and is therefore also weak. Black can menace it by massing his forces on the open Queen Bishop file, and also by bringing one Knight to K5 and the other to Q4. What makes the situation all the more critical is that most of White's Pawns are on black squares, which creates an additional white-square weakness—a kind of "sympathetic toothache" in relation to the weakness of White's QB4 square.

White's remaining Bishop—a black-square operator—is of no earthly use as regards the job of guarding the white squares. Worse yet, this Bishop is definitely hampered by White Pawns on black squares.

We conclude our summary by observing that Black, who has no weaknesses, will have the initiative and an aggressive policy. White, who has a weak Pawn and weak squares, will be strictly on the defensive.

| 1 .... | Q-B5! |
|---|---|

Black's first task is to keep White's weaknesses firmly fixed. If White is given the opportunity, he will play B-R3 and then QR-B1 and try to advance P-B4.

By physically occupying the weak square, Black makes certain that the weaknesses will persist.

| 2 QxQ | .... |
|---|---|

If White avoids the exchange (say by 2 Q-B2), his weaknesses still remain and his Queen is purely passive for the rest of the game.

| 2 .... | RxQ |
|---|---|

Note that this Rook cannot be driven away by White.

| 3 P-QR4 | N-Q4 |
|---|---|

Black attacks, White must defend.

| 4 B-Q2 | N/Q2-B3 |
|---|---|
| 5 KR-B1 | KR-B1 |
| 6 R-R3 | N-K5 |

The previous note still applies. Note that all the Black pieces are on white squares—rather cruelly emphasizing the fact that these squares are completely beyond White's reach.

| 7 B-K1 | P-B4 |
|---|---|
| 8 P-R5 | P-QN4 |
| 9 R-N1 | P-QR3 |
| 10 R/N1-N3 | K-B2 |
| 11 P-N3 | P-R3 |
| 12 P-R4 | K-N3 |

Now White has no Pawn moves left, nor can he move any of the defenders of his weak Queen Bishop Pawn. Black's iron grip on the white squares has, if anything, been intensified by 8 ... P-QN4. The situation now arrived at is characteristic of positions in which an organic weakness exists: *the defender is steadily pushed back until his mobility reaches the vanishing point.*

White must now move his King, but where? If 13 K-B1 (or 13 K-N2), Black plays ... N-K6ch followed by 14 ... N-QB7 with crushing effect.

| 13 K-R2 | P-N5! |
|---------|-------|

This dynamic thrust concludes the period of peaceful maneuvering.

| 14 PxP | R-B7 |
|--------|------|
| 15 R-K3 | .... |

The deadly *pin* by Black's Rook forces this win of the Exchange.

| 15 .... | NxR |
|---------|-----|
| 16 RxN | R-N7 |
| 17 K-N2 | R/B1-B7 and wins |

Black's combination of positional and material advantage is overwhelming. What was important and characteristic about this example was that *Black's pressure on the organic weakness led to irresistible pressure on White's game as a whole.*

Diagram 195          Diagram 196

In the position of Diagram 196 we have Bishops on opposite colors. This reminds us of Diagram 184, for there, as here, White had a Bishop which was very strong on the black squares, while Black had a Bishop which was hemmed in by its own Pawns on white squares.

In the play from Diagram 184, White's King had undisputed sway over the black squares because the Black Bishop had no control over these squares. Similarly, in Diagram 196, White has undisputed sway over the black squares. But White has an additional advantage: he gets the jump in occupying and mastering *the only open line:* the Queen Bishop file. As Black needs one more move to get out his Bishop, his laggard development makes it impossible for him to fight for the open file. From what we have said, White's first move "plays itself":

|   |   |
|---|---|
| 1 KR-B1!          . . . . | |

Thus seizing the open Queen Bishop file and also threatening QxNP. (The immediate 1 QxNP is a mistake because of 1 ... B-R3 winning the Exchange.)

| 1 . . . . | B-R3 |
| 2 R-B7!          . . . . | |

Greatly increasing his command of the board. He not only controls the only open file, he also dominates the seventh rank as well.

| 2 . . . . | Q-K1 |
| 3 Q-R3!          . . . . | |

More play on the black squares.

If Black replies 3 ... P-R5, White strengthens the pressure with 4 R-K7, Q-N3; 5 B-K5 (still the weak-square motif!), R-B2; 6 R-QB1 and Black is on the point of collapse. For example: 6 ... R-QB1; 7 RxRch, BxR; 8 R-K8ch and mate next move.

| 3 . . . . | B-B1 |
| 4 Q-Q6!          . . . | |

Still on the weak squares! Comparing this position with Diagram 196, we can see how much Black's situation has deteriorated.

| 4 . . . . | R-B2 |
| 5 R/R1-QB1 | B-Q2 |
| 6 R-N7 | P-R3 |
| 7 P-KR3!          . . | |

Before engaging in further Rook maneuvers, White removes any danger of a possible *back-rank mate*.

| 7 . . . . | R-QB1 |
| 8 RxR | BxR |
| 9 R-N8          . . . . | |

Black's position is more difficult than ever. He dares not play 9 ... R-Q2, for instance, as then the *pin* on Black's Bishop becomes decisive: 10 Q-B5, R-Q1; 11 B-B7!, R-Q2; 12 BxP and it is all over.

| 9 . . . . | K-R2 |
| 10 Q-B5! | R-B1 |

11 **Q-B2ch!**                    ....

Black's position becomes ever more critical. If now 11 ... K-N1; 12 B-Q6! wins at once.

Also if 11 ... P-N3; 12 Q-B7ch, K-N1; 13 B-K5! (threatens mate), Q-B2; 14 RxB winning a piece.

Note White's instructive—and relentless—play on the weak black squares.

11 ....                           **K-R1**

The neatest variation of all is 11 ... Q-N3; 12 RxB!, RxR; 13 QxR and now 13 ... Q-N8ch does *not* force a *back-rank mate*—thanks to 7 P-KR3!

12 **B-Q6!**                      ....

Still operating on the weak black squares!

12 ....                           **R-N1**
13 **B-K5!**                      ....

Planning a clever finish.

13 ....                           **P-R5**
14 **RxB!**                       **QxR**
15 **Q-N6!**                      **Resigns**

Black is helpless against the threat of 16 QxRP mate (his King Knight Pawn is *pinned*).

Again, thanks to 7 P-KR3!, Black has no *back-rank mate* in the final position.

These two examples tell us a great deal about the play against weak squares. For the weakness of such squares is a kind of "psychosomatic" ailment; it is always accompanied by other symptoms, other weaknesses. The player who is exploiting these weaknesses has at his disposal the "change-of-front" policy which worked so successfully in the earlier endgames. Thus, in the play evolving from Diagrams 195 and 196, the player with the initiative attacks first on the Queen-side, then on the King-side, and shifts back and forth as he feels out the weak spots.

The defender, necessarily hampered in mobility, is not so spry. Sooner or later, he finds that the threats are too much for him.

**Encirclement Maneuvers Against Weaknesses.** We have spoken of weak Pawn and weak squares as "organic weaknesses." They are *structural* defects, inherent in the nature of a given position. There are times, to continue the medical analogy, when they induce a creeping paralysis in the defender's position. In such situations, the aggressor's excess control of the board is such that he can proceed to crush and stifle the last bit of resistance. These brutal terms are used advisedly, for the process is one of reducing the defender to complete immobility.

In Diagram 197, the full gravity of Black's situation is not immediately apparent. The Achilles' heel of his position is the Queen Knight Pawn; should it fall, White has a powerful, advanced, passed Pawn on the sixth rank. In addition, the position of White's Rook on the seventh rank would in itself be decisive.

|  |  |
|---|---|
| 1 Q-B3! | P-B3 |

Forced; but now the whole second rank is opened up for later attack. Another point to be noticed about this position is that White's Queen Pawn is passed. At this stage it is adequately blockaded; but, should Black's forces become overextended, the Pawn will advance ruthlessly.

|  |  |
|---|---|
| 2 N-Q2! | .... |

The gradual concentration of White's forces on the Queen-side is most instructive.

|  |  |
|---|---|
| 2 .... | N-B5 |

Threatening the murderous *forking* check ... N-K7ch. But this is easily parried.

|  |  |
|---|---|
| 3 K-B1 | N-K3 |

Black strives feverishly to transfer his forces to the Queen-side as well. The reply 4 PxN is feeble because of 4 ... QxN.

|  |  |
|---|---|
| 4 N-B4! | Q-Q2 |
| 5 R-R5! | N-Q5 |
| 6 B-R4! | .... |

Note the steady infiltration of White's forces.

|  |  |
|---|---|
| 6 .... | Q-B1 |
| 7 R-R7 | .... |

It has taken very few moves to demonstrate the hopelessness of Black's game. His Queen Knight Pawn is untenable, as he cannot play ... R-Q2.

| 7 .... | P-B4 |
|--------|------|
| 8 N-R5 | K-R1 |
| 9 NxP | PxP |

Black's position is in a state of collapse. Thus, if he tries 9 ... R-N1; there follows 10 P-Q6, B-Q1; 11 P-Q7, Q-N1; 12 QxP, etc.

| 10 NxR | BxN |
|--------|-----|
| 11 P-N7 | Resigns |

On 11 ... Q-B2; 12 B-B6 is one of White's many winning lines. It is always interesting to look into the basis for an encirclement strategy. Black had weaknesses, White did not. White's Bishop was mobile, Black's was not. White's Rook was aggressive, Black's was passive. White's Queen supported the invasion, Black's Queen was deluged with minor defensive chores. Add up these factors, and the total is: encirclement.

Diagram 197          Diagram 198

Diagram 198 has certain familiar features: Black's black squares are painfully weak, all his Pawns being on white squares.

Black's Bishop is consequently reduced to virtual immobility. And, as we know from the endgame following Diagram 182, the White Knights have tremendous power.

White must seek to increase his command of the board. This may be done by P-N5 or by P-R4-5. Both of these advances would create new lines of invasion for his Rooks. However, neither maneuver is feasible at the moment, so White increases the pressure in other ways:

     1 R/R3-KB3!      ....

Threatening 2 NxB, RxR; 3 RxR, RxB; 4 R-B8ch, K-N2; 5 R-N8 mate!—a graphic proof of Black's helplessness.

|     |           |         |
| --- | --------- | ------- |
| 1   | ....      | NxN     |
| 2   | RxN!      | RxR     |
| 3   | KPxR!     | ....    |

This move creates a far-advanced, securely guarded passed Pawn. It also opens White's K5 square for powerful occupation by his King or Knight.

|     |           |         |
| --- | --------- | ------- |
| 3   | ....      | R-K1    |
| 4   | N-B7ch    | K-N1    |
| 5   | N-K5      | ....    |

The occupation takes place with gain of time, as the *forking* check P-B7ch is threatened.

|     |           |         |
| --- | --------- | ------- |
| 5   | ....      | R-Q1    |
| 6   | K-N2!     | ....    |

The King is brought to the center before decisive steps are taken.

|     |           |         |
| --- | --------- | ------- |
| 6   | ....      | K-B1    |
| 7   | P-R4      | ....    |

Creating the potential threat of P-KR5 for opening the King Rook file.

|     |           |         |
| --- | --------- | ------- |
| 7   | ....      | B-K1    |

Now the Bishop is ideally placed to meet the King-side threat (P-KR5) and the Queen-side threat (P-QN5). But this "ideal" state cannot last very long.

|     |           |         |
| --- | --------- | ------- |
| 8   | K-B3      | B-B2    |
| 9   | K-B4      | ....    |

A possible finish now is 9 ... B-K1; 10 N-Q3, K-N1; 11 K-K5, K-B2; 12 N-B4, B-Q2; 13 P-KR5! Here we have the famous "change-of-front" policy. Black is in this case helpless against the threatened 14 PxPch, PxP; 15 R-KR1 followed by 16 R-R7ch with completed infiltration.

So Black tries a different way.

|     |           |         |
| --- | --------- | ------- |
| 9   | ....      | K-K1    |
| 10  | R-QN1!    | ....    |

"Change-of-front"—this time to the Queen-side.

| 10 .... | K-B1 |
| 11 P-N5! | RPxP |
| 12 PxP | B-K1 |

Or 12 ... PxP; 13 RxP, R-N1; 14 N-Q7ch winning the Rook.

| 13 PxP | BxP |

If 13 ... PxP; 14 R-N7 wins very quickly. Again and again we see the advantages of White's enormous plus in mobility: whatever course the game takes, there is always some way for him to infiltrate.

| 14 NxB | PxN |
| 15 K-K5 | Resigns |

After 15 ... R-K1; 16 R-N7 wins—another way is 16 K-Q6, etc.

These examples of encirclement prove conclusively that the combination of weak Pawns and weak squares must necessarily have a crippling effect. Once you are aware of this, it is a relatively easy process to devise means to exploit the enemy's weakness. What makes the exploitation particularly easy is that his passivity deprives him of any chance of effective counterplay.

## SUMMARY

Positional advantage can take two forms:

1. Simple, positive advantage: superior Pawn center or superior development. In this case, there is much that we can learn from the nature of the Pawn formation. Study of the Pawn formation enables us to appraise the present situation, and to plan for the future.

2. More complex advantages, based on the opponent's strategical weakness or weaknesses. Here the study of the Pawn formation is more important than ever. The weak points in the hostile position dictate the further course of the game. Where the uninitiated player is completely at a loss as to how to proceed, the positional landmarks tell the experienced player how he is to continue. An isolated Pawn is to be attacked; an open line is to be occupied; a passed Pawn is to be supported and pushed; superior mobility is to be increased, or to be applied in the direction of reducing the opponent's terrain; and so on.

In each case, we find that there are *positional* landmarks and signposts which make it easy for us to get our bearings and plan our future course. The result is that much of the guesswork is taken out of the play, and is replaced by purposeful planning and executing. Haphazard moves played on the basis of blind instinct tend to disappear, and thoughtful, forceful moves indicate that you are making genuine progress as a chessplayer.

# 7

# THE PRINCIPLES
# OF GOOD OPENING PLAY

Good opening play is basic to the desire and ability to play chess well. A bad opening may ruin your chances from the very start. A good opening gives you a good send-off for the middle game, or at least leaves you on an equal footing with your opponent.

## BASIC PRINCIPLES

The inexperienced, untaught player is greatly handicapped in the opening. Not only is he unfamiliar with the openings; he is even a stranger to the idea that there are definite rules for playing the opening well. True, they are rules of thumb; but they are based on an enormous amount of experience gathered over a period of centuries. Knowledge of these rules will do a great deal to improve your opening play.

**Fight for the Center.** In the previous chapter we saw the importance of having a strong Pawn center; we also came to realize the hopelessness of a player's plight when he has to contend with a powerful Pawn center. The time to secure the advantage of a powerful Pawn center is in the opening. Likewise, the time to break up a potentially powerful hostile Pawn center is also in the opening.

Diagram 199 shows a position from Ponziani's Opening (page 168), in which it is Black's move. White has set up a formidable-looking center. Black has to be very careful in making his reply.

Thus, if he plays 1 ... PxP; his King Knight is driven to a bad square after 2 P-K5.

If Black tries 1 ... NxKP; he finds that after 2 P-Q5, N-N1; 3 B-Q3, his position is also unattractive, as it is difficult to get his Queen Knight to an effective square.

Nor does holding the center by 1 ... B-Q3? answer the question. In that event, Black cannot advance his Queen Pawn and consequently cannot develop his Queen Bishop.

The right way, however, is 1 ... P-Q4! In this way Black fights vigorously for his share of the center, opens up lines of development for his pieces, and has good chances of liquidating White's center altogether. Here is one possibility: 2 QPxP, KNxP. Black's Knight is magnificently posted at K5 and he is actually ahead in development! Another possibility is 2 KPxP, QxP. Then if 3 PxP, QxQch; 4 KxQ, N-KN5. Black regains his Pawn with a marked positional advantage.

Summing up, we see that in the position of Diagram 199, White has various ways to go wrong—that is, compromise his game at the very start. But he has one way of playing correctly—a way of playing that will permit him to face the future with confidence.

Diagram 199                    Diagram 200

 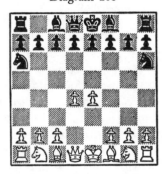

**Play Developing Moves.** We have already seen in the previous chapter the harmful effect of a poor development. Neglected development of one's forces during the opening stage will often permit your opponent to exact a crushing toll later on. Whatever project he undertakes, he will be able to apply more force than you can muster for defense. Thus you will be overborne by his superior weapons.

And these weapons can be qualitative as well as quantitative. Developing your pieces is not merely a matter of counting up how many pieces you have played out. What also matters is, do your pieces occupy good squares? Do they have useful tasks in prospect? Are they in the center or near it? There are certain kinds of "negative" development that are almost as bad as no development.

Here is a case in point, from Diagram 200. White has played out both center Pawns, and has a good development in prospect. Of course, the fact that he has not been opposed in the center also speaks well for his chances.

Black also has made developing moves. But what moves! Both Knights are at the edge of the board, out of touch with the center, and very likely will be out of play for the balance of the game. Here is "negative" development at its worst, without forethought or foresight.

In playing developing moves, you must ask yourself what the developed piece is likely to accomplish? in what plan can it participate? what offensive or defensive purpose can it serve? does it obstruct other forces? is it exposed to enemy attack? When you have good answers to these and similar questions, you will know that you are on the right track in selecting a move.

**Avoid Cramped Positions.** So far we have had two positive rules. Now we come to four negative ones. The one about avoiding cramped positions is sensible enough in the light of what we have already learned. In cramped positions we have little freedom of action; little choice; and perhaps worst of all, little pleasure! Why choose a line of play which leaves little scope for imagination and crushes our spirits with its severe problems and unrewarding cares?

In Diagram 201, for example, Black has played the Hungarian Defense (page 169) and has saddled himself with a position which would have baffled Houdini. Black's pieces are cramped; they cannot be freed; they cannot be given any respectable scope. White can simply proceed to tie up Black systematically, depriving him of more and more terrain until he will finally have to cry "Uncle!" Obviously, this is no way to play chess; yet Black has brought this tragedy on himself with his first few moves.

Diagram 201                    Diagram 202

**Don't Grab Material.** Generally speaking, it is best not to pick posies in the opening in the form of a stray Pawn here and there. The time lost in making such captures may prove very costly. Careful analysis will sometimes show that the Pawns could have been taken safely; but the inexperienced player will generally find that such fine-spun analysis is beyond his abilities—and the actual test of over-the-board play is too taxing for an inexperienced player. He is likely to panic when he realizes the difficulties which he has created for himself; worse yet, he may not even be fully aware of the magnitude of his troubles!

The safe rule, then, is to avoid temptation. But there are times when such captures can be indulged in safely: after a careful study of the consequences, leading to the conclusion that the capture is feasible. It is a procedure which can be recommended only to hardy souls.

Diagram 202 gives us an instance—from the Danish Gambit (page 163). Black has stopped to capture two Pawns and in consequence he is considerably behind in development. But his position is very solid, and White, for all his brilliant development, has no way of piercing Black's armor. This is mainly attributable, by the way, to Black's sturdy Knight at his QB4 square. What can White do? He cannot play Q-N3. If he tries P-K5, then Black has a more than adequate reply in ... P-Q4. Nor can White occupy his Q5 square, as Black has forestalled him with ... P-QB3.

In due course, Black will catch up in development, and then his two plus Pawns are bound to tell in his favor. But again it must be stressed that Pawn-snatchers rarely find themselves in such admirably secure situations.

**Don't Attack Prematurely.** Beginners are all too fond of "one-piece attacks." An attack should be undertaken, as a rule, only when one's development has been completed or well advanced. Merely to make threatening gestures, or to advance in a sporadic or thoughtless sally, is not to attack. The logical consequence of these "attacks" is that they generally have a blunderbuss recoil on the "attacker." Considerable loss of time—sometimes of material—will be the consequence; not to mention hurt pride and loss of face! So: *attack only with adequate force, after due preparation, and against targets which have some vulnerable quality about them.*

**Avoid Creating Weaknesses.** The consequences of being afflicted with an organic weakness—isolated Pawn, weak-square complex, and the like—have been studied in quite a few examples. Such weaknesses should naturally be avoided. This is particularly true of the opening, where a mistake of this kind will compromise a player's position for the rest of the game. As a rule, the creation of such weaknesses, when not due to sheer ignorance of their consequences, may be traced back to some opening mistake which led inevitably to a further concession in the form of an organic weakness. Knowledge of these organic weaknesses will be helpful to most players in avoiding such mistakes in the opening.

The reader should be thoroughly conversant with these six basic rules for opening play, even if he never bothers to study the openings in any detail. Applying these basic rules in his games will greatly enhance his prospects for the remainder of the game, and enable him to avoid many of the pitfalls which beckon to the unwary.

## THE OPENINGS

An opening consists of a standardized pattern of beginning moves. The specific opening as such is generally identifiable from its first two or three moves, sometimes, even, from its very first move. There are about forty well-known openings in modern play, most of them several centuries old. After the first two or three moves, the play admits of a great many alternative lines. This leads to a degree of diversity and complexity which is beyond the average player's grasp.

The problem, then, in teaching the openings is to know where to draw the line between a great mass of detail and an all too simplistic pruning of vitally important information. As far as the beginner is concerned, the encyclopedic compendium, bristling with fearsome columns of endless variations, is just as useless as a bright collection of optimistic platitudes.

The method of presenting the openings in the following chapters is based on a compromise. The attempt has been made to give the average player a fairly comprehensive picture of the openings, eliminating a great many alternatives which are hardly likely to occur in his games. When an opening is considered bad for White, the student is shown a good line for Black, instead of being burdened with a miniature treatise on that opening. Similarly, if an opening is bad for Black, the student is shown a promising continuation for White.

There are other practical considerations. There is little point, for example, in devoting a great deal of space to an opening which is obsolete. The greatest amount of space has therefore been reserved for openings which are popular in modern play. Psychological factors also play a role. Mere technical analysis does not tell the reader too much. He needs to know what kind of openings suits what kind of temperaments. He needs to be reminded constantly what kind of middle-game play is likely to evolve from a given opening. A great deal of attention has been given, in the following chapters, to this kind of need.

The large number of openings makes it difficult for the student to get a clear picture of their groupings and distinctions. To eliminate this confusion, the openings have been presented in groups.

**Double King Pawn Openings.** These are the openings in which White begins with 1 P-K4 and Black replies with 1 ... P-K4. Historically, these are the openings which have received the most attention, and up to about 1900 they actually monopolized the opening repertoire. It is significant that the Double King Pawn opening which has come to be considered the strongest for White—the Ruy Lopez—was the last to be studied in detail and to achieve widespread popularity. These openings are still considered the most suitable for study by a neophyte.

**Single King Pawn Openings.** In these openings, White plays 1 P-K4 and Black replies with some move *other than* 1 ... P-K4. Most of these openings are as venerable as the ones in the Double King Pawn category. However, the Single King Pawn openings required several centuries to become popular. For a long time, it was considered craven or unsporting to avoid 1 ... P-K4. In modern play this rather naïve point of view no longer prevails.

**Double Queen Pawn Openings.** Openings in which White plays 1 P-Q4 and Black replies 1 ... P-Q4 belong in this category. The Queen's Gambit Declined is one of the most venerable of openings, being mentioned in fifteenth-century manuscripts. Yet this opening, the most popular of modern times, was seen very rarely before 1900. The inexperienced player does well to familiarize himself with the King Pawn openings before tackling the rather taxing Queen Pawn openings, with their more refined positional considerations.

**Single Queen Pawn Openings.** In this group we find openings in which 1 P-Q4 is answered by some move *other than* 1 ... P-Q4—usually 1 ... N-KB3. These openings are definitely modern, if not "modernistic." The student does well to steer clear of them until he feels at home in the more orthodox openings.

**Eccentric Openings.** These are openings in which neither 1 P-K4 nor 1 P-Q4 is adopted. They are distinctly out of the ordinary, as far as the average player is concerned. The play is rather tortuous and complex, involving problems which rarely confront players outside the master class.

For the reader's convenience, each of these five groups will be considered in separate chapters. The order in which they appear roughly suggests the order in which they should be studied.

# 8

# DOUBLE KING PAWN OPENINGS

These are the openings which will absorb most of the reader's interest for some time to come. Generally speaking, they stress tactics more than strategy, and are therefore more suitable for the average player. The feeling for strategy, for position play, for quiet and subtle maneuvering, is one which develops only with experience.

The simpler openings are given first. As Black can equalize in them most readily, they are not too fashionable in modern play. But the reader should experiment with them, so that he will be thoroughly familiar with their qualities and basic ideas.

The basic idea of all opening play is *the struggle for expansion in the center*. Hence, in openings in which both players advance their King Pawn two squares, the early play will often be concerned with the advance of the Queen Pawn or King Bishop Pawn, partly to open lines of development, partly to try to remove the hostile King Pawn. This thought is the key to most of the openings in this chapter.

We proceed from simple openings to complex ones. That is why the Ruy Lopez, the strongest but also the most demanding of the lot, comes last, and receives what may seem to be a disproportionate amount of space. The Ruy Lopez will probably be the opening which will become your favorite; but it should not be the first one you adopt!

**Center Game.** An inferior opening for White; the early development of his Queen leads to loss of time and a congested development.

*1 P-K4, P-K4; 2 P-Q4, PxP; 3 QxP, N-QB3; 4 Q-K3, N-B3; 5 N-QB3, B-N5; 6 B-Q2, Castles; 7 Castles, R-K1!*

Black has developed rapidly and to the point. Now ... P-Q4 is a potent liberating threat.

**Danish Gambit.** White boldly sacrifices two Pawns. He hopes to obtain an overwhelming development with prospects of rapid attack.

*1 P-K4, P-K4; 2 P-Q4, PxP; 3 P-QB3, PxP; 4 B-QB4, PxP; 5 QBxP, P-QB3!; 6 N-QB3, P-Q3; 7 N-B3, N-Q2!; 8 Castles, N-B4!*

Black has accepted both Pawns, defending tenaciously and preparing judiciously to break the attack later on by offering exchanges. (See the discussion in connection with Diagram 202.)

**Bishop's Opening.** White's second move does not attack anything; Black can therefore take the initiative.

*1 P-K4, P-K4; 2 B-B4, N-KB3!; 3 P-Q3, P-B3!; 4 P-B4, PxP; 5 QBxP, P-Q4; 6 PxP, NxP.*

Black has excellent prospects.

**Vienna Game.** This is another opening that permits Black to counter dynamically in the center.

**A.** 3 P-B4 Variation—*1 P-K4, P-K4; 2 N-QB3, N-KB3; 3 P-B4, P-Q4!; 4 BPxP, NxP; 5 N-B3, B-K2; 6 P-Q4, Castles; 7 B-Q3, P-KB4!; 8 PxP e.p., BxP!*

Black's Knight is magnificently centralized at his K5 square. White can win a Pawn, but only at the cost of losing his Queen Pawn in return. Black has come out of the opening nicely.

**B.** 3 B-B4 Variation—*1 P-K4, P-K4; 2 N-QB3, N-KB3; 3 B-B4, N-B3; 4 P-Q3, N-QR4; 5 B-N3, NxB; 6 RPxN, B-N5.*

Black has a satisfactory development, and his Bishop-pair may become quite effective later on. (For the involved play that may ensue on 3 ... NxP!?, see the discussion of Diagram 98.)

**King's Bishop's Gambit.** All forms of the King's Gambit have the object of securing a broad Pawn center for White and organizing a powerful attack along the King Bishop file. Black's best policy is to speed his development and hit back in the center.

*1 P-K4, P-K4; 2 P-KB4, PxP; 3 B-B4, N-KB3!; 4 N-QB3, P-B3!; 5 Q-B3, P-Q4!; 6 PxP, B-Q3!; 7 P-Q3, B-KN5!; 8 Q-B2, Castles!*

Black has the initiative and a beautiful position. There is no sign of a White attack.

**King's Knight Gambit.** Here too Black's best course is to concentrate on development.

**A.** 3 ... N-KB3 Variation—*1 P-K4, P-K4; 2 P-KB4, PxP; 3 N-KB3, N-KB3; 4 N-B3, P-Q4!; 5 PxP, NxP; 6 NxN, QxN; 7 P-Q4, B-K2; 8 P-B4!, Q-K5ch; 9 K-B2, B-KB4!; 10 P-B5, N-B3!; 11 B-N5, Q-Q4!; 12 BxP, Castles QR!*

(See Diagram 203.) Black has the initiative, White's Queen Pawn being backward on an open file.

Diagram 203                     Diagram 204

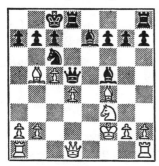 

**B.** 3 ... P-KN4 Variation—*1 P-K4, P-K4; 2 P-KB4, PxP; 3 N-KB3, P-KN4; 4 B-B4, B-N2.*

(The famous Muzio Gambit goes 4 ... P-N5; 5 Castles!?, PxN; 6 QxP, and White has a furious attack.)

*5 Castles, P-Q3; 6 P-Q4, P-KR3; 7 P-B3, N-QB3.*

(See Diagram 204.) White's best chance is now to try to force open the King Bishop file with 8 P-KN3. The canny reply is 8 ... P-N5; 9 N-R4, P-B6; keeping the file closed, and with a complicated game in prospect. However, Variation A is more promising for Black.

**Kieseritzky Gambit.** This offshoot of the King's Knight's Gambit is an unsuccessful attempt to exploit the advanced state of Black's King-side Pawns.

*1 P-K4, P-K4; 2 P-KB4, PxP; 3 N-KB3, P-KN4; 4 P-KR4, P-N5.*

(At this point the Allgaier Gambit—dangerous but not sound—is possible after 5 N-N5, P-KR3; 6 NxP, KxN; etc.)

*5 N-K5, N-KB3!; 6 B-B4, -Q4!; 7 PxP, B-N2; 8 P-Q4, N-R4!*

A very comfortable position for Black. He has returned the extra Pawn in exchange for a fine development and attacking possibilities.

**King's Gambit Declined.** For those who favor common sense and sobriety, declining the gambit is the indicated course.

*1 P-K4, P-K4; 2 P-KB4, B-B4.*

(See the discussion of this position on page 47.)

*3 N-KB3, P-Q3; 4 B-B4, N-KB3; 5 N-B3, N-B3; 6 P-Q3, B-K3; 7 B-N5, P-QR3; 8 BxNch, PxB; 9 P-B5, B-B1.*

Black stands well; he has the Bishop-pair and prospects of playing ... P-Q4 after protecting his King Pawn.

**Falkbeer Counter Gambit.** This is a more aggressive, but far more risky, method of declining the gambit than 2 ... B-B4.

*1 P-K4, P-K4; 2 P-KB4, P-Q4; 3 KPxP, P-K5; 4 P-Q3!, N-KB3; 5 Q-K2!, QxP; 6 N-QB3, B-QN5; 7 B-Q2, BxN; 8 BxB.*

Black has been repulsed. His King Pawn is in danger, and he is on the defensive.

**Greco Counter Gambit.** Here, also, Black counterattacks prematurely and is soon thrust back into an uncomfortable defensive position.

*1 P-K4, P-K4; 2 N-KB3, P-KB4.*

(The gambit move. White's reply threatens 4 Q-R5ch.)

*3 NxP, Q-B3; 4 P-Q4, P-Q3; 5 N-B4, PxP; 6 N-B3, Q-N3; 7 B-B4, N-KB3; 8 N-K3, B-K2; 9 B-B4, P-B3; 10 P-Q5!*

White is far ahead in development. Black's forces are disorganized and his King Pawn is weak.

**Philidor's Defense.** Again White plays the powerful developing move 2 N-KB3, which has the additional advantage of being aggressive and making room for castling. Black has a sorry choice between giving up Pawn control of the center (Variation A), and maintaining Pawn control of the center (Variation B)—being burdened in either event with a congested, unpromising position.

Diagram 205

Diagram 206

**A.** 3 ... PxP Variation—*1 P-K4, P-K4; 2 N-KB3, P-Q3; 3 P-Q4, PxP; 4 QxP!, N-QB3; 5 B-QN5!, B-Q2; 6 BxN, BxB; 7 N-B3, N-B3; 8 B-N5, B-K2; 9 Castles QR.*

(See Diagram 205.) Black's surrender of the center has left his pieces with no mobility to speak of, in contrast to White's splendidly posted forces.

**B.** 3 ... N-Q2 Variation—*1 P-K4, P-K4; 2 N-KB3, P-Q3; 3 P-Q4, N-Q2; 4 B-QB4!*

(See Diagram 206. Black's constricted position creates difficulties for him. Thus, the immediate 4 ... B-K2?; will not do because of 5 PxP!, NxP; 6 NxN, PxN; 7 Q-R5 with a *double attack* that wins a Pawn. Or 4 ... B-K2?; 5 PxP, PxP?; 6 Q-Q5 with a gruesome *mate threat.*)

*4 ... P-QB3; 5 N-B3, B-K2; 6 Castles, KN-B3; 7 P-QR4!, Castles; 8 Q-K2.*

Black suffers from a cramped position that requires a great deal of patience and staying power. White's policy will be to keep Black tied up—7 P-QR4!, for example, prevented Black from gaining room on the Queen-side with ... P-QN4.

**Petroff's Defense.** Again White plays the powerful developing move 2 N-KB3, and again Black counterattacks. But here his counterattack is based on a developing move, and is therefore reasonably sound.

*1 P-K4, P-K4; 2 N-KB3, N-KB3.*

(The counterattack. The reply 3 P-Q4 gives Black an easy game after 3 ... PxP!; 4 P-K5, N-K5; 5 QxP, P-Q4!; etc.)

*3 NxP, P-Q3.*

(The dangers of 3 ... NxP? are explained in the discussion of Diagram 121.)

*4 N-KB3, NxP.*

(Now White gets no more than equality from 5 Q-K2, Q-K2; 6 P-Q3, N-KB3; etc.)

*5 P-Q4, P-Q4; 6 B-Q3, B-K2; 7 Castles, N-QB3; 8 P-B4, N-QN5!; 9 PxP, NxB; 10 QxN, QxP.*

Black's development is a bit in arrears; but he has the Bishop-pair and is free from organic weaknesses. The position may therefore be considered satisfactory for Black.

**Scotch Game.** This opening really wastes White's powerful developing move 2 N-KB3, as White advances too rapidly in the center. The result is that on his fourth move, Black can gain useful time by merely developing. Thus White loses whatever advantage is conferred by the first move.

**A.** *4 ... N-B3 Variation—1 P-K4, P-K4; 2 N-KB3, N-QB3; 3 P-Q4, PxP; 4 NxP, N-B3.*

(See Diagram 207. Black gains time by counterattack on White's King Pawn.)

Diagram 207                     Diagram 208

*5 N-QB3, B-N5; 6 NxN, NPxN; 7 B-Q3, P-Q4!; 8 PxP, Q-K2ch!*

White can do nothing better now than exchange Queens (9 **Q-K2,** etc.), leaving a drawish endgame.

**B.** *4 ... B-B4 Variation—1 P-K4, P-K4; 2 N-KB3, N-QB3; 3 P-Q4, PxP; 4 NxP, B-B4.*

(See Diagram 208. Black gains time by counterattacking White's Knight at the Q4 square.)

*5 B-K3, Q-B3; 6 P-QB3, KN-K2; 7 N-B2, BxB; 8 NxB, Castles; 9 B-K2, P-Q3; 10 Castles, B-K3.*

Black's development is quite comfortable; his position is satisfactory.

**Ponziani's Opening.** Whereas White advances too hastily in the Scotch, he advances too sluggishly in the Ponziani. Black reacts effectively with ... N-KB3 and ... P-Q4—moves that combine development and counterattack in ideal fashion. (See also the discussion in connection with Diagram 199.)

*1 P-K4, P-K4; 2 N-KB3, N-QB3; 3 P-B3, N-B3!; 4 P-Q4, P-Q4!; 5 B-QN5, KPxP; 6 NxP, B-Q2; 7 PxP, NxN; 8 BxBch, QxB; 9 QxN, QxP.*

A characterless position with no hope of initiative for either side.

**Hungarian Defense.** Played to avoid the Giuoco Piano (see below), this defense leaves Black with a bleakly constricted game. It is not an inspiring line of play.

*1 P-K4, P-K4; 2 N-KB3, N-QB3; 3 B-B4, B-K2.*

(Black's third move gives the defense its name.)

*4 P-Q4, P-Q3.*

(Surrender of the center by 4 ... PxP gives Black a lifeless game on the order of Philidor's Defense.)

*5 P-Q5!, N-N1; 6 B-Q3!, N-KB3; 7 P-B4, Castles; 8 P-KR3!*

Black's game is fatally cramped. See the discussion of Diagram 201 for the likely sequel.

**Giuoco Piano.** The Giuoco Piano is the first really logical opening we have tackled. White attacks the King Pawn with 2 N-KB3, Black defends with 2 ... N-QB3. Now White plays 3 B-B4, exerting strong pressure in the center and aiming at Black's vulnerable KB2 square. With this effective development established, White is ready to build a strong Pawn center. Black can maintain equality if he fights back energetically.

**A.** Black gives up the center for counterattack—*1 P-K4, P-K4; 2 N-KB3, N-QB3; 3 B-B4, B-B4; 4 P-B3, N-B3.*

Diagram 209         Diagram 210

(The typical developing, counterattacking move.)

*5 P-Q4, PxP.*

(In reply to 6 P-K5, Black has the forceful reply 6 ... P-Q4!)

*6 PxP, B-N5ch.*

(The passive 6 ... B-N3? invites complete rout by 7 P-K5 and 8 P-Q5.)

(See Diagram 209. White's safest course is now 7 B-Q2, BxBch; 8 QNxB, P-Q4!; with equality.)

*7 N-B3!?, NxKP; 8 Castles!?*

(This is a wild line in which Black can easily go wrong: 8 ... NxN; 9 PxN, BxP?; 10 B-R3!!, with a winning attack.)

*8 ... BxN!; 9 P-Q5!?, N-K4; 10 PxB, NxB; 11 Q-Q4, P-KB4!*

(And not 11 ... N/B5-Q3?; 12 QxNP, Q-B3; 13 QxQ, NxQ; 14 R-K1ch, and White has a winning game.)

*12 QxN/B4, P-Q3.*

Black is quite safe, and he remains a Pawn ahead.

**B.** Black holds the center—*1 P-K4, P-K4; 2 N-KB3, N-QB3; 3 B-B4, B-B4; 4 P-B3, Q-K2; 5 P-Q4, B-N3.*

(See Diagram 210. Black intends to maintain his King Pawn as a strong point on K4.)

*6 Castles, N-B3; 7 R-K1, P-Q3; 8 P-KR3!, Castles; 9 N-R3!, N-Q1; 10 B-Q3, P-B4; 11 N-B4, B-B2; 12 PxKP!, PxP; 13 N-K3!*

White's position is distinctly superior, as he can *centralize* his Queen Knight effectively on Q5, and he has good prospects of controlling the open Queen file. For the consequences of this line of play, see the discussion of Diagram 190.

**C.** White plays conservatively in the center—*1 P-K4, P-K4; 2 N-KB3, N-QB3; 3 B-B4, B-B4; 4 P-Q3, N-B3; 5 N-B3, P-Q3; 6 B-K3, B-N3.*

(After 6 ... BxB; 7 PxB, etc., White's open King Bishop file may give him attacking chances.)

*7 P-KR3, B-K3; 8 B-N3.*

A quiet, colorless position: even game. This is a good line for inexperienced players, as they are not too likely to head into complications.

The lesson derived from the Giuoco Piano is that when White develops purposefully and then plays to build up a powerful Pawn center, Black must react energetically. In the Ruy Lopez (page 175), the problem is stated in even starker terms.

**Evans Gambit.** White sacrifices a Pawn in the purely speculative hope of gaining time for development.

*1 P-K4, P-K4; 2 N-KB3, N-QB3; 3 B-B4, B-B4; 4 P-QN4, BxNP; 5 P-B3, B-K2!*

(After 5 ... B-B4; 6 P-Q4, PxP; 7 PxP, B-N3; 8 Castles, P-Q3; 9 N-B3, White has a promising lead in development for his Pawn.)

*6 P-Q4, N-QR4!; 7 B-Q3, PxP; 8 PxP, P-Q4!; 9 N-B3, PxP; 10 NxP, N-KB3.*

The combination of Black's eighth and tenth moves is our assurance that he is freeing himself. He has an excellent game.

**Evans Gambit Declined.** Refusing the gambit is the sensible course if you want to avoid complications.

*1 P-K4, P-K4; 2 N-KB3, N-QB3; 3 B-B4, B-B4; 4 P-QN4, B-N3; 5 P-QR4, P-QR3; 6 B-N2, P-Q3; 7 P-N5, PxP; 8 PxP, RxR; 9 BxR, N-Q5!*

Black has a fine game, with no trace of attacking possibilities available to White.

**Two Knights' Defense.** This counterattack—or counter gambit—is often adopted to avoid the Giuoco Piano or the Evans Gambit. The opening always leads to lively play, and in adopting it Black should realize that he is committing himself to an enterprising and even risky policy.

**A.** Black's counter gambit—*1 P-K4, P-K4; 2 N-KB3, N-QB3; 3 B-B4, N-B3; 4 N-N5.*

(Hitting out at Black's weak spot: his KB2 square.)

*4 ... P-Q4; 5 PxP.*

(See Diagram 211. Black can now expose himself to the famous "Fried Liver" Attack by playing 5 ... NxP! The Attack begins with the sacrifice 6 NxBP?!, when the moves 6 ... KxN; 7 Q-B3ch, K-K3; 8 N-B3 are indicated. Black's King seems dangerously exposed, yet after

Diagram 211                           Diagram 212

8 ... QN-N5!; 9 Q-K4, P-B3; 10 P-Q4, K-Q2; 11 NxN, PxN; 12 BxP, NxB; 13 QxNch, K-B2; Black is out of danger and his extra piece is stronger than White's Pawns.

Despite the fact that Black can repulse the sacrificial attack, most players prefer to avoid this arduous defensive line and embark on the counter gambit that follows.)

*5 ... N-QR4!?; 6 B-N5ch!, P-B3; 7 PxP, PxP; 8 B-K2, P-KR3; 9 N-KB3, P-K5; 10 N-K5, B-Q3.*

(Black has gained a lot of time, and White wisely decides to return the extra Pawn for reasons that will soon appear.)

*11 P-KB4!, Castles; 12 Castles!, BxN; 13 PxB, Q-Q5ch; 14 K-R1, QxKP; 15 P-Q4!*

(See Diagram 212.) White's position is decidedly superior. He has an open King Bishop file and the Bishop-pair for attacking purposes. Black has weak Queen-side Pawns and weak black squares. A splendid example of the value of returning extra material for positional advantage.

**B.** Max Lange Attack—*1 P-K4, P-K4; 2 N-KB3, N-QB3; 3 B-B4, N-B3; 4 P-Q4, PxP; 5 Castles.*

(See Diagram 213. Black's safest course is 5 ... NxP; 6 R-K1, P-Q4. White recovers his Pawns by an ingenious maneuver: 7 BxP, QxB; 8 N-B3. A neat *pin*, this! 8 ... Q-KR4—the simplest—and now 9 NxN, B-K3; 10 B-N5, B-QN5; 11 NxP, QxQ; 12 KRxQ with equal chances.)

*5 ... B-B4; 6 P-K5, P-Q4!; 7 PxN, PxB; 8 R-K1ch, B-K3; 9 N-N5.*

(See Diagram 214. This is the famous Max Lange Attack, one of the

Diagram 213          Diagram 214

most complicated of all the chess openings. If now 9 ... QxP?; 10 NxB, PxN; and the *double attack* 11 Q-R5ch wins a piece for White.)

*9 ... Q-Q4; 10 N-QB3, Q-B4.*

(If 10 ... PxN??; 11 QxQ and Black's Bishop at K3, being *pinned,* cannot recapture.)

*11 N/B3-K4, Castles QR!; 12 N/N5xB, PxN; 13 P-KN4, Q-K4; 14 PxP, KR-N1.*

White continues logically with 15 B-R6, but after 15 ... B-N5!; 16 R-K2, P-Q6!; Black's counterplay, being *centralized,* should triumph.

In general, the Two Knights' Defense leads to lively, interesting play; only those reasonably familiar with its intricacies should venture on it.

**Four Knights' Game.** This conservative opening is ideal for timid players. It is anathema to lovers of lively chess because of its symmetrical "drawing" variations. For example: 1 P-K4, P-K4; 2 N-KB3, N-QB3; 3 N-B3, N-B3; 4 B-N5, N-Q5; 5 NxN, PxN; 6 P-K5, PxN; 7 PxN. There are equally dull perspectives after 1 P-K4, P-K4; 2 N-KB3, N-QB3; 3 N-B3, N-B3; 4 B-N5, B-N5; 5 Castles, Castles; 6 BxN, QPxB; 7 NxP, BxN; 8 QPxB, NxP; etc.

**A.** Black keeps his Bishops—*1 P-K4, P-K4; 2 N-KB3, N-QB3; 3 N-B3, N-B3; 4 B-N5, B-N5; 5 Castles, Castles; 6 P-Q3, P-Q3; 7 B-N5.*

(White's most aggressive course. There is nothing to be gained from the symmetrical 7 N-K2, N-K2; 8 N-N3, N-N3; etc. See Diagram 215.)

*7 ... N-K2.*

(The *counterpin* 7 ... B-N5?; is bad because White reinforces his *pin* with 8 N-Q5!)

Diagram 215                    Diagram 216

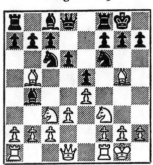      

*8 BxN, PxB; 9 N-KR4, N-N3; 10 NxN, RPxN; 11 P-B4, B-QB4ch;*
*12 K-R1, K-N2.*

Black has fine attacking chances with his Bishop-pair and open King
Rook file.

**B.** Black parts with a Bishop—*1 P-K4, P-K4; 2 N-KB3, N-QB3; 3*
*N-B3, N-B3; 4 B-N5, B-N5; 5 Castles, Castles; 6 P-Q3, BxN; 7 PxB,*
*P-Q3; 8 B-N5, Q-K2.*

(Black intends to retain his King Pawn at K4 after White's P-Q4.
In order to make his K4 square a strong point, Black gives it additional
protection with his Queen.)

*9 R-K1, N-Q1; 10 P-Q4, N-K3; 11 B-QB1, P-B4!*

Black does not fear 12 PxP, PxP; 13 NxP? because of the *discovered*
*attack* 13 ... N-B2!; winning a piece. Black has a fine game, as White's
Bishops have little scope.

**C.** Rubinstein Variation—*1 P-K4, P-K4; 2 N-KB3, N-QB3; 3 N-B3,*
*N-B3; 4 B-N5, N-Q5; 5 NxP!, Q-K2; 6 P-B4, NxB; 7 NxN, P-Q3;*
*8 N-KB3, QxPch; 9 K-B2!, N-N5ch; 10 K-N1!, K-Q1.*

(See Diagram 216. Both Kings have been disturbed; but White can
achieve the equivalent of a normal castled position.)

*11 P-Q3, Q-B3; 12 QN-Q4, Q-N3; 13 P-KR3, N-B3; 14 K-R2.*

Black's position is disorganized, his King insecure, and his Bishop-
pair does not count for much in this situation.

To summarize, the Four Knights' holds no terrors for Black if he defends correctly as in Variations A and B. On the other hand, Variation C is too venturesome, and is not to be recommended for Black.

**Three Knights' Game.** This opening has little independent value of its own, its chief significance lying in the avoidance of the Four Knights' Game by Black, or the Petroff by White.

*1 P-K4, P-K4; 2 N-KB3, N-QB3; 3 N-B3, B-N5; 4 N-Q5, N-B3!; 5 NxB, NxN.*

(White's Bishop-pair is of little value here—for example 6 **P-Q4,** **P-Q4!**—or 6 B-B4, P-Q4; 7 PxP, P-K5!; etc.)

*6 NxP, Q-K2; 7 P-Q4, NxKP; 8 P-QB3, N-QB3; 9 NxN, QPxN.*

Even game. Black has made good use of the familiar equalizing moves ... N-KB3 and ... P-Q4.

The other form of the Three Knights'—1 P-K4, P-K4; 2 N-KB3, N-KB3—takes a similarly uneventful course after 3 N-B3, B-N5; 4 NxP, Castles!; 5 B-K2, R-K1; etc.

**Ruy Lopez.** This opening is without doubt the strongest of the group which begins 1 P-K4, P-K4; 2 N-KB3, N-QB3. The continuation 3 B-N5 (menacing 4 BxN and 5 NxP) is an improvement on the Giuoco Piano. We see here a struggle for control of the center—White attacks, Black defends.

Sooner or later Black will have to guard his King Pawn with ... P-Q3, so that the standard freeing move ... P-Q4 is generally impractical and often impossible.

With White's pressure established in the center to Black's discomfort, White is ready to advance in the center with P-Q4—very often prepared by P-B3 to support the thrust with the Queen Pawn. In many variations of the Ruy Lopez, Black finds himself compelled to capture the Queen Pawn with his King Pawn—that is, *to give up the center.* But in that event, experience has shown, White's game is much freer and his pieces have more scope than Black's.

The first great question that arises after 3 B-N5 is this: is White really threatening to win a Pawn at once? The answer is No! For example: 3 ... P-QR3; 4 BxN, QPxB; 5 NxP, and now Black can regain his Pawn by the *double attack* 5 ... Q-Q5 or 5 ... Q-N4.

On this simple tactical finesse rests the most important and best defense to the Ruy Lopez. This is the Morphy Defense, which begins with 3 . . P-QR3. *It allows Black to drive off White's King Bishop so that it no longer menaces Black's Queen Knight.* This removes a great deal of pressure on Black's game, so that he has a more-or-less free choice between what has been called the Strong-Point Variation (maintaining his Pawn at the K4 square), and the Counterattack Variation (seeking counterplay by capturing White's King Pawn).

The Strong-Point Variation is the more conservative, solid and cramped—an improved version of Black's hold-the-line procedure in the Philidor Defense (page 166). The Counterattack Variation is the more enterprising of the two; it is also more risky, and involves the creation of positional weaknesses.

**A.** Strong-Point Variation: Black maintains the center—*1 P-K4, P-K4; 2 N-KB3, N-QB3; 3 B-N5, P-QR3; 4 B-R4, N-B3.*

(The familiar counterattacking move.)

Diagram 217          Diagram 218

(See Diagram 217. If White protects his King Pawn with 5 P-Q3, then Black is not subject to pressure and has an easy game after 5 ··· P-Q3; 6 P-B3, P-KN3; 7 QN-Q2, B-N2.

Also satisfactory for Black is 5 N-B3, P-QN4; 6 B-N3, B-K2; 7 Castles, P-Q3. Then we get the Noah's Ark Trap after 8 P-Q4?, NxQP; 9 NxN, PxN; 10 QxP??, P-B4; followed by ··· P-B5; winning White's Bishop. Here we see the power of the ··· P-QR3 and ··· P-QN4 maneuver to drive back White's Bishop.)

*5 Castles, B-K2.*

(The characteristic move of the Strong-Point Variation; 5 ·· NxP gives us the Counterattack Variation.

The alternative 5 ··· B-B4 looks more aggressive, but after 6 P-B3 followed by P-Q4, Black's King Bishop is not happy.)

*6 R-K1, P-QN4.*

(Now that White has firmly guarded his King Pawn, Black must prevent BxN followed by NxP.)

*7 B-N3, P-Q3; 8 P-B3, Castles.*

(White can now play 9 P-Q4, but then the *pin* 9 ... B-N5 is bothersome. Hence he prevents the *pin*.)

*9 P-KR3, N-QR4!; 10 B-B2, P-B4; 11 P-Q4, Q-B2.*

(See Diagram 218. Black's last three moves have completed his basic formation in the Strong-Point Variation. By driving off White's King Bishop, Black gains time for an expansion maneuver on the Queen-side which makes ... Q-B2 possible, and with it the maintenance of his strong point at his K4 square.)

*12 QN-Q2, N-B3.*

(The point of this excellent move is that 13 N-B1 loses a Pawn because of 13 ... BPxP; 14 PxP, PxP; when White cannot recapture without losing a piece. This induces White to barricade the center.)

*13 P-Q5, N-Q1; 14 P-QR4, R-N1; 15 P-B4!, P-N5; 16 N-B1, N-K1; 17 P-KN4, P-N3; 18 B-R6, N-KN2.*

With the center blockaded, Black need not worry about guarding his strong point at the K4 square. His position is cramped, but he has maneuvering space. White will try to open lines on the King-side. Black will stand pat and await developments. Not an easy game for either player, and one that calls for patience on both sides. This rather stodgy defense does not appeal to aggressive-minded players.

**B.** Strong-Point Variation: Counterattack with 8 ... P-Q4?!—*1P-K4, P-K4; 2 N-KB3, N-QB3; 3 B-N5, P-QR3; 4 B-R4, N-B3; 5 Castles, B-K2; 6 R-K1, P-QN4; 7 B-N3, Castles; 8 P-B3, P-Q4?!*

(Now we see why Black avoided the regulation 7 ... P-Q3. He is playing a gambit which, if not met correctly, can give him promising attacking chances.)

*9 PxP, NxP; 10 NxP, NxN; 11 RxN, P-QB3; 12 P-Q4!, B-Q3; 13 R-K1, Q-R5; 14 P-N3, Q-R6; 15 R-K4!*

(Black's attack is not yet over, but White has survived the worst. His extra Pawn will eventually tell in his favor.)

**C.** Strong-Point Variation: White's early P-Q4—*1 P-K4, P-K4; 2 N-KB3, N-QB3; 3 B-N5, P-QR3; 4 B-R4, N-B3; 5 Castles, B-K2, 6 P-Q4.*

(An attempt to upset the Strong-Point Variation. The Black King Pawn must disappear, and with it the whole concept of maintaining a strong point at Black's K4 square. This is a kind of well-prepared Scotch Game: White plays P-Q4 *after due preparation*.)

*6 ... PxP.*

(See Diagram 219. If now 7 R-K1, P-QN4; 8 B-N3, P-Q3; 9 NxP??, NxN; 10 QxN, P-B4 followed by ... P-B5 winning the Bishop—the Noah's Ark Trap again!)

*7 P-K5, N-K5; 8 NxP, NxN; 9 QxN, N-B4.*

The position is about even. Black will get the Bishop-pair, but White has a noticeable lead in development.

**D.** Strong-Point Variation: White's early Q-K2—*1 P-K4, P-K4; 2 N-KB3, N-QB3; 3 B-N5, P-QR3; 4 B-R4, N-B3; 5 Castles, B-K2; 6 Q-K2.*

(White guards his King Pawn and thus compels Black to do likewise. However, if 6 ... P-Q3; 7 P-B3, Castles; 8 P-Q4, Black's game is rather constricted.)

*6 ... P-QN4; 7 B-N3, P-Q3; 8 P-B3, Castles; 9 P-Q4, B-N5; 10 R-Q1.*

White's position is preferable because his game is freer.

**E.** Strong-Point Variation: Steinitz Defense Deferred—*1 P-K4, P-K4; 2 N-KB3, N-QB3; 3 B-N5, P-QR3; 4 B-R4, P-Q3.*

Diagram 219          Diagram 220

(See Diagram 220. This defense has many favorable features. The early ... P-QR3 makes it possible to drive away White's annoying King Bishop in some variations, thus easing the pressure on Black's strong point, his K4 square. Also, the Noah's Ark Trap may turn up!

Secondly, the delay in developing Black's King Knight leaves open the possibility of a later ... KN-K2, or else ... P-KB4 for counter-attack, or ... P-KB3 supporting the strong point at his K4 square.

Now for White's possible replies: 5 P-Q4 may lead to a modified Noah's Ark Trap: 5 ... P-QN4!; 6 B-N3, NxP; 7 NxN, PxN; 8 QxP?, P-QB4! [Noah's Ark!]; 9 Q-Q5, B-K3; 10 Q-B6ch, B-Q2; 11 Q-Q5, P-B5; winning the Bishop in familiar style.

At first sight 5 P-B4 looks strong, as it sets up a powerful grip on the center and prevents ... P-QN4. The right reply is 5 ... B-N5!; with a *pin* that exerts pressure on White's Q4 square.

Finally, after 5 BxNch, PxB; 6 P-Q4, Black can support the strong point at K4 with 6 ... P-B3! This leaves Black with a solid center, and his Bishop-pair is an additional asset.)

*5 P-B3, B-Q2.*

(The counterplay with 5 ... P-B4; will not do: 6 PxP, BxP; 7 P-Q4!, P-K5; 8 N-N5, P-Q4; 9 P-B3!, and White opens up the game advantageously.)

*6 P-Q4, P-KN3; 7 B-KN5, P-B3; 8 B-K3, N-R3!; 9 Castles, B-N2; 10 P-KR3, N-B2; 11 QN-Q2, Castles.*

Black's position, compact rather than constricted, has a great deal of latent power. This is one of the most satisfactory lines for Black in the Ruy Lopez.

**F.** Strong-Point Variation: Exchanges for the endgame—*1 P-K4, P-K4; 2 N-KB3, N-QB3; 3 B-N5, P-QR3; 4 BxN, QPxB.*

(White has exchanged in the hope of obtaining a theoretical advantage for the endgame.)

*5 P-Q4, PxP; 6 QxP, QxQ; 7 NxQ, B-Q2.*

(As in Diagram 177, White has a very favorable Pawn position. But in practice we find that Black's Bishop-pair is an important factor in his favor.)

*8 B-K3, Castles; 9 N-Q2, N-K2; 10 Castles QR, R-K1; 11 KR-K1, N-N3.*

Black has at least an even game.

**A.** Counterattack Variation with 9 ... B-K2 and 10 P-QR4!—*1 P-K4, P-K4; 2 N-KB3, N-QB3; 3 B-N5, P-QR3; 4 B-R4, N-B3; 5 Castles, NxP; 6 P-Q4.*

Diagram 221

Diagram 222

(See Diagram 221. White has lost a Pawn and now offers a second one. Why?

One of the basic points of the Counterattack Variation is that unless Black returns the extra Pawn, he will find himself in serious trouble. Thus, if now 6 ... PxP; the clearest line of refutation is 7 R-K1—*pinning!*—P-Q4; 8 B-KN5!, and Black's shaky position on the King file is cause for concern.)

6 ... *P-QN4; 7 B-N3, P-Q4; 8 PxP, B-K3; 9 P-B3.*

(See Diagram 222. Another characteristic position in the Counterattack Variation. White's last move was played to save his precious King Bishop from exchange and also to support a possible N-Q4 preparing for P-KB3 and P-KB4.

Black has attained a degree of freedom practically unknown to us in this opening; all his pieces function, or will function, actively. The price Black pays is that his position is somewhat loose—exposed to tactical threats, as we shall see. And, of course, the White Pawn wedge at K5 is useful in the formation of a King-side attack, as Black cannot post a protective Knight at his KB3 square.)

9 ... *B-K2; 10 P-QR4!*

(Probably White's strongest move. It hits at the Queen-side, but its effect will be felt all over the board.)

10 ... *P-N5; 11 N-Q4!, NxKP; 12 P-KB4, B-N5; 13 Q-B2.*

(If now 13 ... N-N3; 14 PxP, BxP; 15 N-B6 and wins.)

*13 ... P-QB4; 14 PxN, PxN; 15 PxQP, Castles.*

The likely continuation is 16 B-K3, B-K3; 17 N-Q2, NxN; 18 QxN. White has greater mobility, attacking chances, prospects of creating weaknesses in Black's King-side. The King Bishop file is White's great trump.

**B.** Counterattack Variation with 9 ... B-QB4—*1 P-K4, P-K4; 2 N-KB3, N-QB3; 3 B-N5, P-QR3; 4 B-R4, N-B3; 5 Castles, NxP; 6 P-Q4, P-QN4; 7 B-N3, P-Q4; 8 PxP, B-K3; 9 P-B3, B-QB4.*

Diagram 223        Diagram 224

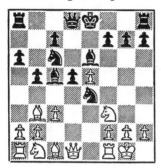 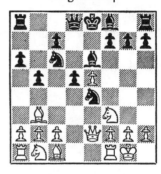

(See Diagram 223. The development of Black's King Bishop is more aggressive than 9 ... B-K2; but aggressiveness is not always desirable. There are several drawbacks to the Bishop's position at QB4. It prevents the rounding out of Black's Queen-side formation with ... P-QB4. It deprives Black's advanced Knight of a possible retreat to his QB4 square. Finally, the Bishop is usually exchanged, whereupon Black loses whatever benefit he might have had from ... B-QB4.)

*10 Q-Q3, Castles; 11 B-K3, BxB; 12 QxB, N-K2; 13 B-B2, P-KB4; 14 PxP e.p., RxP; 15 N-Q4!*

Despite his favorable development, Black's prospects are inferior. His black squares (note particularly his QB4 square) are weak, and his remaining Bishop is a "bad" Bishop.

**C.** Counterattack Variation with 9 Q-K2!—*1 P-K4, P-K4; 2 N-KB3, N-QB3; 3 B-N5, P-QR3; 4 B-R4, N-B3; 5 Castles, NxP; 6 P-Q4, P-QN4; 7 B-N3, P-Q4; 8 PxP, B-K3; 9 Q-K2!*

(See Diagram 224. White wants to play the logical R-Q1 in order to concentrate on Black's somewhat insecure Queen Pawn. He therefore dispenses with the conventional 9 P-B3, as he does not fear the coming exchange of his King Bishop.)

*9 ... N-B4; 10 R-Q1!, P-N5.*

(After 10 ... NxB; 11 RPxN, Q-B1; White has a very promising sacrifice in 12 P-B4!—for example 12 ... QPxP; 13 PxP, BxP; 14 Q-K4!, with a probably winning attack.)

*11 B-K3, NxB; 12 RPxN, Q-B1; 13 P-B4, QPxP; 14 PxP.*

White retains persistent pressure on the Queen-side, for example by playing QN-Q2-N3 and B-B5.

Our study of the Morphy Defense favors the Strong-Point Variation for Black, especially in the Steinitz Defense Deferred form. Black's freedom of action in the Counterattack Variation is deceptive, as his Pawn weaknesses are disquieting.

# 9

# SINGLE KING PAWN OPENINGS

In these openings Black avoids answering 1 P-K4 with 1 ... P-K4. This leads to positions which give an inexperienced player the impression that Black does not have a fair share of center control. The absence of a Black Pawn on K4 often permits White to work up a King-side attack based on the presence of his Pawn on K5 or KB5.

However, Black has his compensations. In the first place, he has avoided ... P-K4 in order to deprive White of playing whatever opening he intended to adopt. So Black has the satisfaction of having steered the game into his own favorite channels.

The struggle for the center still goes on. Black has not played ... P-K4, but he has other moves to fight for the center. Generally he plays ... P-Q4 (prepared by ... P-K3 or ... P-QB3). Where White plays P-K5 and supports the advanced King Pawn with P-Q4, Black has a fine counter with ... P-QB4. This leads to struggles for center supremacy which are as absorbing as they are critical.

Generally speaking, the rule in this type of opening is that White has a King-side initiative, while Black counters strongly on the other wing. It is a formula which makes for fascinating chess.

**French Defense.** This is above all a defense played to avoid whatever opening White has in mind when playing 1 P-K4. What does Black gain in return? The French Defense is tenacious and resourceful, an admirable weapon for conservative and patient players.

In almost all variations of the French, White has more terrain and King-side attacking chances. But Black usually has a stable position in the center and fair prospects of counterplay. The chief drawback in most of Black's formations is the difficulty of developing his Queen Bishop, which may become a "bad" Bishop if hemmed in by too many Black Pawns on white squares.

After 1 P-K4, P-K3; 2 P-Q4, P-Q4; it is rather pointless for White to play 3 PxP (the Exchange Variation), for after 3 ... PxP; Black frees his game, creates a diagonal for his problem Bishop and has a symmetrical position with considerable likelihood of a draw.

**A.** McCutcheon Variation with 4 ... B-N5—*1 P-K4, P-K3; 2 P-Q4, P-Q4; 3 N-QB3, N-KB3; 4 B-KN5, B-N5.*

The play thus far is an excellent example of the fight for the center which is characteristic of the French. White gets nowhere with 5 PxP, PxP; so he tries an aggressive line.

*5 P-K5, P-KR3.*

(Forced, in view of the fact that Black's *pinned* Knight cannot move.)

*6 B-Q2, BxN; 7 PxB, N-K5; 8 Q-N4, P-KN3.*

(This weakens the black squares, no longer guarded by Black's King Bishop. But 8 ... K-B1 loses the castling privilege and keeps Black's King Rook out of play.)

*9 B-B1!?, NxQBP.*

Diagram 225                    Diagram 226

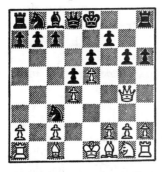 

(See Diagram 225. White's Pawn sacrifice preserves his Queen Bishop for effective action on the black squares.)

*10 B-Q3, P-QB4; 11 PxP, Q-B2; 12 B-K3, N-Q2.*

White still preserves considerable pressure after 13 Q-Q4. His Bishops and his strength on the black squares create a serious problem for Black. Note that the Black Bishop is yet to be developed.

**B.** Classical Variation with 4 ... B-K2—*1 P-K4, P-K3; 2 P-Q4, P-Q4; 3 N-QB3, N-KB3; 4 B-KN5, B-K2.*

(Though this move is less obviously aggressive than 4 ... B-N5, it fights equally stubbornly for control of the center by *unpinning* Black's King Knight and thereby threatening to capture White's King Pawn.

The alternative 4 ... PxP; 5 NxP, B-K2; leads to a quieter, rather lifeless, game.)

*5 P-K5, KN-Q2; 6 BxB, QxB; 7 Q-Q2, Castles; 8 P-B4, P-QB4; 9 N-B3, N-QB3.*

(See Diagram 226. Note how Black always uses the advance of the Queen Bishop Pawn to obtain more playing space for his forces. He intends to dissolve White's formidable-looking Pawn center with ... P-B3. The combination of ... P-QB4 and ... P-KB3 for this purpose is one of the most popular motifs in the French Defense.)

*10 Castles, P-B3; 11 KPxP, NPxP!*

Black preserves a powerful Pawn center which gives him at least equal chances.

**C.** Classical Variation: Alekhine's Attack—*1 P-K4, P-K3; 2 P-Q4, P-Q4; 3 N-QB3, N-KB3; 4 B-KN5, B-K2; 5 P-K5, KN-Q2; 6 P-KR4!*

(A puzzling move to meet properly. Accepting the proffered Pawn is pretty much out of the question, as after 6 ... BxB; 7 PxB, QxP; 8 N-R3, White has open lines and a lasting lead in development for his Pawn.)

*6 ... P-QB4!*

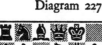

Diagram 227         Diagram 228

 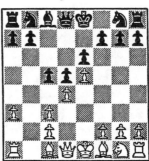

(See Diagram 227. Black has played the thematic freeing move!)

*7 BxB, KxB!*

(The natural-looking 7 ... QxB needlessly complicates matters because of the reply 8 N-N5.)

*8 P-B4, PxP; 9 QxP, N-QB3; 10 Q-Q2, P-QR3; 11 Castles, P-QN4; 12 N-B3, N-N3.*

Black has a playable game, despite his somewhat insecure King.

**D.** Counterattack Variation with 3 ... B-N5—*1 P-K4, P-K3; 2 P-Q4, P-Q4; 3 N-QB3, B-N5.*

(By pinning the Queen Knight, Black takes up the fight for the center in a different form from the one studied previously. White can relieve the tension in the center by 4 PxP, PxP; but the exchange gives Black an easy game.)

*4 P-K5!, P-QB4!*

(The advance of White's King Pawn is his most aggressive course, and Black's reply is the familiar reaction to P-K5. Now White plays to get rid of Black's valuable King Bishop. If he succeeds, the black squares in Black's camp will be very weak.)

*5 P-QR3, BxNch; 6 PxB.*

(See Diagram 228. Black's chief difficulty is that his remaining Bishop is condemned to have very little mobility, whereas White's Bishops can become very powerful—particularly on the black squares. To add to Black's troubles, he will be exposed in many cases to a powerful King-side attack—as for example after 6 ... N-K2; 7 Q-N4, N-B4; 8 N-B3, P-KR4; 9 Q-B4, with a very aggressive position for White.)

*6 ... Q-B2; 7 N-B3, N-K2; 8 P-KR4!, B-Q2; 9 P-R5, P-KR3.*

(White cannot be permitted to play P-R6, creating a fatal weakness in Black's black-square position on the King-side.)

*10 P-N4!, B-R5; 11 B-Q3, N-Q2; 12 P-N5, QR-B1; 13 R-QR2!*

White is fully protected against Black's indirect attack against the White Pawn at QB2. Black's pressure on the Queen Bishop file remains, but White has more freedom and better co-ordination for his pieces. His Bishop-pair will play an important role.

**E.** Tarrasch Variation with 3 N-Q2—*1 P-K4, P-K3; 2 P-Q4, P-Q4; 3 N-Q2.*

(The popularity of this move stems from White's frequent unwillingness to permit the *pinning* move 3 ... B-N5. On the other hand, 3 N-Q2 violates opening principles in that it blocks the development of White's Queen Bishop.)

 3 ... P-QB4!

(Black's tried and true resource. See Diagram 229. He is often left with an isolated Queen Pawn, but the marked freedom of his pieces is ample consolation.)

Diagram 229                    Diagram 230

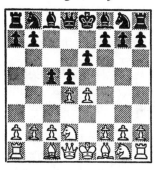        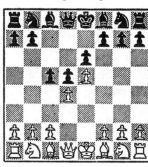

*4 KN-B3, P-QR3!; 5 KPxP, KPxP.*

(Now Black gets an isolated Queen Pawn, but in return he has an open King file and an open diagonal for his "problem child," the Queen Bishop.)

 *6 PxP, BxP; 7 N-N3, B-R2!; 8 B-KN5, N-KB3; 9 KN-Q4, Castles; 10 B-K2, Q-Q3!; 11 Castles, N-B3!; 12 B-K3, B-N1!*

Black has a free, aggressive game, such as rarely falls to his lot in this opening.

 **F.** Nimzovich Variation with 3 P-K5—*1 P-K4, P-K3; 2 P-Q4, P-Q4; 3 P-K5, P-QB4.*

(See Diagram 230. White throws down the gauntlet with a vengeance. By playing the early 3 P-K5, he at once reveals his intention to constrict Black relentlessly. To P-K5 the correct reaction is always ... P-QB4—an attempt to undermine the White Pawn-chain by attacking its base at Q4. White's best course is to support the Pawn-chain.)

 *4 P-QB3, N-QB3; 5 N-B3, Q-N3.*

(A hot fight is shaping up in Black's pressure against, and White's support of, White's Q4 square.)

*6 B-K2, PxP; 7 PxP, KN-K2; 8 P-QN3, N-B4; 9 B-N2, B-N5ch.*

(This compels White to renounce castling, as interposition will cost him the Queen Pawn.)

*10 K-B1, Castles; 11 P-N4, N-R3; 12 R-N1, P-B3!*

The attack on White's Pawn-chain still continues. A fighting game is in prospect.

This concludes our study of the French Defense. With the insight gained into the intricacies of this opening, we realize that Black must depend almost invariably on … P-QB4 for his counterplay; that he must beware of getting a constricted game or a serious weakness on the black squares; and that he must be alert for opportunities to make use of his Queen Bishop.

**Sicilian Defense.** Like the French Defense, the Sicilian Defense is a means of evading White's intended opening after 1 P-K4. Unlike the French, the Sicilian is aggressive in character and almost always leads to sharp play.

The characteristic move 1 … P-QB4 hinders the formation of a White Pawn center. Once White plays P-Q4 and Pawns are exchanged in the center, Black has a half-open Queen Bishop file along which he can exert pressure. In many cases Black fianchettoes his King Bishop, with considerable pressure on the long diagonal. These are definite trumps for Black, and White must look sharp for counterchances.

Even experienced players fail to realize that White's counterplay is chiefly based on the possibility of playing P-KB4 followed by P-B5 or P-K5 according to circumstances. The absence of a Black Pawn (as a rule) at Black's K4 square is what makes this possible. Whenever White is able to advance his King Bishop Pawn two squares, his game immediately takes on an aggressive aspect. This in turn calls for alert play on Black's part, and so we see that neither player can afford to be easygoing.

**A.** Dragon Variation—*1 P-K4, P-QB4; 2 N-KB3, N-QB3; 3 P-Q4, PxP; 4 NxP, N-B3; 5 N-QB3, P-Q3; 6 B-K2, P-KN3; 7 B-K3, B-N2.*

(Black has a satisfactory development. Note particularly how his fianchettoed Bishop strikes along the long diagonal.)

*8 Castles, Castles; 9 N-N3, B-K3; 10 P-B4, Q-B1!*

(An excellent resource against White's contemplated P-B5. See Diagram 231.)

Diagram 231          Diagram 232

Black has a good game in the position of Diagram 231, for example 11 P-KR3, R-Q1; 12 B-B3, B-B5; 13 R-K1, P-QR4; with a complicated struggle in prospect.

Another instance: 11 P-KR3, R-Q1; 12 P-N4, P-Q4! A center thrust is almost always a powerful antidote to a flank attack. Thus we see that 10 ... Q-B1! gives Black a sturdy defense against which it is not easy for White to make headway.

**B.** Scheveningen Variation—*1 P-K4, P-QB4; 2 N-KB3, N-QB3; 3 P-Q4, PxP; 4 NxP, N-B3; 5 N-QB3, P-Q3; 6 B-K2, P-K3.*

(Black discards the fianchetto idea, replacing it with a center Pawn formation at his K3 and Q3 squares. This has the drawback of being rather passive.)

*7 Castles, P-QR3.*

(See Diagram 232. Aside from the Pawn-storming attack which White adopts in the main line, he also has this effective procedure: 8 B-K3, Q-B2; 9 P-B4, B-K2; 10 N-N3, P-QN4; 11 B-B3, B-N2; 12 Q-K1!, Castles. Black soon finds himself under severe pressure after 13 Q-N3!, KR-Q1; 14 QR-Q1, N-Q2; 15 P-B5, etc.)

*8 K-R1, Q-B2; 9 P-B4, B-K2; 10 B-B3, Castles; 11 P-KN4!, B-Q2; 12 P-N5, N-K1; 13 P-QR4, N-R4; 14 P-B5.*

White's attack has assumed menacing proportions, and it is very doubtful whether Black can defend himself adequately.

**C.** 2 ... P-K3 Variation with ... B-N5—*1 P-K4, P-QB4; 2 N-KB3, P-K3; 3 P-Q4, PxP; 4 NxP, N-KB3; 5 N-QB3, N-B3; 6 N/Q4-N5.*

(See Diagram 233. Black's game is very difficult as White trains his

Diagram 233                    Diagram 234

sights on Black's weak Q3 square. The reply 6 ... P-Q3? leads to a bad game after 7 B-KB4! For then 7 ... N-K4? loses a Pawn by 8 Q-Q4!— and 7 ... P-K4; 8 B-N5 leaves Black with a critically weakened position.)

*6 ... B-N5; 7 P-QR3, BxNch; 8 NxB, P-Q4; 9 PxP, PxP; 10 B-Q3.*

White has some positional advantage because of his two Bishops and Black's isolated Queen Pawn.

**D.** 2 N-QB3 Variation—*1 P-K4, P-QB4; 2 N-QB3, N-QB3; 3 P-KN3, P-KN3; 4 B-N2, B-N2; 5 P-Q3.*

(See Diagram 234. White's system is different from the ones we have seen up to this point. He deliberately keeps the game closed, with the idea of opening up the position at a later, favorable, stage. Black must be careful not to drift into passivity.)

*5 ... P-K3.*

(Another good system is 5 ... P-Q3; 6 KN-K2, R-N1!; 7 B-K3, P-QN4; 8 Q-Q2, N-Q5; and Black stands well.)

*6 B-K3, Q-R4!; 7 KN-K2, N-Q5; 8 Castles, N-K2.*

The position is more or less even. Black's fianchettoed Bishop is quite effective.

What we have seen of the Sicilian Defense reinforces the feeling that this opening demands vigorous treatment on both sides. It is therefore an ideal opening for aggressive-minded players.

**Caro-Kann Defense.** The Caro-Kann Defense (1 ... P-QB3) has many of the virtues of the French Defense (1 ... P-K3). It involves less risk, and also yields less winning chances. Whereas the Sicilian (1 ...

P-QB4) fights from the very start against White's desire to set up a Pawn center, the Caro-Kann—like the French—allows White to form a Pawn center, and then meets it head-on with a Pawn center set up by Black. (The prevailing scheme is: 1 P-K4, P-QB3; 2 P-Q4, P-Q4.)

As you will see, Black's Queen Bishop is developed satisfactorily in almost every variation of the Caro-Kann. This is a plus feature as compared with the French, in which this Bishop is often hemmed in.

On the other hand, the Caro-Kann is rather colorless, and a bit of a bore for those with a lively temperament!

**A.** 3 N-QB3 Variation with 3 ... PxP and 4 ... N-Q2—*1 P-K4, P-QB3; 2 P-Q4, P-Q4.*

(White now has the problem of deciding how to operate in the center. Should he exchange Pawns, push on his King Pawn, or support his King Pawn?

The advance 3 P-K5 looks impressive, but has little sting. After the excellent reply 3 ... B-B4!; Black no longer has anything to fear; the development of his Queen Bishop is taken care of.)

*3 N-QB3, PxP; 4 NxP.*

(Black can now play 4 ... N-B3; but after 5 NxNch, he gets a doubled Pawn, with the kind of potential endgame disadvantage that we studied in the play beginning from Diagram 177. He therefore chooses a move which avoids Pawn weaknesses—at the cost of leading to a somewhat constricted game.)

*4 ... N-Q2; 5 N-KB3, KN-B3; 6 N-N3, P-K3.*

(One consequence of Black's selection of this conservative line is that

| Diagram 235 | Diagram 236 |
|:---:|:---:|
|  |  |

his Queen Bishop's development will be delayed considerably. See **Diagram 235**.)

*7 B-Q3, B-Q3; 8 Castles, Castles; 9 Q-K2, Q-B2; 10 N-K4, B-B5.*

Offering an exchange which will ease his game somewhat. White's game is freer and his development more rapid; but Black's position is very solid.

**B.** 3 N-QB3 Variation with 3 … PxP and 4 … B-B4—*1 P-K4, P-QB3; 2 P-Q4, P-Q4; 3 N-QB3, PxP; 4 NxP, B-B4.*

(Note the rapid and easy development of this Bishop.)

*5 N-N3, B-N3; 6 P-KR4, P-KR3; 7 N-B3, N-Q2; 8 B-Q3.*

(See Diagram 236. White has decided to get rid of the enemy Bishop, which is annoyingly well posted.)

*8 … BxB; 9 QxB, P-K3; 10 B-Q2, KN-B3; 11 Castles QR, Q-B2; 12 K-N1, Castles; 13 P-B4!*

White has greater freedom of action, while Black is well equipped for solid defense—but no more. A characteristic Caro-Kann verdict!

**C.** Exchange Variation with 4 P-QB4—*1 P-K4, P-QB3; 2 P-Q4, P-Q4; 3 PxP, PxP.*

(Once the Pawns have been exchanged, White must choose between an aggressive or conservative course in the center. Quiet continuations do not offer much, for example: 4 B-Q3, N-QB3; 5 P-QB3, N-B3; 6 B-KB4, P-KN3; 7 N-B3, B-N2; 8 P-KR3, Castles; 9 Castles, N-KR4!; and Black has an excellent game.)

*4 P-QB4, N-KB3; 5 N-QB3, N-B3.*

(Now White must put more pressure on the center—as he does with his next move. 6 N-B3 is too easygoing because of the *pinning* reply 6 … B-N5!)

*6 B-N5, P-K3.*

(Black can also play 6 … PxP; 7 BxP, P-K3; along the lines of the Queen's Gambit Accepted—see page 209.)

*7 N-B3, B-K2; 8 P-B5, Castles.*

(If White plays 9 B-N5 now, preparing to castle, Black liberates himself with 9 … N-K5!; 10 BxB, NxB. It then turns out that White's imposing Pawn structure is difficult to maintain against Black's undermining technique—. . . P-QN3; etc.)

    *9 R-B1, N-K5!; 10 BxB, QxB; 11 B-K2, R-Q1!; 12 Castles, P-K4!*

After this interesting freeing maneuver, prospects are about even. A likely sequel is 13 NxKP, N/B3xN; 14 PxN, NxN; 15 RxN, P-Q5!; when White's Queen-side Pawn majority is balanced by Black's formidable passed Pawn.

These representative variations give us a good idea of the character of the Caro-Kann. It is a defense that is solid—and stolid! Offering Black little chance for initiative, it seeks to deprive White of his initiative as well. It is an excellent resource for patient, conservative players who want to avoid risk and are not too troubled by the somewhat colorless nature of the Caro-Kann.

**Alekhine's Defense.** This defense (1 P-K4, N-KB3) is as bold as the Caro-Kann is stodgy. In fact, the consensus of opinion is that Alekhine's Defense is too daring. Its underlying idea is to menace White's King Pawn at once, provoking the advance of that Pawn—and other White Pawns as well—in the hope of later demonstrating that the Pawns have been weakened by their advance.

This sounds fine in theory, but in actual practice it will be found that if White combines sobriety with energy, his Pawn thrusts will result in a most uncomfortable position for Black. The fact, by the way, that Black's King Knight often winds up at Black's QN3 square is a telling point against the defense. This is generally a poor post for a Knight, giving him little influence on the vital center squares.

    **A.** Three Pawns' Variation—*1 P-K4, N-KB3; 2 P-K5, N-Q4; 3 P-QB4, N-N3; 4 P-Q4, P-Q3.*

<table>
<tr><td>Diagram 237</td><td>Diagram 238</td></tr>
</table>

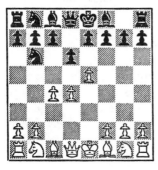

(See Diagram 237. White can now continue with 5 P-B4, and if 5 ...
PxP; 6 BPxP, N-B3; 7 B-K3. This is the most aggressive but also the
riskiest course. For inexperienced players the more modest text method
is more suitable.)

*5 PxP, KPxP.*

(The alternative 5 ... BPxP; leaves Black with a poor game after
6 P-Q5!, P-N3; 7 B-K3!, B-N2; 8 B-Q4!, when Black can hardly avoid
parting with his valuable fianchettoed Bishop.)

*6 N-QB3, N-B3; 7 B-K3, B-K2; 8 B-Q3, Castles; 9 KN-K2!, B-N5;
10 Castles, R-K1; 11 P-KR3, B-R4; 12 Q-Q2.*

White's development is free and harmonious. The poor position of
Black's Knight at QN3 is a distinct drawback for Black.

**B.** 4 N-KB3 Variation—*1 P-K4, N-KB3; 2 P-K5.*

(The colorless 2 N-QB3 is most simply answered by 2 ... P-K4;
transposing into the Vienna Game—page 164.)

*2 ... N-Q4; 3 P-Q4, P-Q3; 4 N-KB3.*

(See Diagram 238. White's intention is clear—he avoids advancing
Pawns unduly and concentrates on development.)

*4 ... B-N5; 5 B-K2, N-QB3; 6 Castles, P-K3; 7 P-B4, N-N3; 8 PxP,
PxP; 9 P-QN3, B-K2.*

(Again Black has been left with the stranded Knight at his QN3
square.)

*10 B-K3, Castles; 11 N-B3, P-Q4.*

(The "dead" position of Black's Knights goads him to action.)

*12 P-B5, N-Q2; 13 P-N4!*

White's Queen-side majority of Pawns, plus his superior development,
gives him a decided plus.

To sum up: Alekhine's Defense is most suited to the needs of stronger
players who are handling the Black pieces against weaker opponents.
Black's loss of time (especially the exile of the Knight at QN3) has no
compensating advantages. As we have seen, Black is rarely able to profit
by the anticipated weakening of White's Pawn center. Verdict: a
dubious defense, not to be recommended.

**Center Counter Defense.** This defense is definitely questionable, as it involves an early Queen development by Black with resulting difficulties in development.

*1 P-K4, P-Q4; 2 PxP, QxP; 3 N-QB3, Q-QR4.*

(This loss of time, as has been pointed out, is enough to discredit the defense. The drawbacks are similar to those of the Center Game—see page 163.

Note that in the French Defense Black *prepares* for ... P-Q4 by playing ... P-K3; while in the Caro-Kann Defense Black prepares for ... P-Q4 by playing ... P-QB3.)

*4 P-Q4, N-KB3.*

(The seemingly energetic 4 ... P-K4; only exposes the Queen to further attack after 5 PxP, QxKPch; 6 B-K2, with 7 N-B3 in the offing.)

*5 N-B3, B-N5; 6 P-KR3!, B-R4.*

(A dilemma for Black. After 6 ... BxN; 7 QxB, White has an easy two-Bishop game and more terrain.)

*7 P-KN4!, B-N3; 8 N-K5!, P-B3.*

(White's unorthodox play was threatening serious danger to Black's Queen by 9 N-B4, etc. Hence Black has prepared a retreat with his last move.)

*9 P-KR4!, N-K5; 10 B-Q2, Q-N3.*

(After 10 .. NxB; 11 QxN, White threatens P-R5. Then, after 11 ... P-B3; 12 NxB, PxN; 13 B-Q3, Black's King-side is seriously weak.)

*11 NxB, NxN; 12 BxN, RPxN.*

White continues 13 Q-Q2, P-K3; 14 Castles, with the twin advantages of the Bishop-pair and greater freedom of action.

The Center Counter is clearly inferior for Black and has no virtues that make it worth recommending.

**Nimzovich Defense.** The basic idea of this defense is very similar to that of Alekhine's Defense: the enticement of White's center Pawns to advance in the hope of weakening them. In practice, White's Pawns prove quite sturdy and Black is apt to have a constricted game.

**A. 2** ... P-Q4 Variation—*1 P-K4, N-QB3; 2 P-Q4, P-Q4; 3 N-QB3, P-K3.*

(Black avoids the gambit 3 ... PxP; 4 P-Q5, N-K4; 5 P-B3!, which gives White a rapid development for his Pawn.)

*4 N-B3, B-N5; 5 P-K5, BxNch.*

(Hoping to weaken White's Pawn structure.)

*6 PxB, N-R4; 7 P-QR4, N-K2; 8 B-Q3, P-QN3; 9 N-Q2!, P-QB4; 10 Q-N4, P-B5; 11 B-K2, N-B4; 12 N-B3.*

White's position is much more aggressive, and his Queen Bishop will have a magnificent post at QR3. Seriously hampered by the immobility of his Bishop, Black's game is anything but inviting.

**B.** 2 ... P-K4 Variation—*1 P-K4, N-QB3; 2 P-Q4, P-K4; 3 PxP, NxP.*

(The early deployment of Black's Knight is reminiscent of Alekhine's Defense—page 193. In this opening the advanced Knight is generally driven to a poor post at the KN3 square.)

*4 N-QB3, B-B4.*

(Or 4 ... N-KB3; 5 P-B4, N-B3; 6 P-K5, N-KN1; 7 N-B3!, P-Q3; 8 B-N5!, and White's position is markedly freer.)

*5 P-B4, N-N3; 6 N-B3, P-Q3; 7 B-B4, B-K3; 8 Q-K2, BxB; 9 QxB, Q-Q2; 10 P-B5.*

White has a very promising game, based on his superior development. Black's position is passive and devoid of counterplay. The position of his Knight at KN3 is particularly unfortunate.

We conclude, then, that the French Defense is sound, tenacious and not lacking in counterplay; the Sicilian is enterprising but somewhat risky; the Caro-Kann is safe albeit colorless. The Alekhine Defense, Center Counter Defense and Nimzovich Defense all have questionable aspects which disqualify them from serious consideration.

# 10

# DOUBLE QUEEN PAWN OPENINGS

The Double Queen Pawn openings have been described as "the chamber music of chess." This comment is a tribute to their subtlety and to the delicate nuances of positional judgment in which they abound.

In these openings, the emphasis is less on immediate attack and more on long-range preparation. This requires patience—and understanding of the goals involved. That is why the aspiring student is advised to devote his attention to the King Pawn openings at the start, leaving the more complex Queen Pawn lines for later examination and assimilation.

Friends and acquaintances may tell you that the Queen Pawn openings are "stodgy" or less interesting than those beginning with 1 P-K4. This is part of a prejudice that dies hard. The openings commencing with 1 P-Q4 are admittedly more complex, but they are full of fight and unusually rich in "chessy" ideas. The greatest masters of modern times have shown a decided preference for 1 P-Q4 precisely because of the many opportunities the resulting play has given them for the display of their magnificent capabilities.

If you begin playing 1 P-Q4 *when you are ready for it*, you will derive from it some of the most delightful rewards that fall to a chessplayer's lot.

**Queen's Gambit Declined.** This opening rivals the Ruy Lopez in popularity. The appeal of the gambit is obvious: after 1 P-Q4, P-Q4; White plays 2 P-QB4, ostensibly with a view to destroying Black's Pawn-hold on the center and thus obtaining a monopoly in the center with P-K4. At the same time, White creates for himself the possibility of opening the Queen Bishop file.

If Black is to maintain a Pawn in the center, he must play 2 ... P-K3 (closing his Queen Bishop's diagonal), or 2 ... P-QB3 (taking away his Queen Knight's best square). In either case, Black's development suffers, his game may become cramped, his freedom postponed indefinitely. Black has ways of freeing his game, but unless he is thoroughly alive to his opportunities, he may find himself with a permanently inferior position, or else exposed to a devastating attack which he cannot meet with the required elasticity and resourcefulness.

Inexperienced players, who manage to get by in the King Pawn openings with fair success, generally find themselves in serious trouble in the variations of the Queen's Gambit Declined. Black's difficulties generally stem from the Queen Bishop's lack of mobility. This is natural enough, in situations where he has Pawns on K3, Q4 and QB3 (all white squares). The logical solution for Black is to play ... P-QB4 with proper preparation. This has a liberating effect on his game, and also creates the possibility of an open line for Black's Rooks.

The liberating possibilities of ... P-QB4 are so important that, with one or two notable exceptions, Black must avoid blocking this Pawn by playing ... N-QB3 before advancing the Pawn.

**Queen's Gambit Declined: 2** ... P-K3 Defense—As we have already learned, Black is likely to have a cramped game during the opening stage. With careless, mediocre play on his part, this may lead to a crisis in the middle game. (In Diagrams 179, 191, 192, 196 and 198 we have instances of the kinds of difficulties which may beset Black in this opening in the event of consistently inferior play.)

If Black is aware of his difficulties, he knows that he must try to free himself in due course with ... P-QB4 or ... P-K4. The emancipating thrust with the Queen Bishop Pawn is the easier of the two to achieve.

Failure on Black's part to free himself will leave him a more or less passive victim of White's machinations. In some cases White's superior mobility will provide him with the makings of a powerful King-side attack. Oftentimes White can post his King Knight very formidably at K5; or he may attack along the vital diagonal QN1-KR7 (see Diagram 274). Another purely positional measure is the opening and occupation of the fully open Queen Bishop file or the half-open Queen Bishop file (see Diagram 196). Chess literature abounds in many a famous victory achieved through these and related methods.

**A.** Orthodox Defense—*1 P-Q4, P-Q4; 2 P-QB4, P-K3; 3 N-QB3, N-KB3; 4 B-N5, QN-Q2.*

(This is the setting for one of the oldest traps in the openings: 5 PxP, PxP; 6 NxP?? Black sacrifices his Queen and ends up a piece to the good: 6 ... NxN!!; 7 BxQ, B-N5ch!; 8 Q-Q2, BxQch; 9 KxB, KxB.)

*5 P-K3, B-K2; 6 N-B3, Castles; 7 R-B1!*

(A powerful move because it has an inhibiting effect on Black's playing ... P-QB4. But without that freeing Pawn move the future of Black's Queen Bishop is dark indeed.)

7 ... *P-B3; 8 B-Q3, PxP; 9 BxBP, N-Q4.*

(Black seeks exchanges to free his cramped game.)

*10 BxB, QxB; 11 Castles, NxN; 12 RxN, P-K4.*

Diagram 239                    Diagram 240

(See Diagram 239. Having played the standard liberating move—... P-K4—Black can just about hold his own after 13 PxP, NxP; 14 NxN, QxN; 15 P-B4!, Q-K5!)

*13 Q-B2!*

This leaves White with a freer and therefore preferable position.

**B.** Cambridge Springs Defense—*1 P-Q4, P-Q4; 2 P-QB4, P-K3; 3 N-QB3, N-KB3; 4 B-N5, QN-Q2; 5 P-K3, P-B3; 6 N-B3, Q-R4.*

(See Diagram 240. This is the move from which the Defense derives its name. Black's idea is to *pin* White's Queen Knight, taking advantage of the fact that White's Queen Bishop is unable to return to Q2.

White cannot afford to be careless, for example 7 B-Q3?, PxP; 8 BxBP, K-N5!; and Black wins some material because of the *double attack* on White's Queen Knight and Queen Bishop. White therefore *unpins* his Queen Knight.)

*7 N-Q2, PxP; 8 BxN, NxB; 9 NxP, Q-B2.*

Black's position is now somewhat cramped, but he has a real future because of his Bishop-pair. Later on he will succeed in playing .. P-QB4, bringing his Queen Bishop to life.

**C.** Exchange Variation—*1 P-Q4, P-Q4; 2 P-QB4, P-K3; 3 N-QB3, N-KB3; 4 B-N5, QN-Q2; 5 P-K3, P-B3; 6 PxP.*

(This exchange is also played as early as the third, fourth or fifth moves—or sometimes later on. It appears here in its clearest form. Black's method of recapture is determined by his desire to create an open line for his Queen Bishop.)

*6 ... KPxP; 7 B-Q3, B-K2; 8 Q-B2!*

(The alternative 8 N-B3 is inexact, as Black frees himself with 8 ... N-K5!; which gives him a fine game.)

Diagram 241                    Diagram 242

(See Diagram 241. And now, after 8 Q-B2!, Black cannot play 8 ... N-K5?; which loses a Pawn after 9 BxB, etc.)

*8 ... Castles; 9 N-B3, R-K1; 10 Castles KR, N-B1; 11 QR-N1!*

Herein is revealed the basic motif of the Exchange Variation: White proposes to advance his Queen Knight Pawn to QN5 with a view to inducing Black to play ... BPxNP. In that case, Black's Queen Pawn will be isolated and subject to attack, and White will be able to operate on the open Queen Bishop and Queen Knight files with his heavy pieces.

If Black stands pat after P-N5 and allows White to exchange Pawns, the end product will be a backward Queen Bishop Pawn on the open file. In recent years, the Exchange Variation has become one of White's most feared weapons. To counteract this danger, a vital simplifying defense has been devised for Black.

**D.** Lasker's Variation—*1 P-Q4, P-Q4; 2 P-QB4, P-K3; 3 N-QB3, N-KB3; 4 B-N5, B-K2; 5 P-K3, Castles; 6 N-B3, P-KR3; 7 B-R4, N-K5!*

(The key-move of the defense.)

*8 BxB, QxB.*

(See Diagram 242. White has no way of gaining an advantage. Thus if 9 NxN, PxN; 10 N-Q2, P-K4!; 11 NxP?, PxP; 12 QxP??, R-Q1; and Black wins a piece!)

*9 PxP, NxN; 10 PxN, PxP.*

(This is the best development we have yet seen for Black in the Queen's Gambit Declined. He has freed his position considerably and he has an open diagonal for the Queen Bishop.)

*11 Q-N3, R-Q1; 12 P-B4, PxP; 13 BxP, N-B3; 14 Q-B3, B-N5.*

With this Bishop aggressively developed, Black's worries are over. Because of its simplicity and relatively small number of variations, this defense should be a favorite with all inexperienced players. Few defenses are as effective in squelching White's initiative.

**E. Prague Variation**—*1 P-Q4, P-Q4; 2 P-QB4, P-K3; 3 N-KB3, N-KB3; 4 N-B3, P-B4!*

Diagram 243          Diagram 244

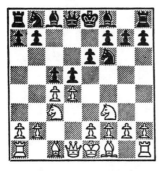    

(See Diagram 243. Black frees his game with the early ... P-B4. The reply 5 P-K3 leads to a fairly symmetrical position with even chances.)

*5 BPxP, NxP!; 6 P-K4, NxN; 7 PxN, PxP; 8 PxP, B-N5ch!*

(Simplification eases Black's task.)

*9 B-Q2, BxBch; 10 QxB, Castles; 11 B-B4, N-B3; 12 Castles, P-QN3; 13 KR-Q1, B-N2.*

White has a powerful Pawn center, Black has the Queen-side majority of Pawns. The position is approximately even. This is a recommended defense.

**F.** Tarrasch Defense—*1 P-Q4, P-Q4; 2 P-QB4, P-K3; 3 N-QB3, P-QB4; 4 BPxP!, KPxP.*

(Note that Black does not have the resource of ... NxP as in Variation E. He is therefore likely to be burdened with an isolated Queen Pawn.)

*5 N-B3, N-QB3; 6 P-KN3!*

(See Diagram 244. White intends to fianchetto his King Bishop—a formidable weapon against Black's weak Queen Pawn.)

*6 ... N-B3; 7 B-N2, B-K2; 8 Castles, Castles; 9 PxP!, BxP; 10 N-QR4, B-K2; 11 B-K3, N-K5; 12 R-B1.*

White's pressure on the Queen Pawn and the magnificent square at Q4 give him a definitely superior position. Black's free development does not make up for the weakness of his Queen Pawn.

A brief summary of these six defenses with ... P-K3 is in order. The most promising lines for Black are Variations B (Cambridge Springs), D (Lasker), and E (Prague).

Variation F (Tarrasch) is to be avoided, as it creates a lasting organic weakness in Black's game.

Variations A (Orthodox) and C (Exchange) are playable for Black but unrewarding, as they subject him to considerable pressure and an arduous draw at best.

**Queen's Gambit Declined:** Slav Defense—The characteristic move of this defense is 2 ... P-QB3. Very often Black develops his Queen Bishop to KB4, enabling the Bishop to take an active part in the game or be exchanged. This is a welcome relief from the difficulties encountered with the Bishop in the ... P-K3 defenses.

However, as we shall see later on, Black often considers it necessary to play ... QPxBP before bringing out this Bishop. This surrender of the center forces him to fight aggressively for his share of the center.

Generally speaking, the freeing move ... P-QB4, if played at all, will appear rather late in the day.

An important segment in the Slav group is formed by the Semi-Slav defenses. In these, the characteristic moves are ... P-QB3 *and* ... P-K3, so that as a rule the problem of developing the Queen Bishop again comes to the fore. However, some unusually interesting techniques have been worked out to minimize this difficulty.

**A.** Slav Accepted with 5 P-QR4 and 9 ... B-KN5—*1 P-Q4, P-Q4; 2 P-QB4, P-QB3; 3 N-KB3, N-B3; 4 N-B3, PxP.*

(This deferred acceptance of the gambit strikes Black as unavoidable; for if 4 ... B-B4; 5 PxP, PxP; 6 Q-N3!, and Black's defense is cumbersome.)

*5 P-QR4.*

(He can also play 5 P-K3, for after 5 ... P-QN4; 6 P-QR4, he will recover his Pawn—for example 6 .. P-QR3; 7 PxP, BPxP; 8 NxP!, etc.)

*5 ... B-B4; 6 P-K3, P-K3; 7 BxP, B-QN5.*

Diagram 245                    Diagram 246

     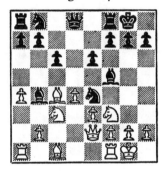

(See Diagram 245. Black's last move is played to restrain P-K4 by threatening ... BxN in the event of P-K4.)

*8 Castles, Castles; 9 Q-K2, B-N5; 10 P-R3, BxN; 11 QxB, QN-Q2; 12 R-Q1, P-K4!*

The basic idea is that if 13 PxP, NxP! The likely continuation is 13 P-Q5, BxN!; 14 PxP!, P-K5!; 15 Q-B5, B-K4!; 16 PxN, Q-B2. This variation is tricky, but Black can hold his own with good play.

**B.** Slav Accepted with 5 P-QR4 and 9 ... N-K5—*1 P-Q4, P-Q4; 2 P-QB4, P-QB3; 3 N-KB3, N-B3; 4 N-B3, PxP; 5 P-QR4, B-B4; 6 P-K3, P-K3; 7 BxP, B-QN5; 8 Castles, Castles; 9 Q-K2, N-K5.*

(See Diagram 246. Black has physically prevented P-K4. Can White drive off the intruder?)

*10 B-Q3!*

(After this enterprising sacrifice, Black must give way. If 10 ...

NxN; 11 PxN, BxP; 12 R-N1, White has a splendid post for his Queen Bishop at QR3; Black's advanced Bishop is dangerously exposed, and his prospects of development are poor.)

*10 ... BxN; 11 PxB!, NxQBP; 12 Q-B2, BxB; 13 QxB, N-Q4; 14 B-R3.*

White's vastly superior development, coupled with his overwhelming center (after P-K4), gives him a very favorable position.

**C.** Slav Accepted with 5 P-QR4 and 8 P-KN3—*1 P-Q4, P-Q4; 2 P-QB4, P-QB3; 3 N-KB3, N-B3; 4 N-B3, PxP; 5 P-QR4, B-B4; 6 N-K5.*

(White intends to recapture the gambit Pawn with this Knight.)

Diagram 247        Diagram 248

(See Diagram 247. If Black tries 6 ... P-K3 now, White can play 7 P-B3!, B-QN5; 8 NxP/B4, Castles; 9 B-N5!, P-B4; 10 PxP, QxQch; 11 KxQ, BxP; 12 P-K4!, B-KN3; 13 N-K5, etc. This gives him a favorable ending because of his two Bishops against Bishop and Knight after 14 NxB.)

*6 ... QN-Q2; 7 NxP/B4, Q-B2; 8 P-KN3!*

(Preparing for B-B4, and for the effective fianchetto of the other Bishop.)

*8 ... P-K4; 9 PxP, NxP; 10 B-B4, N/B3-Q2; 11 B-N2, P-B3; 12 Castles, R-Q1; 13 Q-B1!, B-K3; 14 N-K4!*

Black hoped to minimize the *pin* with his last move, but White keeps up the pressure. The point is that if 14 ... BxN; 15 QxB, NxQ; 16 BxQ, and White has a distinctly favorable two-Bishop endgame. In any case, White retains the initiative.

The Slav Accepted, in the forms we have seen it, does not seem very promising for Black. This explains the popularity of a number of variations grouped under the heading of "Semi-Slav." Here Black plays ... P-QB3 and then ... P-K3, hemming in his Queen Bishop, but having certain possibilities of freeing himself. These variations, with their many intricate consequences, have been the subject of intensive research for several decades; the *theoretical* decision is generally in White's favor.

**D.** Semi-Slav: Meran Defense—*1 P-Q4, P-Q4; 2 P-QB4, P-QB3; 3 N-KB3, N-B3; 4 N-B3, P-K3.*

(Black renounces the idea of developing his Queen Bishop by ... B-B4; he intends to fianchetto the Bishop later on.)

*5 P-K3, QN-Q2; 6 B-Q3, PxP; 7 BxBP, P-QN4; 8 B-Q3, P-QR3.*

(Also possible is 8 ... B-N2; 9 P-K4, P-N5!; 10 N-QR4, P-B4! See Diagram 248.)

*9 P-K4.*

(White tries an aggressive advance. If he proceeds peacefully with 9 Castles, P-B4; 10 P-QR4, P-N5; 11 N-K4, Black has nothing to fear after 11 ... B-N2; which gives him a comfortable development.)

*9 ... P-B4!; 10 P-K5, PxP!; 11 NxNP, NxP!*

(A fearfully complicated position! If 11 ... PxN; 12 PxN, Q-N3; 13 PxP, BxP; 14 Castles, B-N2; 15 B-KB4, Castles KR; he finds himself in some difficulty because his King-side is a bit denuded.)

*12 NxN, PxN; 13 Q-B3, B-N5ch!; 14 K-K2, QR-N1.*

(The apparently crushing 15 N-B6 is now parried by 15 ... B-N2!)

*15 Q-N3, Q-Q3!; 16 N-B3, QxQ; 17 RPxQ, B-Q3; 18 NxP, B-Q2.*

The ending is fairly even. However, this defense is too complicated for inexperienced players.

**E.** Semi-Slav: Anti-Meran Variation—*1 P-Q4, P-Q4; 2 P-QB4, P-QB3; 3 N-KB3, N-B3; 4 N-B3, P-K3; 5 B-N5!?*

(Played to avoid the Meran Variation, but the sequel is, if anything, even more complicated!)

*5 ... PxP.*

(Note that with 5 ... QN-Q2; Black can transpose into such lines as the Orthodox Defense, Cambridge Springs or Exchange Variations.)

*6 P-K4, P-N4; 7 P-K5, P-KR3.*

(This and Black's following move are forced.)

*8 B-R4, P-N4; 9 NxKNP!, PxN; 10 BxNP, QN-Q2.*

| Diagram 249 | Diagram 250 |
|:-:|:-:|
|  |  |

(See Diagram 249. This position abounds in wild possibilities. If 11 Q-B3, B-QN2; 12 B-K2, Q-N3!; 13 PxN, P-B4!; and Black has freed himself. White therefore finds a different way to make use of the long diagonal; he intends to fianchetto his King Bishop.)

*11 P-KN3, Q-R4; 12 PxN, P-N5; 13 N-K4, B-QR3!*

A position full of fight, with the outcome undetermined.

**F.** Semi-Slav: Classical Variation—*1 P-Q4, P-Q4; 2 P-QB4, P-QB3; 3 N-KB3, N-B3; 4 N-B3, P-K3; 5 P-K3, QN-Q2.*

(Against the "Stonewall" line 5 ... N-K5; 6 B-Q3, P-KB4; White has a powerful retort in 7 P-KN4!)

*6 B-Q3, B-Q3.*

(In this variation Black avoids the intricacies of the Meran Variation by developing his King Bishop, but his position remains somewhat constricted. After 6 ... B-K2; 7 Castles, Castles; 8 P-QN3!, P-QN3; 9 B-N2, B-N2; White has the advantage of having a more aggressive position for his King Bishop.)

*7 Castles, Castles; 8 P-K4!*

(See Diagram 250. White opens up the game to exploit his superior mobility. If now 8 ... PxBP; 9 BxBP, P-K4; 10 B-KN5!, and White preserves greater freedom of action.)

8 ... *PxKP; 9 NxP, NxN; 10 BxN.*

No matter how Black plays, he will not find it easy to free his game. The immediate 10 ... P-K4?; loses a Pawn: 11 PxP, NxP; 12 NxN, BxN; 13 BxPch!, KxB; 14 Q-R5ch winning a Pawn by *double attack.*

**G.** Slav Defense with ... B-B4—*1 P-Q4, P-Q4; 2 P-QB4, P-QB3; 3 N-KB3, N-B3; 4 P-K3, B-B4.*

(This development disposes of Black's chief difficulty without quite solving all his problems.)

*5 B-Q3, BxB; 6 QxB, P-K3; 7 N-B3, QN-Q2; 8 Castles, B-N5.*

(After 8 ... B-Q3; 9 P-K4, White maintains a somewhat freer game. The text is played to restrain him from playing P-K4.)

*9 B-Q2!*

Diagram 251      Diagram 252

(See Diagram 251. If Black is careless, he will lose a Pawn: 9 ... Castles?; 10 NxP!)

*9 ... B-R4; 10 P-QN4!, B-B2.*

(Or 10 ... BxP; 11 NxP!, NxN; 12 PxN, BxB; 13 PxBP!, and White has a clear advantage.)

*11 P-K4, PxBP; 12 QxBP.*

White has come out of the opening with a markedly freer game.

**H.** Slav Defense: Exchange Variation—*1 P-Q4, P-Q4; 2 P-QB4, P-QB3; 3 PxP, PxP; 4 N-QB3, N-KB3; 5 N-B3, N-B3; 6 B-B4.*

(See Diagram 252. If Black continues 6 ... P-K3; 7 B-K3, B-K2; he may find himself limited to an uncomfortably passive position later on.)

*6 .. B-B4!; 7 P-K3, P-K3; 8 Q-N3, B-QN5!*

(If now 9 N-K5, Q-R4!; with counterattack.)

*9 B-QN5, Castles!*

(So that if 10 BxN, BxNch; 11 QxB, R-B1!; with good counterplay after 12 Q-R3, RxB; 13 QxP, B-Q6!)

*10 Castles, BxN; 11 BxN, BxNP; 12 BxNP, BxR; 13 RxB.*

White also wins the exchange, with a quick draw indicated. A most useful defense.

Black's best bet in the whole range of Slav Defense lines appears to be Variation D—the Meran Variation. If he plays for this variation, he must also be prepared for Variation E—the Anti-Meran Variation. Both of these variations are lively, complicated and full of fight. All forms of the Slav Accepted seem to offer little of value for Black—perhaps because they involve a surrender of the center on his part.

**Albin Counter Gambit.** This is a violent attempt to wrest the initiative from White. White's indicated course is to develop quickly, as retaining the gambit Pawn is less important than development. Thus, he generally allows Black to regain the Pawn, but this loses time for Black and usually gives White the Bishop-pair. Still a further important point is that Black's advanced Queen Pawn may become an object of attack.

*1 P-Q4, P-Q4; 2 P-QB4, P-K4?!; 3 QPxP, P-Q5.*

(This is the gambit move.)

*4 N-KB3, N-QB3.*

(Now White can return the Pawn advantageously with 5 QN-Q2, B-QN5; 6 P-QR3!, BxNch; 7 QxB!, B-N5; 8 P-N4!, BxN; 9 KPxB, NxKP; 10 B-N2, Q-K2; 11 Castles, Castles; 12 P-B4—with a far superior game for White because of his two Bishops against two Knights.)

*5 P-KN3, B-K3; 6 QN-Q2, Q-Q2; 7 B-N2, R-Q1.*

(Castling, instead of Black's last move, is dangerous because experience has shown that White's King Bishop has strong attacking possibilities along the diagonal.)

*8 Castles, KN-K2; 9 Q-R4, N-N3; 10 P-QR3, B-K2.*

(Black cannot win the King Pawn without losing a Pawn of his own in return for it.)

*11 P-QN4, Castles; 12 B-N2.*

White's position is vastly superior—and he has held on to his material advantage.

**Queen's Gambit Accepted.** To those who are weary of the tasks confronting Black in declining the gambit, its acceptance seems to offer a welcome relief. But accepting the gambit results, of course, in new problems. Black surrenders the center, with the consequence that his opponent almost always has greater mobility and generally a faster development. There is also the possibility of White's being able to play P-K4, which gives him a powerful game in the center. Black must play with great precision if he is not to succumb to a quick attack.

Having captured in the center, Black has at least succeeded in opening the long diagonal, and will generally fianchetto his Queen Bishop. However, in one popular variation, he develops his Queen Bishop to KN5. As is to be expected, this leaves him exposed to attack on the Queen-side.

**A.** 4 ... P-K3 Variation—*1 P-Q4, P-Q4; 2 P-QB4, PxP; 3 N-KB3, N-KB3; 4 P-K3, P-K3.*

(Trying to retain the gambit Pawn is pointless: 4 ... P-QN4; 5 P-QR4, P-B3; 6 P-QN3!, etc.)

*5 BxP, P-B4; 6 Castles, P-QR3; 7 Q-K2, N-B3.*

Diagram 253                Diagram 254

(See Diagram 253. The simplest way for White to obtain a positional advantage here is 8 PxP!, BxP; 9 P-QR3!, P-QN4; 10 B-R2, B-N2; 11 P-QN4, B-K2; 12 B-N2, Castles; 13 QN-Q2! This last move is the point of the variation. White's Queen Knight heads for the QB5 square—a powerful post. Thus, after 13 ... Q-N3; 14 N-N3, KR-Q1; 15 QR-B1, QR-B1; 16 N-B5, the dominant position of this Knight gives White a definitely superior game.)

*8 R-Q1, P-QN4.*

(Black hopes for 9 B-Q3—or 9 B-N3, when he can continue 9 ... P-B5!; 10 B-B2, N-QN5!; followed by ... NxB; with a comfortable two-Bishop game.)

*9 PxP!, Q-B2; 10 B-Q3.*

(If now 10 ... N-QN5; White has 11 P-QR4!, NxB; 12 QxN, P-N5; 13 P-B6!, and the advanced Pawn has a paralyzing effect on Black's game—if 13 ... QxBP??; 14 Q-Q8 mate!)

*10 ... BxP; 11 P-QR4!*

(And now if 11 ... PxP; 12 RxP, N-QN5; 13 B-N5ch!, B-Q2; 14 BxBch, NxB; 15 B-Q2, and Black's position is very difficult.)

*11 ... P-N5; 12 QN-Q2, Castles; 13 N-N3, B-K2; 14 P-K4!*

White will play out his Queen Bishop followed by QR-B1, leaving Black with a very uncomfortable position.

**B.** 4 ... B-N5 Variation—*1 P-Q4, P-Q4; 2 P-QB4, PxP; 3 N-KB3, P-QR3.*

("Threatening" ... P-QN4 and thus provoking White's reply, which allows a *pin* by Black.)

*4 P-K3, B-N5; 5 P-KR3, B-R4; 6 BxP, P-K3; 7 Q-N3!*

(See Diagram 254. Aside from the threat QxNP, White wants to play N-K5.)

*7 ... BxN; 8 PxB, P-QN4; 9 B-K2, P-QB4; 10 P-QR4!, P-N5; 11 PxP, BxP.*

White has weakened Black's Queen-side Pawns in familiar fashion and secured the QB4 square for his pieces. With the Bishop-pair and the open King Knight file at his disposal, he has the makings of a very strong position.

Thus we see that after accepting the gambit Black generally suffers from a shortage of terrain. The early opening-up of the game is likely to turn out unsatisfactorily for him.

# 11

# SINGLE QUEEN PAWN OPENINGS

These openings are based on what seems at first sight a very strange idea. Black refrains from playing ... P-Q4, either temporarily or permanently. He thus obtains an elastic position by not committing himself in the center, but he does have to find a way to contend with White's threat to monopolize the center with P-K4. There are two ways to accomplish this. One is to play ... P-Q4 later on; the other is to permit P-K4 and form a countercenter with ... P-Q3 and ... P-K4.

One of the great advantages of these defenses is that Black rarely has trouble with the development of his Queen Bishop, which, as we have seen, is Black's paramount difficulty in the Queen's Gambit.

The defenses which we are about to study are generally aggressive in spirit and thereby eliminate another source of discomfort which Black generally experiences in the Queen's Gambit Declined. It is logical, however, to start defending with ... P-Q4 first before proceeding to the defenses in this chapter. You cannot really appreciate the merits of the defenses beginning with 1 ... N-KB3, for example, without being familiar with Black's problems arising from 1 P-Q4.

**Nimzoindian Defense.** This defense starts with the moves 1 P-Q4, N-KB3; 2 P-QB4, P-K3; 3 N-QB3, B-N5. The *pinning* move of the Bishop is designed to restrain White's immediate P-K4. (See Diagram 255.)

You may confidently anticipate that the resulting play will revolve in some form or other around the control of White's K4 square. As we have noted, Black can either play ... P-Q4 later on (to restrain White's P-K4); or he may form a countercenter with ... P-Q3 and ... P-K4. Still a third method is to play an early ... P-QB4, hoping by this diversion to discourage White from committing himself unduly with P-K4.

The Nimzoindian Defense has the theoretical drawback that Black's King Bishop is almost invariably exchanged for White's Knight. This gives White the Bishop-pair and, with inexact play on Black's part, will result in strong attacking chances for White. In addition, when White

Diagram 255                    Diagram 256

recaptures with his Knight Pawn, he supports the Queen Pawn and may be able to build up a powerful Pawn mass. This too contributes to the prospects of White's securing a strong initiative.

But Black has counterplay; for White often has Pawn weaknesses on the Queen Bishop file, and in general Black's development is rapid enough to enable him to put up a good fight. So, weighing up all the factors involved, we find that the Nimzoindian Defense is a fighting game with chances for both sides.

**A.** 4 Q-B2 Variation with 4 ... P-Q4—*1 P-Q4, N-KB3; 2 P-QB4, P-K3; 3 N-QB3, B-N5; 4 Q-B2, P-Q4.*

(The simplest way to prevent P-K4.

See Diagram 256. If White tries 5 P-QR3, BxNch; 6 QxB, N-K5; 7 Q-B2, N-QB3; 8 N-B3, P-K4!?; he finds himself in a highly complicated line. So he chooses a less risky variation.)

*5 PxP, QxP; 6 N-B3, P-B4; 7 B-Q2, BxN.*

(Black exchanges in order to be able to maintain his Queen at her *centralized* position.)

*8 BxB, PxP; 9 NxP, P-K4; 10 N-B3, N-B3; 11 P-K3, Castles; 12 B-K2, B-N5.*

White's Bishop-pair gives him a slightly better game. But Black has developed rapidly and freely.

**B.** 4 Q-B2 Variation with 4 ... N-B3—*1 P-Q4, N-KB3; 2 P-QB4, P-K3; 3 N-QB3, B-N5; 4 Q-B2, N-B3.*

(This is played with the object of forming a countercenter with .  . P-Q3 and ... P-K4.)

*5 N-B3, P-Q3; 6 B-Q2, P-K4; 7 P-QR3, BxN; 8 BxB, Q-K2; 9 PxP, PxP.*

(Black has succeeded in establishing himself in the center, but again White has the Bishop-pair.)

*10 P-K3, P-QR4!*

(An important move to prevent White from seizing too much ground with P-QN4.)

*11 P-R3!*

This prevents ... B-N5 and forces Black's Bishop to develop rather modestly. As in the previous variation, White has somewhat more mobility because of his two Bishops; but Black has developed comfortably.

**C.** 4 Q-B2 Variation with 4 ... P-B4—*1 P-Q4, N-KB3; 2 P-QB4, P-K3; 3 N-QB3, B-N5; 4 Q-B2, P-B4; 5 PxP.*

(Black tries counterattack against White's center, but Black's resulting backward Queen Pawn on the open file inspires some skepticism. Note, by the way, that 5 P-Q5? is all wrong—it simply loses a Pawn because of the *pin*.)

*5 ... Castles.*

(The alternative method 5 ... N-B3; 6 N-B3, BxP; 7 B-N5, N-Q5; 8 NxN, BxN; 9 N-N5!, gives White powerful pressure along the Queen file.)

*6 N-B3, N-R3!*

(An interesting if roundabout way to get more pressure against White's K4 square.)

*7 B-Q2.*

(After 7 P-QR3, BxNch; 8 QxB, NxP; 9 P-QN4, N/B4-K5; Black's more active development compensates for White's Bishop-pair.)

*7 ... NxP; 8 P-QR3, BxN; 9 BxB, N/B4-K5.*

And again Black's active development gives him a hold on the center. Black's methods in this variation are very interesting.

**D.** 4 P-K3 Variation—*1 P-Q4, N-KB3; 2 P-QB4, P-K3; 3 N-QB3, B-N5; 4 P-K3, P-Q4.*

(White's rather modest fourth move is intended to store up energy for a future struggle for the center. Despite its appearance of simplicity, it can lead to a hard fight.)

*5 B-Q3, Castles; 6 P-QR3, BxNch; 7 PxB.*

Diagram 257              Diagram 258

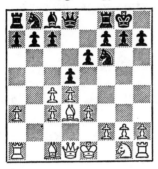     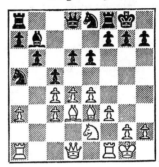

(See Diagram 257. Now Black can go seriously wrong with 7 ... P-B4; 8 BPxP!, KPxP; 9 B-Q3, P-QN3; 10 N-K2, B-R3; 11 BxB, QxB. In that case, White soon works up a powerful attack based on the possibility of P-B3! and P-K4!)

*7 ... PxP!; 8 BxBP, P-B4!*

(Black's sequence has taken most of the starch out of White's contemplated attacking formation, and Black has good play on the Queen Bishop file against White's Queen Bishop Pawn, which may turn out to be a weakness.)

*9 N-B3, Q-B2!*

Black has an excellent game. White's Queen Bishop Pawn is troublesome, and the situation of both his Bishops is awkward.

**E.** 4 P-QR3 Variation—*1 P-Q4, N-KB3; 2 P-QB4, P-K3; 3 N-QB3, B-N5; 4 P-QR3.*

(A dashing move. White provokes the immediate exchange, in order to bolster his center and obtain the Bishop-pair, with an attack in view.)

*4 ... BxNch; 5 PxB, P-B4!*

(Black fights back in the center, reserving the possibility of menacing White's doubled Queen Bishop Pawns.)

*6 P-K3, P-QN3; 7 B-Q3, B-N2; 8 P-B3, N-B3.*

(More pressure on White's center.)

*9 N-K2, Castles; 10 P-K4, N-K1!*

(Allowing himself to be *pinned* by B-N5 would be too constricting.)

*11 B-K3, P-Q3; 12 Castles, N-R4!*

Black announces his counterplay. See Diagram 258. As circumstances permit, he will play ... B-R3 and ... Q-Q2-R5; training his guns on White's weak doubled Pawns.

In every one of these variations Black has ceded the Bishop-pair to his opponent, but has managed—by active counterplay, to maintain a promising game. Thus the Nimzoindian Defense lives up to its reputation as a fighting line.

**Queen's Indian Defense.** This defense involves the fianchetto of Black's Queen Bishop to control his important K5 square. White likewise struggles for control of this square, but the fact that he plays 3 N-KB3 (instead of 3 N-QB3) leaves him with a real fight on his hands. The experience of many years with this defense indicates that White's best weapon against the fianchetto is a counterfianchetto which participates in the fight for control of the center.

The Queen's Indian is, by the way, tactically less dangerous for Black than the Nimzoindian; in the Queen's Indian, White's Bishop at KN2 aims at the Queen-side, ruling out possibilities of King-side attack. Also, White rarely secures a powerful Pawn center in the Queen's Indian—another factor that makes formidable attacks unlikely. Nevertheless, White usually obtains a slight but persistent initiative.

**A.** 4 P-KN3 Variation with 5 ... B-K2—*1 P-Q4, N-KB3; 2 P-QB4, P-K3; 3 N-KB3, P-QN3; 4 P-KN3, B-N2; 5 B-N2, B-K2; 6 Castles, Castles; 7 N-B3.*

(White prepares to fight the pressure on his K4 square. If Black replies 7 ... P-Q4; then 8 N-K5! gives White a powerful *pin*, and leaves Black with a cramped game.)

*7 ... N-K5; 8 Q-B2, NxN; 9 QxN.*

See Diagram 259. The struggle for control of the center still goes on! Black has the problem of forming a countercenter (... P-Q3 and ... P-K4), and his Knight is undeveloped. White therefore has very fair

Diagram 259                         Diagram 260

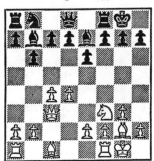          

chances of seizing the initiative. An example: 9 ... P-Q3; 10 **Q-B2**, **P-KB4**; 11 P-Q5!, PxP; 12 N-Q4! (another *pin*) with a splendid game for White. Or 11 ... P-K4; 12 P-K4!, PxP; 13 N-Q2!, followed by 14 NxP—when Black's Bishop is in a bad way.

**B.** 4 P-KN3 Variation with 5 ... B-N5ch—*1 P-Q4, N-KB3; 2 P-QB4, P-K3; 3 N-KB3, P-QN3; 4 P-KN3, B-N2; 5 B-N2.*

(See Diagram 260. The flank thrust 5 ... P-B4—good in principle, bad in this context—is refuted by 6 P-Q5!, PxP; 7 N-R4! Again the *pin* functions effectively. White monopolizes the center while Black's fianchettoed Bishop is frozen out.)

*5 ... B-N5ch; 6 B-Q2, BxBch; 7 QxB!*

(Stronger than 7 QNxB, as White's Queen Knight is more aggressive at the QB3 square.)

*7 ... Castles; 8 N-B3, P-Q3.*

(Not 8 ... N-K5; 9 Q-B2!, NxN?; 10 N-N5! with a *double attack* based on a mate threat! In that case, White wins the Exchange.)

*9 Q-B2, Q-K2; 10 Castles, P-B4.*

(Black must chop down White's Pawn center a bit.)

*11 QR-Q1, PxP; 12 NxP, BxB; 13 KxB.*

White's position is markedly freer. Black has lost the fight for control of his K5 square, and his position is passive. In general, passivity is the curse of Black's position in the Queen's Indian.

**King's Indian Defense.** This is a fighting defense par excellence. In the Philidor Defense (page 166) and the Hungarian Defense (page 169), we noticed that Black formed a countercenter with … P-Q3 and … P-K4, followed in due course by … B-K2. The common defect of both these defenses is that Black gets a cramped game.

To meet this difficulty, the King's Indian Defense was evolved. Here Black's King Bishop is fianchettoed, giving this piece an effective diagonal when Black exchanges Pawns in the center, and giving him a solid countercenter when White pushes on with P-Q5 in reply to … P-K4. In the latter event Black can hope for counterplay with … P-KB4. Come what may, Black has ample maneuvering space for his forces.

White's chief trump is his more comfortable development. Add to this his strong Pawn center, and you realize that he is bound to enjoy considerable mobility. Occasionally Black is in a position to play … P-Q4; but this usually enhances White's command of the board, as we shall see.

**A.** 3 P-KN3 Variation with … P-Q3 and … PxP—*1 P-Q4, N-KB3; 2 P-QB4, P-KN3; 3 P-KN3, B-N2; 4 B-N2, Castles; 5 P-K4, P-Q3; 6 N-K2, P-K4.*

(White has also fianchettoed his King Bishop, one of the most effective methods of proceeding against this defense.)

*7 Castles, QN-Q2; 8 QN-B3, P-B3.*

(Creates later counterplay by making … Q-N3 possible in some cases, or by supporting the advance … P-Q4 in due course.)

*9 P-KR3!*

(Solidifies White's position by preventing … N-N5 in reply to a possible B-K3.)

*9 … PxP; 10 NxP.*

Black has opened the fianchettoed Bishop's diagonal and hopes for counterattack against White's center and his Pawns on the K4 and QB4 squares. But White has a powerful resource in his free development; and the weakness of Black's Queen Pawn often makes itself felt.

Here is an example of Black's counterplay (in which Black has played 9 P-N3 instead of 9 P-KR3): 10 … R-K1; 11 B-N2, Q-N3!; 12 Q-Q2, N-B4; 13 KR-K1, P-QR4!; 14 QR-N1, P-R5!; with a fine game.

Diagram 261                          Diagram 262

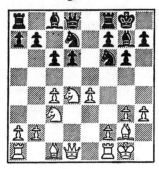 

However, in the position of Diagram 261, White has not weakened his position with P-N3. Here are some possibilities from Diagram 261:

I  10 ... R-K1; 11 B-K3, N-B4; 12 Q-B2, P-QR4; 13 QR-Q1, followed by KR-K1 with a beautiful position for White.

II  10 ... R-K1; 11 R-K1, N-B4; 12 B-B4! The pressure on Black's Queen Pawn is very uncomfortable.

III  10 ... N-N3; 11 P-N3, P-Q4 (very attractive, but White can refute it); 12 KPxP, PxP; 13 B-R3!, R-K1; 14 P-B5!, and Black's plan has been defeated.

In general, White's freedom of action should outweigh Black's possibilities of counteraction.

**B.** 3 P-KN3 Variation with ... P-Q3 and P-Q5—*1 P-Q4, N-KB3; 2 P-QB4, P-KN3; 3 P-KN3, B-N2; 4 B-N2, Castles; 5 P-K4, P-Q3; 6 N-K2, P-K4; 7 P-Q5.*

(This push produces a totally different picture from the Pawn position in the previous variation. Here the Pawn position is stabilized. Black will play for ... P-KB4. White may do the same, or he may strive for P-QN4 and P-B5, smothering Black on the Queen-side; or White may advance on both wings. In any event, the role of Black's King Bishop is considerably minimized.)

*7 ... P-QR4.*

(A characteristic move to restrain White's P-QN4 and support the coming posting of Black's Queen Knight at his QB4 square.)

*8 Castles, QN-Q2; 9 QN-B3, N-B4; 10 P-KR3, N-K1; 11 B-K3, P-B4; 12 PxP, PxP; 13 P-B4.*

A fierce struggle is in prospect. White's practical chances are superior, as he still has in reserve the Queen-side advance P-QR3 followed by P-QN4.

**C.** 3 P-KN3 Variation with ... P-Q4—*1 P-Q4, N-KB3; 2 P-QB4, P-KN3; 3 P-KN3, B-N2; 4 B-N2, P-Q4.*

This system has definite drawbacks. The idea is to desist from forming a countercenter with ... P-Q3 and ... P-K4; and to try to demonstrate that White's Pawn center is weak.

*5 PxP, NxP; 6 P-K4!, N-N3; 7 N-K2, Castles; 8 Castles.*

(See Diagram 262. The defect of this defensive system is that Black has no foothold in the center and consequently cannot develop his forces effectively.)

*8 ... N-B3.*

(This attack on White's center is fruitless. The same is true of 8 ... P-QB4; 9 P-Q5, N-R3; 10 P-QR4!)

*9 P-Q5, N-N1; 10 QN-B3, P-QB3; 11 Q-N3, PxP; 12 PxP, N/N1-Q2; 13 P-QR4!*

White has a very superior development and considerably greater command of the board. Black's Knights are particularly ineffective. As we have seen in Alekhine's Defense, a Knight has very little scope at his QN3 square. The fianchettoed Bishop's strong diagonal is a minor consolation.

In the King's Indian, then, theory is all in White's favor. In practical play, however, Black often makes a good fight of it.

**Gruenfeld Defense.** Black's defensive system in this opening is based on a combination of ... P-KN3 and ... P-Q4 (1 P-Q4, N-KB3; 2 P-QB4, P-KN3; 3 N-QB3, P-Q4). White generally gets an imposing Pawn center; but Black hopes to exert sharp pressure against it—generally by a combination of his fianchettoed Bishop striking along the diagonal and the flank thrust ... P-QB4.

Black's resources are numerous, and White's Pawn center is sometimes vulnerable. White's trumps are his more rapid development and his greater command of the board.

**A.** 4 PxP Variation—*1 P-Q4, N-KB3; 2 P-QB4, P-KN3; 3 N-QB3, P-Q4; 4 PxP.*

(This is the most natural—or the most dogmatic?—line of play. Other suitable moves, though less forceful ones, are 4 B-B4 or 4 P-K3.)

*4 ... NxP; 5 P-K4, NxN; 6 PxN, P-QB4.*

(White has the desired Pawn center, but it is already under pressure. Now White wants to get the most aggressive development which is consistent with the protection of his Pawn center.)

*7 B-QB4, B-N2.*

(Note the pressure on the long diagonal against White's Queen Pawn.)

*8 N-K2!*

(More elastic than 8 N-B3, which would allow a *pin* by ... B-N5 later on, in turn menacing White's Queen Pawn indirectly. Also, White provides for a possible P-B4 later on, with aggressive tendencies.)

*8 ... Castles; 9 Castles, PxP; 10 PxP, N-B3; 11 B-K3.*

Diagram 263         Diagram 264

See Diagram 263. Black has put more pressure on the Queen Pawn, White has given it more protection. This is a crucial position, but it seems that White's free development is adequate to meet the pressure—even at the cost of sacrificing the Exchange by P-Q5—if need be.

**B.** 5 Q-N3 Variation—*1 P-Q4, N-KB3; 2 P-QB4, P-KN3; 3 N-QB3, P-Q4; 4 N-B3, B-N2; 5 Q-N3.*

(This enterprising move involves a certain amount of risk, as is almost always the case when the Queen is developed early in the game. But White is willing to pay the price in order to force a clarification of the center.)

*5 ... PxP; 6 QxBP, Castles; 7 P-K4, B-N5.*

(Again Black has given up the center, and again he plays to undermine White's formation.)

*8 B-K3, N/B3-Q2.*

(The Knight unmasks the fianchettoed Bishop's diagonal.)

*9 Q-N3, N-N3.*

(See Diagram 264. Another crucial situation. White's greater command of the board should again outweigh the pressure on his Queen Pawn.)

*10 R-Q1, N-B3; 11 P-Q5, N-K4; 12 B-K2.*

White's center position is quite secure and exercises a stifling grip on Black's game. Note once more the unfavorable placement of the Black Knight at QN3.

The theoretical verdict on the Gruenfeld, then, is that White's greater command of the board outweighs Black's pressure on the center. But, as in the case of the King's Indian, this is a good defense in practical play.

**Blumenfeld Counter Gambit.** With his fourth move Black offers a Pawn in order to obtain a powerful-looking center. White's simplest course is to ignore the proffered Pawn and go about his business of developing his forces effectively.

*1 P-Q4, N-KB3; 2 P-QB4, P-K3; 3 N-KB3, P-B4; 4 P-Q5, P-QN4?!*

(Black hopes to evade the constricting effects of White's last move after 5 QPxP, BPxP; 6 PxP, P-Q4; etc. But White ignores the gambit.)

*5 B-N5!*

Black has gone out on a limb with his weakening Pawn moves, and his development must suffer accordingly. White has a fine initiative in all variations.

**Budapest Defense.** This is another counter gambit which is most effectively answered by simple development. Examination of games lost by White in this opening almost always yields the conclusion that White failed to make the most of his opportunities for development. The moral is obvious: Concentrate on development!

*1 P-Q4, N-KB3; 2 P-QB4, P-K4!?; 3 PxP.*

Diagram 265                Diagram 266

(See Diagram 265. Black can now try 3 ... N-K5;—a baffling move that has resulted in many brilliant victories for him! Straight development is White's best course, for example: 4 N-KB3, N-QB3; 5 QN-Q2, N-B4; 6 P-KN3. Black can now regain his Pawn with ... Q-K2; but this would lose time. He therefore prefers an outright gambit continuation: 6 ... P-Q3; 7 PxP, QxP; 8 B-N2, B-B4; 9 P-QR3, P-QR4; 10 Castles, Castles; 11 P-QN4! Quite right: White returns the Pawn for a powerful attack.)

*3 ... N-N5; 4 P-K4!, NxKP; 5 P-B4, N/K4-B3.*

(This retreat is best; after 5 ... N-N3; the Knight is sadly out of play.)

*6 P-QR3, P-QR4; 7 B-K3, N-R3; 8 N-KB3, B-B4; 9 Q-Q2, P-Q3; 10 N-B3, Castles; 11 B-Q3, BxB; 12 QxB, N-B4; 13 Castles QR.*

White will play KR-K1 with a notably freer development. Black's prospects are dreary. These variations bear out the comment that White does well to concentrate on development.

**Dutch Defense.** This defense arises from the moves 1 P-Q4, P-KB4; or—to avoid Variation B below—from the sequence 1 P-Q4, P-K3; 2 P-QB4, P-KB4. (Note that in the latter case, White can transpose into the French Defense—see page 183—with 2 P-K4, etc.)

In playing ... P-KB4; Black's idea is of course to control his important K5 square. However, this often results in Pawn weaknesses which White can exploit effectively.

**A.** P-KN3 Variation—*1 P-Q4, P-KB4; 2 P-KN3, N-KB3; 3 B-N2, P-K3.*

(See Diagram 266. Considerable experience with this opening has shown that White's fianchetto gives his King Bishop powerful pressure on Black's center. Black has a choice of ... P-Q3;—aiming at an eventual ... P-K4;—or ... P-Q4; leading to the "Stonewall" formation.

White in turn can choose between N-KB3, with pressure on the K5 square—and N-KR3, followed by N-B4, likewise with pressure on the center. Theory favors White in all these lines.)

*4 N-KB3.*

(After 4 N-KR3, P-Q4; 5 Castles, B-Q3; 6 P-QB4, P-B3; Black has the Stonewall Pawn formation. The sequel might be: 7 N-B3, QN-Q2; 8 Q-Q3, N-K5; 9 P-B3!, NxN; 10 PxN. White has a powerful thrust in P-K4, and his King Knight will have a fine post at KB4.

Likewise favorable for White is 4 N-KR3, B-K2; 5 Castles, Castles; 6 P-B4, P-Q3; 7 N-B3, Q-K1; 8 P-K4, PxP; 9 N-B4!, P-B3; 10 N/B3xP, NxN; 11 BxN, P-K4. Black can complete his development only at the cost of burdening himself with Pawn weaknesses in the center.)

*4 ... B-K2; 5 Castles, Castles; 6 P-B4, P-Q4.*

(Black decides in favor of the Stonewall line. After 6 ... P-Q3; 7 N-B3, Q-K1; 8 R-K1!, Q-R4; 9 P-K4!, White has a beautiful game. Black will have lasting difficulties with his development and with his Pawn formation.)

*7 P-N3, P-B3; 8 N-B3, Q-K1; 9 Q-B2, Q-R4.*

(Note this characteristic Queen maneuver, played in the hope of obtaining a King-side attack.)

*10 N-K5, QN-Q2; 11 N-Q3!, P-KN4; 12 P-B3!*

White intends a powerful smash at the center with P-K4. White has a lasting initiative and a big lead in development.

Thus we see that the P-KN3 Variation is always in White's favor—theoretically, at least. In practice, however, it offers Black fair chances if he is a resourceful player and is familiar with the fine points of the defense.

**B.** Staunton Gambit—*1 P-Q4, P-KB4; 2 P-K4, PxP; 3 N-QB3, N-KB3.*

(White's gambit is difficult to meet unless Black wisely concentrates on development and does not mind returning the gambit Pawn promptly if doing so furthers his development.)

*4 B-KN5, N-B3!*

Black must develop!

If now 5 P-Q5, N-K4; 6 Q-Q4, N-B2; 7 BxN, KPxB; 8 NxP, P-KB4!;
9 N-N3, P-KN3!; 10 P-KR4, B-R3!

Or 5 P-B3, P-K4!; 6 P-Q5, N-Q5; 7 PxP, B-K2; 8 B-QB4, P-Q3!;
9 KN-K2, N-N5!

In both cases, we see Black developing rapidly and preparing a coun-
terinitiative. For the cautiously inclined, 1 ... P-K3 is the recommended
course—to avoid the gambit.

**Benoni Counter Gambit.** We have seen in numerous openings that
the move ... P-QB4 gives Black good counterplay. When adopted on
the first move, however, in reply to 1 P-Q4, it allows White to push by
(2 P-Q5). Black is then burdened with an unwieldy Pawn position and
an inharmonious development.

*1 P-Q4, P-QB4; 2 P-Q5!, P-K4; 3 P-K4, P-Q3.*

(Black's difficulty is twofold: his King Bishop is a "bad" Bishop,
blocked by his Pawns at the K4 and Q3 squares. Secondly, his Queen
Knight has been deprived of its best post, the QB3 square.)

*4 B-Q3, N-K2.*

(Also unsatisfactory for Black is 4 ... P-QR3; 5 P-QR4!, N-K2;
6 N-K2, N-N3; 7 N-R3!, B-K2; 8 N-QB4!, Castles; 9 Castles, N-Q2; 10
B-Q2, P-N3; 11 P-QB3, R-N1; 12 P-QN4!, when White has a lasting
initiative on the Queen-side.)

*5 N-K2, P-B4.*

(The only counterplay.)

*6 P-KB4!, BPxP; 7 BxP, N-Q2; 8 Castles, N-KB3; 9 QN-B3!*

White has a far superior development. Obviously these variations are
anything but appealing for Black.

### SUMMARY

A brief summary of the defenses in this group is now in order. The
Nimzoindian Defense is the most enterprising, the most interesting and
the most successful in practice. The Queen's Indian is rather dreary and
involves Black in a dour struggle for equality. On the other hand, the
King's Indian yields interesting chess, rich in possibilities despite the
theoretical drawbacks for Black. The Gruenfeld Defense is similarly

promising, for in practice White often overreaches himself in attaching too much value (and too little protection!) to his Pawn center.

The Blumenfeld Counter Gambit is basically unsound from the point of view of compromised Pawn structure and neglected development. The Budapest Defense has higher claims to respectability, but straight development is adequate to establish White's superiority. Both the Dutch Defense and the Benoni Counter Gambit suffer from defective Pawn structures in the Black camp. But in the Dutch Defense this difficulty does not preclude Black's obtaining a fair and sometimes even aggressive development; whereas in the Benoni Counter Gambit the instances where Black is able to develop reasonably are rare indeed.

This brings us to the "eccentric" openings—eccentric in that they do not involve P-K4 or P-Q4 on White's first move.

# 12

## ECCENTRIC OPENINGS

To avoid any misunderstanding, let us make clear at once that the openings in this group are definitely not recommended for adoption by the average player. They are discussed here so that he will have some idea of how to play against them when he has the Black pieces.

These openings are really suitable for adoption only by highly experienced players. As 1 P-K4 and 1 P-Q4 give the average player his best chance for easy, quick and effective development, he is strongly advised to cling to the openings involving a central Pawn move. The openings in the present chapter do not call for an initial center Pawn move, and only an experienced player can adopt these openings without incurring dangerous delays in development.

Another difficulty characteristic of these openings is that in many cases the opening moves are such that one opening can be *transposed* into another. This puts a premium on detailed knowledge of the openings, and thereby creates another stumbling block for the inexperienced player.

There is still another feature common to these openings. They stress positional aspects: maneuvering, wing control of the center, delayed advance of the center Pawns, waiting policy for a long-deferred breakthrough, and the like. This is "deep stuff," and most players prefer a type of game which is more active.

**Reti Opening.** In this opening White always fianchettoes the King Bishop, and sometimes the Queen Bishop as well. As a rule the center Pawns are held back, the idea being to control the center through the action of one or both fianchettoed Bishops. As an aid in achieving this objective, White plays an early P-QB4 to engage Black's center Pawns. When first introduced in the early Twenties, this opening scored some sensational victories, but it has since been shorn of most of its terrors.

**A. 2** ... P-QB3 Variation—*1 N-KB3, P-Q4.*

(Black can be just as coy as his opponent by playing 1 ... N-KB3.

Then the possibilities of transposition are endless, as 2 P-B4, P-QN3; 3 P-Q4 turns into the Queen's Indian; 2 P-B4, P-KN3; 3 P-Q4 gives us the King's Indian; while 2 P-Q4, P-Q4; 3 P-B4 gives us the Queen's Gambit. And this by no means exhausts the possibilities of transposing!)

*2 P-B4, P-QB3.*

(White can now transpose into the Slav Defense by 3 P-Q4. Instead, being intent on playing the Reti Opening, he stops to guard his Queen Bishop Pawn.)

*3 P-QN3, N-B3; 4 P-N3, B-B4!*

(The characteristic developing move of Black's system.)

*5 B-KN2, QN-Q2; 6 B-N2, P-K3; 7 Castles.*

Diagram 267                          Diagram 268

 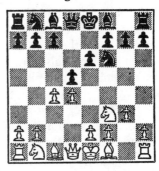

See Diagram 267. An extremely revealing position. Black has made perfectly orthodox Pawn moves in the center, whereas White is trying to control the center by means of the diagonal action of his Bishops. Black has reason to be quite satisfied with his position, as may be seen from these sample variations:

I   7 ... B-Q3; 8 P-Q4, Castles; 9 N-B3, Q-K2; 10 P-QR3, P-QR4!; 11 N-KR4, B-KN5. Black stands well.

II   7 ... P-KR3 (creating a retreat for his Queen Bishop); 8 P-Q3, B-K2; 9 QN-Q2, Castles; 10 R-B1, P-QR4; 11 P-QR3, R-K1; 12 R-B2, B-Q3; 13 Q-R1, Q-K2. Here we have in extreme form White's attempt to control the center by "hypermodern" means. Black is not impressed, and strives for ... P-K4.

**B. 2 ... P-Q5 Variation**—*1 N-KB3, P-Q4; 2 P-B4, P-Q5; 3 P-K3, N-QB3!*

(Black has committed himself irrevocably by advancing his Queen Pawn. Theoretically it is now supposed to be a target for White's forces; but the fact of the matter is that the advanced Pawn is a stumbling block for White's further development.

Rather than be hampered by the Pawn, White exchanges now. This brings Black's Queen out at an early stage, but Black comes to no harm —an indication that the opening has misfired. Incidentally, White does not even get to fianchetto his King Bishop—another indication of the disorganizing effects of 2 ... P-Q5.)

*4 PxP, NxP; 5 NxN, QxN; 6 N-B3, B-N5!*

(Black has a fine game. The backwardness of the White Pawn on the Queen file is a serious organic weakness.)

*7 Q-R4ch, B-Q2!; 8 Q-N3, Q-K4ch!; 9 B-K2, B-B3; 10 Castles, Castles.*

White has been completely outplayed.

As long as Black is reasonably careful about his Pawn center, he has little to fear from the Reti Opening.

**Catalan System.** This is an offshoot of the Reti Opening and the Queen's Gambit. White plays P-Q4 and fianchettoes his King Bishop as well. With minimum care, Black can obtain a satisfactory game. As in the Reti Opening, transpositions occur with great frequency. Thus, the position of Diagram 268 can be reached in a great variety of ways, beginning with 1 P-Q4 or 1 P-QB4 or 1 N-KB3.

*1 P-Q4, N-KB3; 2 P-QB4, P-K3; 3 N-KB3, P-Q4; 4 P-KN3.*

See Diagram 268. Of the various equalizing methods at Black's disposal, here are two:

I   4 ... PxP; 5 Q-R4ch, B-Q2!; 6 QxBP, B-B3 (neutralization of White's fianchetto); 7 B-N2, B-Q4; 8 Q-B2, N-B3; 9 Q-Q1, B-N5ch. Black has an easy game, with at least equality.

II   4 ... B-K2; 5 B-N2, Castles; 6 Castles, P-B4; 7 BPxP (hoping for transposition into the Tarrasch Defense—page 202—which we know is less advantageous for Black), NxP!; 8 P-K4, N-N3; 9 N-B3, PxP; 10 NxP. White's position is a shade more comfortable, but Black does well enough with 10 ... N-B3; 11 NxN, PxN; 12 Q-K2, P-K4. Black will achieve a satisfactory development.

Black's chief problem in the Catalan is perhaps psychological—a placid position may lull him into making careless moves. But if he is alert in keeping the center under control, he has little to fear.

**English Opening.** White's first move (1 P-QB4), while not a center Pawn move, nevertheless does have considerable significance as regards control of the center. Specifically, it aims at control of White's Q5 square. Black can fight back by playing 1 … P-QB3 or 1 … P-K3, keeping that center square under observation and heading for a likely transposition into the Queen's Gambit after 2 P-Q4, P-Q4. Or Black can refuse to commit himself by playing 1 … N-KB3, holding out the possibility of transposing into a great many openings!

Another method is to answer 1 P-QB4 with 1 … P-QB4. But this is questionable policy, as such symmetrical positions are generally uninteresting and at the same time leave Black with little scope for creative play. This is an almost infallible recipe for defeat!

The move which chiefly gives the English Opening status as an individual opening is the reply 1 … P-K4. This is open to the objection that it "weakens" somewhat Black's Q4 square, exposing that square to further pressure through a fianchetto of White's King Bishop. While all this seems far-fetched, it seems to be borne out by the following variations.

**A.** Fianchetto Variation with … P-Q4—*1 P-QB4, P-K4; 2 N-QB3, N-KB3; 3 P-KN3, P-Q4.*

Black tries to free his game before the White Bishop reaches KN2.

*4 PxP, NxP; 5 B-N2.*

| Diagram 269 | Diagram 270 |
|:---:|:---:|
|  |  |

See Diagram 269. White's Bishop strikes along the diagonal with considerable power. Some sample variations:

I  5 … N-N3; 6 P-Q3, B-K2; 7 N-R3! (one of the rare instances where this development is good), Castles; 8 Castles, N-B3; 9 P-B4!,

R-N1; 10 PxP!, NxP; 11 N-B4! White has a marked strategic advantage: strong pressure on the Q5 square, open files, an intact Pawn center.

II 5 ... B-K3; 6 N-B3, N-QB3; 7 Castles, B-K2; 8 P-Q4! (opening up the game favorably), PxP; 9 NxP, N/Q4xN; 10 PxN, NxN; 11 PxN, P-QB3; 12 R-N1! White obviously has greater freedom of action.

**B.** Fianchetto Variation with ... P-Q3—*1 P-QB4, P-K4; 2 N-QB3, N-QB3; 3 P-KN3, P-KN3; 4 B-N2, B-N2; 5 P-K3!, P-Q3.*

(White has a firm grip on the Q5 square, and he is also able to establish a Pawn center of his own.)

*6 KN-K2, KN-K2; 7 P-Q4, PxP; 8 PxP, Castles; 9 Castles.*

Black is really embarrassed for a workable plan, as he has no foothold in the center. White will eventually fianchetto his other Bishop as well, or play N-K4 in conjunction with B-N5. Black is condemned to passivity.

**C.** Four Knights' Variation with P-Q4—*1 P-QB4, P-K4; 2 N-QB3, N-KB3; 3 N-B3, N-B3; 4 P-Q4.*

(See Diagram 270. Again White is able to maintain a slight edge. The seemingly aggressive reply 4 ... P-K5 is unsatisfactory after 5 KN-Q2, NxP; 6 N/Q2xP, N-K3; 7 P-KN3, NxN; 8 NxN, when White remains with a noticeably freer game.)

*4 ... PxP; 5 NxP, B-N5; 6 B-N5, P-KR3; 7 B-R4, BxNch.*

(This seems advisable, partly to loosen White's grip on his Q5 square, partly to weaken White's Pawn structure.)

*8 PxB, N-K4.*

Anticipating 9 P-K3, N-N3; 10 B-N3, N-K5; depriving White of his Bishop-pair and remaining with fairly even chances.

However, White has two tricky continuations which still leave the game up in the air:

I 9 P-B4!?, intending to answer 9 ... NxBP?; with 10 P-K4!, which yields White a formidable attack.

II 9 N-N5!?, so that if 9 ... NxBP?; 10 Q-Q4!, with the twofold threat of 11 QxN/B4 and 11 Q-K5ch (after 10 ... N-N3).

From all these variations, we see that the English Opening must be taken seriously. It gives White many promising chances, especially against an inexperienced player.

**Nimzovich Attack.** White plays for an early fianchetto of his Queen Bishop, aiming at control of the long diagonal, particularly the K5 square. Black has little difficulty in maintaining at least equality, as may be seen from the following variations:

I   1 N-KB3, P-Q4; 2 P-QN3, N-KB3; 3 B-N2, P-B4; 4 P-K3, N-B3; 5 B-N5, Q-N3!; 6 BxNch, QxB; 7 P-Q3, P-KN3!; 8 QN-Q2, B-N2. Black has the Bishop-pair, and the pressure on the long diagonal is neutralized.

II   1 N-KB3, P-Q4; 2 P-QN3, P-QB4; 3 B-N2, P-B3!; 4 P-K3, P-K4. Black builds up a solid Pawn center, nullifying the action of White's fianchettoed Bishop.

**Bird's Opening.** White's opening move 1 P-KB4 often leads to positions very similar to those of the Dutch, with colors reversed. Black has an easy time of it by fianchettoing his King Bishop, as White's first move is not conducive to a natural, quick development. The alternative method (1 ... P-K4; 2 PxP, P-Q3; 3 PxP, BxP;—known as From's Gambit) is needlessly risky.

*1 P-KB4, N-KB3; 2 P-K3, P-KN3.*

Black has a good game, as may be seen from these variations:

I   3 P-QN3, B-N2; 4 B-N2, P-Q3! (keeping the vital K4 square under Pawn control); 5 Q-B1, Castles; 6 N-KB3, N-B3; 7 B-K2, B-N5; 8 Castles, P-K4. Black has the initiative.

II   3 N-KB3, P-Q4; 4 B-K2, B-N2; 5 Castles, P-B4; 6 P-Q3, N-B3; 7 Q-K1, Castles; 8 Q-R4, Q-B2. This line is an echo of the Dutch Defense (page 222). Black will continue ... P-K4; with an excellent game.

White can also adopt a Stonewall formation, by playing 4 P-Q4, for example, in Variation II. However, as we know from our study of the Dutch Defense, this formation is less formidable than its name!

Of these eccentric openings, then, the Reti Opening and Catalan System leave Black with several comfortable equalizing methods. This is also true of the Nimzovich Attack and Bird's Opening. On the other hand, the English Opening merits serious consideration as a promising line for White. In fact, as has been indicated, Black's most judicious course against 1 P-QB4 may be transposition into some more familiar opening by 1 ... N-KB3 or 1 ... P-K3 or 1 ... P-QB3.

# 13

# ILLUSTRATIVE GAMES

In the previous chapters we have learned a great deal about chess: how all the men move, how the object of the game is achieved, how the forces act in combination; how to play the endgame, how to make a material advantage tell; how to attack, how to exploit weaknesses in the enemy formation; how to play the openings, how to distinguish and appraise the most important opening lines.

All this material is valuable and useful, but to drive these lessons home, you must see how these ideas and precepts work out in *real games*. In the games that follow, you can see the clash of wills right in the opening; you can observe how each player makes his plans for the middle game; how blunders are committed, and punished; how the possibility of attack arises and how it is exploited; how the defender fights back and tries to keep his position intact.

To see all this happening in an actual game is invaluable for the student. Chess is not all study and contemplation; practice and hard struggle are just as—if not even more—important. Once you have played over these games, you will be inspired to try your hand at actual play too. When you play your own games, you will enjoy them. You'll make mistakes, but you'll learn from them. Practice may not make perfect, but it does help!

## ATTACK BASED ON SUPERIOR MOBILITY

### Queen's Gambit Declined

#### New York, 1933

| White | Black |
|-------|-------|
| A. S. Denker | B. Siff |

| 1 P-Q4 | N-KB3 |
| 2 P-QB4 | P-K3 |
| 3 N-QB3 | P-Q4 |

| 4 B-N5 | B-K2 |
| 5 P-K3 | N-K5 |

As Black's position is somewhat constricted, he seeks exchanges which will ease his position.

| 6 BxB | QxB |
| 7 PxP | NxN |
| 8 PxN | PxP |

Black has freed his game considerably. His Bishop has a clear path of development, and he is even ahead in development!

| 9 N-B3 | .... |

Diagram 271

Now Black should continue 9 ... Castles; 10 Q-N3, Q-Q3; 11 P-B4, PxP; 12 BxP, N-B3; 13 Q-B3, B-N5 with a satisfactory solution of his opening problems.

| 9 .... | N-Q2? |

But this is all wrong. Black chooses a less active development of his Knight ( ... N-Q2 instead of ... N-B3) and blocks the development of his Bishop. Thus he voluntarily cuts down his own mobility.

| 10 P-B4 | PxP |
| 11 BxP | P-QR3 |

On 11 ... Q-N5ch (*double at-*

*tack*), White parries with 12 N-Q2, guarding his menaced Bishop.

| 12 Castles | Castles |

Now Black hopes to continue with ... P-QB4 and ... P-QN4 followed by ... B-N2, when his development will be complete. But White nips this plan in the bud.

| 13 Q-B2 | P-QB4 |
| 14 QR-B1! | .... |

This threatens 15 PxP, NxP; 16 BxPch (*double attack*) followed by 17 QxN winning a Pawn.

| 14 .... | PxP |

The contemplated 14 ... P-QN4 will not do because of 15 B-Q5! attacking the Rook; this *discovered attack* wins the Queen Bishop Pawn.

| 15 PxP | .... |

The right way to retake. White opens the King file for his Rooks and also reserves the possibility of playing N-K5 with powerful effect.

| 15 .... | N-B3 |

But now 15 ... P-QN4 is better, in order to develop the Bishop.

| 16 KR-K1! | Q-Q3 |
| 17 N-K5! | .... |

White's forces co-operate beautifully. If now 17 ... QxQP?; 18 NxP!, RxN; 19 R-K7 and the *pin* enables White to win the Rook, with the Exchange ahead—unless Black tries 19 ... N-Q4; 20 RxR, KxR; 21 R-Q1. In that case White wins the Knight and a Pawn as well, winding up the transaction with a Pawn to the good.

| 17 .... | P-QN4 |
| 18 B-N3 | B-N2 |

This allows a very pretty combination based on the superior mobility of White's pieces.

The alternative was 18 ... B-K3; 19 BxB, PxB (19 ... QxB? allows the *discovered attack* 20 N-N6 winning the Exchange); 20 Q-B6 and the endgame weakness of Black's King Pawn and Queen Rook Pawn will decide the issue against him.

Diagram 272

| 19 NxP! | RxN |
| 20 BxRch | KxB |
| 21 Q-B7ch | Q-Q2 |

Or 21 ... QxQ; 22 RxQch (*double attack*) followed by 23 RxB and, as in the actual play, White is the Exchange and a Pawn ahead.

| 22 QxQch | NxQ |
| 23 R-B7 | B-B1 |

The only possible reply to White's *double attack*.

| 24 KR-QB1! | .... |

This is what White had in mind on move 19. Black's helplessness is striking: he cannot save his Bishop, as 24 ... N-N3 is ruled out because the Knight is *pinned*.

| 24 .... | K-K3 |
| 25 RxB | RxR |
| 26 RxR | P-QR4 |

White's material advantage gives him an easy win.

| 27 K-B1 | P-R5 |
| 28 K-K2 | K-Q3 |
| 29 K-Q3 | N-N3 |
| 30 R-B5 | Resigns |

After 30 ... P-N5; 31 R-QN5, N-Q4; 32 K-B4, Black's Knight must move. White plays 33 RxP and soon wins the Queen Rook Pawn as well. Faced with this hopeless prospect, Black does not care to continue.

This game is an impressive example of the value of superior mobility.

## SACRIFICIAL ATTACK AGAINST A WEAKENED KING-SIDE

### Queen's Gambit Declined

New York, 1910

| White | Black |
|-------|-------|
| J. R. CAPABLANCA | C. JAFFE |

| 1 P-Q4 | P-Q4 |
|--------|------|
| 2 N-KB3 | N-KB3 |
| 3 P-K3 | P-B3 |
| 4 P-B4 | P-K3 |

A perfectly good move here is 4 ... B-B4, for reasons that will soon become clear.

| 5 N-B3 | QN-Q2 |
|--------|-------|
| 6 B-Q3 | .... |

Now this Bishop has a powerful attacking diagonal—which could have been avoided by Black's playing 4 ... B-B4.

| 6 .... | B-Q3 |
|--------|------|
| 7 Castles | Castles |
| 8 P-K4 | .... |

This advance in the center greatly increases the scope of White's pieces.

| 8 .... | PxKP |

Black can still obtain an excellent game with 8 ... PxBP; 9 BxP, P-K4 with a fair amount of freedom for his forces.

| 9 NxP | NxN |
|-------|-----|
| 10 BxN | .... |

Diagram 273

Now Black would like to free his game by 10 ... P-K4. But this laudable idea would be defeated by 11 PxP, NxP; 12 NxN, BxN; 13 BxPch!, KxB; 14 Q-R5ch (*double attack*) and 15 QxB. This transaction leaves Black a Pawn short; hence, 10 ... P-K4 is out of the question.

| 10 .... | N-B3 |
|---------|------|
| 11 B-B2 | .... |

Planning 12 Q-Q3 followed by 13 B-N5—with a view to BxN and QxP mate!

| 11 .... | P-KR3 |

He sees through White's plan and therefore prevents B-N5. But White has achieved his first objective: *he has provoked a weakening of Black's King-side.*

12 P-QN3      P-QN3
13 B-N2       B-N2
14 Q-Q3       ....

Note the brutal diagonal threat to Black's King. Black must be on his guard against the opening of the long diagonal.

Consider, for example, this possibility: 14 ... Q-B2; 15 P-B5!, B-K2 (or 15 ... PxP; 16 PxP and wins); 16 P-Q5!, and White wins because of the double threat 17 BxN or 17 P-Q6.

14 ....        P-N3

Guarding against the threat on the diagonal. But now he has advanced two Pawns in front of his King, and the castled position has become quite vulnerable.

15 QR-K1      ....

Now Black must be on guard against the smash-up of his castled position by RxP.

15 ....        N-R4

This takes care of the threat—for a while. The point is that 16 RxP? can be answered by 16 ... N-B5 (*fork*) and Black wins.

16 B-B1!      ....

White guards against ... N-B5 and also attacks Black's King Rook Pawn.

[*See Diagram 274*]

Diagram 274

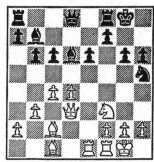

16 ....        K-N2

It is clear that 16 ... N-B5 will not do: 17 BxN, BxB; 18 RxP! and if 18 ... PxR; 19 QxPch and mate next move.

16 ... B-B5; 17 RxP!, BxB is also unsatisfactory for Black: 18 RxPch! (but not 18 RxB?, N-B5 again *forking* Queen and Rook), and Black is helpless:

I   18 ... K-R1; 19 R-N8ch! followed by 20 Q-R7 mate.

II  18 ... N-N2; 19 R-Q6! winning the Queen because of the mating threat.

III 18 ... PxR; 19 QxPch, N-N2; 20 N-K5 with a winning attack.

17 RxP!       ....

Threatening 18 RxPch and a quick mate.

17 ....        N-B3

Capturing the Rook allows mate in two moves.

18 N-K5!      ....

He leaves the Rook *en prise*, relying on the variation 18 ... PxR; 19 QxPch, K-R1; 20 QxPch, K-N1; 21 Q-N6ch, K-R1; 22 R-K1, Q-K1; 23 Q-R6ch, K-N1; 24 R-K3 and the intervention of White's Rook on the third rank is decisive.

18 ....                  P-B4

Allowing a quick finish, but 18 ... BxN; 19 RxB is hopeless for Black, as he is behind in material and position.

**19 BxPch!**            ....

The King-side weakness takes its toll.

19 ....                  KxB
**20 NxBPch!!**          **Resigns**

The only reply to the *forking check* is 20 ... RxN, whereupon 21 QxP mate ends it all. A very impressive example of how to exploit a weakened King-side.

## SACRIFICIAL ATTACK TO OPEN A FILE

### Alekhine's Defense

London, 1949

| White | Black |
|---|---|
| H. GOLOMBEK | E. BROWN |
| 1 P-K4 | N-KB3 |
| 2 P-K5 | N-Q4 |

In adopting this line of play (see p. 193), Black wants to provoke a general advance of White's Pawns: 3 P-QB4, N-N3; 4 P-Q4, P-Q3; 5 P-B4—on the doubtful theory that White's advanced Pawns are vulnerable to counterattack. White decides to "play it safe."

| 3 N-QB3 | NxN |
|---|---|
| 4 NPxN | P-Q4 |

Now he contradicts himself. The text stabilizes White's King Pawn at K5, whereas 4 ... P-Q3; 5 P-

KB4, P-KN3 followed by ... B-N2 leaves a fluid center. The resulting struggle would give Black fair prospects.

| 5 P-KB4 | P-K3 |
|---|---|

Bad, as it locks in his Queen Bishop and thus reduces Black to passivity. The less revealing ... P-KN3 followed by ... B-N2 gives Black a more elastic position.

| 6 N-B3 | P-QB4 |
|---|---|
| 7 P-Q4 | P-QN3 |

Black has condemned his Queen Bishop to inactivity (5 ... P-K3). He therefore contemplates exchanging this virtually useless Bishop by ... B-R3.

This plan is certainly plausible, but it does little to oppose the ominous concentration of White pressure on the King-side. Two better plans suggest themselves:

I  7 ... B-K2 followed by 8 ... Castles to get the Black King into a reasonably safe haven.

II  7 ... P-B5 to deprive White's King Bishop of its best square: Q3.

| 8 B-Q3 | B-R3 |
|---|---|
| 9 Castles | BxB |
| 10 QxB | .... |

Now Black must be on his guard against P-B5, which will open the King Bishop file for action against the Black King.

| 10 .... | P-B5 |
|---|---|
| 11 Q-K2 | .... |

At this point, 11 ... P-B4 suggests itself as a purely mechanical safety measure. But it would not do at all: 12 PxP e.p.! (see page 25), QxP; 13 P-B5!, QxBP; 14 N-N5 and Black's game is in ruins. Such dynamic continuations are always likely when center files can be opened against an uncastled King.

| 11 .... | P-N3 |
|---|---|

*[See Diagram 275]*

Black has done what was humanly possible to prevent P-B5. But White refuses to be appeased:

Diagram 275

| 12 P-N4! | .... |
|---|---|

Still intending P-B5. White can permit his King to be somewhat exposed, as Black has no real attacking force at his disposal.

| 12 .... | P-KR4 |
|---|---|

Forcing the issue.

| 13 P-B5! | .... |
|---|---|

Golombek goes right ahead with his plan, even though it involves sacrificing a piece "on spec."

The meek alternative 13 P-N5 would blockade the Pawn position and *ruin White's prospects of opening the King Bishop file.*

| 13 .... | RPxP |
|---|---|
| 14 PxKP! | .... |

He sacrifices the piece because he sees that he will obtain a devastating attack along the open King Bishop file. In addition, he is well aware that the black squares on Black's King-side are weak: they are no longer guarded by Black Pawns and are therefore available for infiltration.

14 ....        PxN

To decline the sacrifice is pointless; after 14 ... PxP; 15 N-N5 Black's position is in shreds.

15 QxKBP!    ....

Threatens 16 QxBP mate.

If now 15 ... Q-R5 (also threatening mate!); 16 PxPch, K-K2 (on other King moves, White wins with 17 QxPch and 18 B-B4); 17 B-R3ch, K-K3; 18 Q-B6ch!, QxQ; 19 RxQch, K-Q2; 20 P-K6ch, K-Q1; 21 RxKNP and Black is helpless against 22 R-N8!

This brings us to the theme of *Pawn promotion*, which will play an important role from now on.

15 ....        P-B4
16 PxP e.p.    ....

Diagram 276

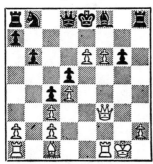

Black has managed to close the terrible file; but White's *advanced,* connected passed Pawns are worth more than a piece.

16 ....        B-Q3
17 B-N5!       ....

With the brutal threat of 18 P-B7ch (*discovered attack*) winning Black's Queen!

17 ....        Q-B2

If instead 17 ... BxPch; 18 K-N2, Q-B2; 19 P-B7ch, K-B1; 20 P-K7ch (again the *Pawn promotion* theme!) and Black must resign.

18 P-B7ch      K-B1
19 Q-B6!       ....

This involves two pretty examples of the *Pawn promotion* idea. The first: 19 ... R-R2; 20 P-K7ch!, BxKP; 21 QxBch!, QxQ; 22 BxQch, KxB; 23 P-B8(Q)ch etc.

19 ....        BxPch
20 K-R1!       B-K4 dis ch

Ordinarily such a *discovered check* is killing...but not here!

21 QxRch       BxQ
22 P-K7ch      Resigns

For if 22 ... QxP; 23 BxQch, KxB; 24 P-B8(Q)ch and wins—the other instance of the *Pawn promotion* motif!

This sparkling little game shows how *a line may be violently forced open by sacrificial means* when the hostile King lacks adequate protection.

## ATTACK AGAINST THE UNCASTLED KING

### Ruy Lopez

#### Match, 1893

| White | Black |
|-------|-------|
| DR. S. TARRASCH | M. TCHIGORIN |
| 1 P-K4 | P-K4 |
| 2 N-KB3 | N-QB3 |
| 3 B-N5 | P-QR3 |
| 4 B-R4 | N-B3 |
| 5 N-B3 | B-N5 |

Both players are bringing out their pieces rapidly, and in the normal course of events they will soon be castling their Kings into safety.

**6 N-Q5** ....

This threatens to win a piece by 7 BxN and 8 NxB. (The technique here is *forcible removal of a defending piece*.)

**6 ....** **B-R4?**

Black sees the threat, and therefore removes the Bishop from its position of jeopardy. But the more conservative 6 ... B-K2 is in order.

Tchigorin is eager to attack; defensive moves are not to his taste. But, as has been stressed in the section on opening play, Black's chief aim in the opening is to maintain the balance of power: early attacks are likely to be disastrous for him.

| 7 Castles | P-QN4 |
|-----------|-------|
| 8 B-N3 | P-Q3 |
| 9 P-Q3 | B-KN5 |

He *pins* White's King Knight and threatens ... N-Q5, which would break up White's Pawns in front of the castled King (see p. 72).

White meets the threat by preventing ... N-Q5.

**10 P-B3** ....

White's King is now quite safe. Black's King is still in the center, and 10 ... Castles is questionable because of 11 B-N5, *pinning* Black's King Knight and threatening to break up his King-side.

Black's correct course is 10 ... P-R3 (preventing the pin by B-N5) followed by ... Castles.

Note, by the way, that the correct Bishop retreat at move 6 ( ... B-K2) would have saved Black all these difficulties.

**10 ....** **N-K2??**

Black misses the point and plays into a fiendish trap.

[*See Diagram 277*]

**11 NxKP!!** ....

Beautiful play: Tarrasch breaks out of the pin by means of an offered Queen sacrifice.

Diagram 277

The main point is: 11 ... BxQ; 12 NxNch, PxN??; 13 BxPch, K-B1; 14 B-R6 mate!

| 11 .... | PxN |

Black can lose prosaically with 11 ... BxQ; 12 NxNch, K-B1; 13 N/K5-Q7ch, QxN (forced); 14 NxQch, K-K1; 15 RxB, KxN—when White's extra Pawn will win the endgame for him sooner or later.

| 12 NxNch | .... |

This is the real point of White's combination: he removes—*with check*—the Knight which is *defending* Black's Queen Bishop. This makes White's next move possible.

| 12 .... | PxN |
| 13 QxB | .... |

White has won back the sacrificed piece. His pieces are more effectively developed, and Black's King still cannot find a safe haven.

| 13 .... | N-N3 |

But not 13 ... QxP??; 14 R-Q1 and Black is lost.

| 14 B-Q5 | QR-N1 |
| 15 P-KB4! | .... |

Tarrasch wants to open the King Bishop file for attack on the hostile King. *Pawn exchanges lead to open lines.*

| 15 .... | P-B3 |

Giving up a second Pawn to create complications.

| 16 BxQBPch | K-K2 |

Now he threatens 17 ... Q-N3ch (*double attack*) winning the Bishop.

| 17 B-Q5 | P-N5 |
| 18 PxKP | Q-N3ch |
| 19 K-R1 | NxP |
| 20 Q-R5 | .... |

Diagram 278

The fatal effects of Black's faulty policy are now particularly glaring.

White's King is safely tucked away in the corner, while Black's King can be subjected to withering attack. White's two Bishops are particularly useful.

In this position White threatens 21 RxP!!, KxR; 22 Q-N5 mate. Or 21 RxP!!, QxR; 22 B-N5 *pinning* and winning Black's Queen.

| 20 .... | N-N3 |
| 21 RxP!! | KxR |

Black's King is badly exposed as a result of White's Rook sacrifice. Black's pieces are mostly idle, so that his academic plus in material has little value.

| 22 B-N5ch | K-N2 |

If 22 ... K-K4; 23 B-K7 dis ch. leads to mate. (A King thus far advanced cannot last very long!)

| 23 Q-R6ch | K-N1 |
| 24 R-KB1 | .... |

Threatening 25 BxP mate. White has been making splendid use of the line-opening initiated with his fifteenth move.

| 24 .... | R-KB1 |
| 25 B-KB6 | .... |

Now the threat is 26 Q-N7 mate. The breach in Black's Pawn structure exposes his King to devastating attack even at KN1.

| 25 .... | QxB |

Even giving up the Queen does not afford relief.

| 26 RxQ | Resigns |

Now he sees that there is nothing to be done against the menace of an "epaulette" mate by 27 RxNch!, RPxR; 28 QxP mate (Black's King Bishop Pawn is *pinned*).

*To the very end, Black suffered from failing to retreat 6 ... B-K2. The safety of his King should have been his paramount consideration.*

## ATTACK ALONG AN OPEN FILE

### Ruy Lopez

U.S. Open Championship, 1938

| White | Black | | |
|---|---|---|---|
| I. A. HOROWITZ | A. MARTIN | | |
| 1 P-K4 | P-K4 | 4 B-R4 | N-B3 |
| 2 N-KB3 | N-QB3 | 5 Castles | B-K2 |
| 3 B-N5 | P-QR3 | 6 Q-K2 | P-Q3 |
| | | 7 P-B3 | B-Q2 |
| | | 8 P-Q4 | Castles |

Diagram 279

White's position is noticeably freer, and his center Pawns make an aggressive impression on the fourth rank. Black's forces are somewhat cramped, yet they have potential power. At the moment, for example, Black threatens to win a Pawn by *discovered attack*: 9 ... PxP; 10 PxP, NxQP!

9 B-B2    ....

By removing his unguarded Bishop, White nullifies the threat.

This position is a perfect example of the principle that *a player with a cramped position must seek exchanges to ease his game*. In this way he gains elbow room for his remaining forces. Black can achieve this by 9 ... PxP!

I 10 PxP, N-QN5; 11 B-N3, B-N4; 12 B-QB4, BxB; 13 QxB, P-Q4!

II 10 NxP, NxN; 11 PxN, B-N4; 12 B-Q3, BxB; 13 QxB, P-Q4; 14 P-K5, N-K5.

In either case, Black obtains a considerable measure of freedom.

| 9 | .... | Q-K1 |
|---|---|---|
| 10 | P-KR3 | R-Q1 |
| 11 | R-K1 | K-R1 |
| 12 | QN-Q2 | N-KN1 |
| 13 | N-B1 | B-B3 |
| 14 | Q-Q1 | QN-K2 |

Black has avoided the simplifying process previously recommended for him. He now finds that the moves of his forces are limited to only three ranks, and there is very little that he can accomplish of a positive nature.

| 15 | N-K3 | P-B4 |
|---|---|---|
| 16 | N-N4 | BxN |

16 ... N-N3 is relatively better.

17 PxB    . . .

*Pawn exchanges result in attacking lines.* White has obtained an open King Rook file as a consequence of the previous exchange, and will soon seek to mount an attack along the newly opened line.

| 17 | .... | N-B3 |
|---|---|---|
| 18 | P-Q5 | .... |

White closes the center, so as to avoid the possibility of any diversionary activity in that sector while he prosecutes his King-side attack.

| 18 | .... | N-N1 |
|---|---|---|
| 19 | P-KN3 | Q-Q2 |
| 20 | P-N5 | B-K2 |
| 21 | N-R4 | P-KN3 |
| 22 | K-N2 | P-B3 |
| 23 | R-R1 | .... |

At last the Rook is on the open file. This has explosive potentialities, as will be seen.

23 ....    K-N2

Black tries to flee, but finds that it is too late. The threat was 24 NxPch (*fork plus pin*), winning the exchange and a Pawn.

Diagram 280

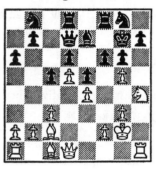

24 N-B5ch!!    PxN

There is no escape. If 24 .. K-R1; 25 RxPch!!, KxR; 26 Q-R1ch, N-R3; 27 QxNch and mate next move. Thus the open file takes its toll.

25 RxPch!!    KxR
26 Q-R5ch    N-R3

Equally disastrous is 26 ... K-N2; 27 P-N6!

27 QxNch    K-N1
28 Q-N6ch    K-R1
29 B-K3    Resigns

He is helpless against the further exploitation of the open file (30 R-R1 mate).

White's magnificent sacrificial combination effectively highlights the value of an open file.

## ATTACK AGAINST QUEEN-SIDE CASTLING

### Vienna Game

New York, 1889

| White | Black |
|---|---|
| D. G. BAIRD | A. BURN |
| 1 P-K4 | P-K4 |
| 2 N-QB3 | N-KB3 |
| 3 P-B4 | P-Q4 |

These last two Pawn-moves promise a lively game: attacking lines will be opened.

| 4 BPxP | NxP |
| 5 Q-B3 | N-QB3 |

Black sets a trap: if 6 NxN, N-Q5!; 7 Q-Q3?, PxN; 8 QxP??, B-KB4 followed by 9 ... NxPch (*forking check*) and 10 ... NxR.

The lesson taught by this trap is that one must beware of too many early Queen-moves coupled with time-wasting Pawn-grabbing.

6 B-N5    ....

White avoids the trap with a

commendable developing move; he *pins* Black's Queen Knight to save his King Pawn.

| 6 .... | NxN |
| 7 NPxN | .... |

White has two open files and the makings of a powerful Pawn center (eventual P-Q4).

Black therefore does well to head discreetly for the endgame: 7 ... Q-R5ch!; 8 P-N3, Q-K5ch; 9 QxQ, PxQ; 10 BxNch, PxB, etc.

| 7 .... | B-K2 |
| 8 P-Q4 | B-K3 |

Black should be thinking of getting his King into safety by castling.

| 9 N-K2 | Q-Q2 |
| 10 Castles | P-B3 |

See the previous note. Black is heading for trouble.

| 11 PxP | BxP |
| 12 B-R3! | .... |

Now Black cannot castle on the King-side, as the rules forbid his King's passage over KB1 (Diagram 55).

| 12 .... | Castles QR |

Obviously the King could not remain on the open King file; but Queen-side castling is likewise extremely dangerous because of the open Queen Knight file.

(Note, by the way, that White has castlèd in good time in perfectly orthodox fashion; his King will never be in danger.)

| 13 Q-Q3 | B-B2 |
| 14 QR-N1 | B-N3 |

In order to drive the Queen off the vital attacking line. Too late!

Diagram 281

| 15 B-R6!! | N-R4 |

Black must decline the Queen sacrifice.

If 15 ... BxQ; 16 BxPch, K-N1; 17 BxN dis ch, K-B1; 18 BxQch followed by 19 PxB and White has won a piece. Now we can appreciate the value of the Queen Knight file for attacking purposes. The open file makes possible a *discovered check* which is devastating.

| 16 BxPch! | NxB |
| 17 Q-R6 | .... |

Threatens mate on the move. The attack on the open file is strengthened by the *pin*.

17 ....          P-B3

This Pawn must be advanced to prevent the threatened mate.

17 ... P-B4 will not do, for then 18 PxP menaces the deadly *Pawn fork* 19 P-B6.

Also hopeless is 17 ... Q-B2; 18 RxN, K-Q2; 19 Q-N5ch, K-K3; 20 Q-B6ch, etc.

18 B-Q6!!          ....

Diagram 282

White is one piece down, and offers another. He now threatens 19 QxRP followed by 20 Q-N8 mate.

18 ....          KR-K1

And not 18 ... QxB??; 19 QxN mate.

19 QxRP!          Q-KB2
20 Q-N8ch          ....

Not the best.

20 N-B4!! wins offhand, for if 20 ... NxB; 21 R-N8 mate; and if 20 ... RxB; 21 Q-R8ch and mate next move. Meanwhile, after 20 N-B4!!, Black is helpless against the threat of 21 Q-N8ch and 22 Q-B7 mate.

20 ....          K-Q2
21 RxNch          K-K3
22 N-B4ch          K-B4
23 NxP dis ch      K-N4
24 B-B4ch          K-R4

With his King still exposed and with three Pawns minus, Black cannot hold out very long in any event.

25 RxQ            RxQ
26 NxBch          PxN
27 RxBP            R-N7
28 RxP            RxBP
29 R-B5ch          K-N5
30 P-R3ch          K-R5
31 K-R2          ....

Threatens 32 B-N3 mate. Black has nothing left but a "spite check."

31 ....          RxPch
32 KxR            R-K7ch
33 K-B3            Resigns

This game demonstrates the foolhardiness of castling right into an open file.

## ATTACK BASED ON PERSISTENT INITIATIVE

### Queen's Gambit Declined

Argentine-Uruguay, 1936

| White | Black |
|-------|-------|
| R. GRAU | C. H. FLEURQUIN |
| 1 N-KB3 | P-Q4 |
| 2 P-B4 | P-K3 |
| 3 P-Q4 | P-QB3 |

Diagram 283

This move always creates the theoretical possibility of ... PxP followed by ... P-QN4 with a plausible attempt to hold the gambit Pawn. That is why many players prefer to answer the text with 4 P-K3, ruling out any of the problems that are raised by ... PxP.

| 4 N-B3 | PxP |
|--------|-----|
| 5 P-QR4 | B-N5 |
| 6 P-KN3 | .... |

6 P-K3, playing to regain the Pawn, is simpler. With the text White announces that he will concentrate on development for the time being, and go after the Pawn later.

| 6 .... | N-B3 |
|--------|------|
| 7 B-N2 | Castles |
| 8 Castles | .... |

Many players would now continue 8 ... BxN; 9 PxB, P-QN4 in order to remain a Pawn ahead—perhaps for good. But after 10 B-QR3, R-K1; 11 N-K5 White is left with a magnificent position.

Black therefore wisely decides to proceed with his own development, relying on White's having to lose time if he is to win back the Pawn. The time so lost may make it possible for Black to take the initiative.

| 8 .... | P-B4! |
|--------|-------|
| 9 B-N5 | N-B3 |
| 10 BxN | QxB |
| 11 N-K4 | Q-K2 |
| 12 PxP | P-B4! |
| 13 N-Q6 | BxP |
| 14 NxBP | P-K4! |

Black is no longer a Pawn ahead, but he has a strong game in the center, he is ahead in development, and his Bishops will soon be functioning efficiently. In short, he has the initiative.

15 P-QN4?!     ....

White doesn't like what he has, and he decides to complicate in the hope of confusing his opponent.

Thus, if 15 ... NxP, Black's King Pawn falls.

Or if 15 ... BxNP; 16 N/B4xP, NxN; 17 NxN, QxN; 18 Q-N3ch (*double attack*), B-K3; 19 QxB/N4 and the position is about even.

Note that after 15 ... BxNP; 16 N/B4xP, Black must not try the *double attack* 16 ... B-B6? because of the *double attack* 17 Q-N3ch in reply!

| 15 .... | R-Q1! |

Simple and good.

| 16 Q-N3 | N-Q5! |
| 17 NxN | BxN |

Now it turns out that Black need not fear any *discovered checks*. 18 N-N6 dis ch, for instance, is squelched by the counterattack 18 ... B-K3. This shows how good development turns the enemy's threats into mere make-believe.

| 18 QR-B1 | B-K3 |
| 19 P-K3 | .... |

With a view to 19 ... B-N3; 20 P-R5, B-QB2; 21 BxP, QR-N1; 22 P-R6. How does Black meet this threat?

[*See Diagram 284*]

| 19 .... | QR-B1! |

Beautiful play! Black relies on

Diagram 284

the *pin* to regain the lost piece advantageously. Here we see once more how Black's aggressive development gives him an easy initiative.

| 20 PxB | RxP |
| 21 KR-K1 | .... |

He has no way of giving the *pinned* Knight adequate support.

| 21 .... | R/Q5xN |
| 22 RxR | RxR |

Black has seen ahead quite a bit. If now 23 RxP, his Bishop is *pinned* (and 24 QxR is threatened). But there follows the *back-rank attack* and *discovered attack* 23 ... R-B8ch; 24 B-B1, BxQ; 25 RxQ. So far White has held his own, but now comes the fatal *pin* 25 ... B-B5 winning a piece.

| 23 Q-K3 | .... |

White realizes that 23 RxP? costs him a piece.

| 23 .... | P-K5! |

| 24 P-B3 | B-Q4 |
|---------|------|
| 25 Q-Q2 | B-B3 |
| 26 PxP  | QxNP |

An unpleasant situation for White: if 27 QxQ, RxQ; 28 PxP, BxB; 29 KxB, RxP and Black's connected passed Pawns win easily for him.

| 27 Q-Q8ch | Q-B1 |
|-----------|------|
| 28 R-Q1   | PxP! |
| 29 Q-B7   | .... |

Apparently threatening the *pin* 30 R-Q8 with crushing effect, as 30 ... B-K1? loses because of 31 QxRch, etc.

| 29 .... | P-K6! |
|---------|-------|

Black calmly disregards the "threat," as he has an ace in the hole.

| 30 B-B3 | .... |
|---------|------|

Despair. If 30 R-Q8, R-B8ch (*back-rank attack*) and mate follows!

| 30 .... | P-K7! |
|---------|-------|

All nicely timed. If now 31 BxP, Q-B4ch; 32 K-B1, B-N7ch winning White's Queen by *discovered attack*.

| 31 R-K1 | Q-B4ch |
|---------|--------|
| Resigns |        |

For if 32 K-N2, BxBch winning the White Queen by *discovered attack*.

A very pleasing and effective example of the way in which aggressive development almost automatically confers a persistent initiative.

## GRADUAL CONSTRICTION

### Queen's Gambit

France-Belgium, 1948

| White | Black |
|-------|-------|
| A. MUFFANG | P. DEVOS |
| 1 P-Q4 | P-Q4 |
| 2 P-QB4 | PxP |
| 3 N-KB3 | N-KB3 |
| 4 P-K3 | P-K3 |
| 5 BxP | P-B4 |

With his second move, Black has given up Pawn control of the center. He must now exercise care to prevent White from obtaining a stifling monopoly of the center. Hence 5 ... P-B4, which disputes control of the center.

| 6 Castles | P-QR3 |
|-----------|-------|
| 7 P-QR3   | B-K2  |
| 8 Q-K2    | P-QN4 |
| 9 B-R2    | B-N2  |

The fianchetto of the Bishop is very important for Black. It enables him to control his K5 square; in this way he makes up for the disappearance of his Queen Pawn.

| 10 | PxP    | BxP     |
|----|--------|---------|
| 11 | P-QN4  | B-R2    |
| 12 | B-N2   | Castles |

Diagram 285

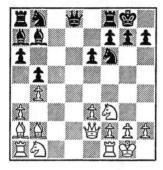

This is a symmetrical position, so that our first thought is that Black has equality. But there is more to it than that. After White makes his next move, he will be *two* moves ahead of Black. This means that somewhere in the first twelve moves, Black has lost a tempo. When did this happen? The answer is interesting: White captured Black's Queen Bishop Pawn in one move, but Black took two moves of his King Bishop to capture White's Queen Bishop Pawn.

The fact, then, that Black is two moves behind in obtaining a completely symmetrical position, means that he must be very careful to maintain the balance of power.

| 13 | QN-Q2 | N-K5? |
|----|-------|-------|

A misstep which has surprisingly serious consequences. He should continue his development with ... QN-Q2.

| 14 | KR-Q1 | .... |
|----|-------|------|

This highlights the gravity of Black's dilemma. White's lead in development takes the form of *prior occupation of the open files* by his Rooks. Black cannot follow suit: he has lost too much time.

| 14 | .... | Q-K2 |
|----|------|------|

White was of course threatening to win a piece with 15 NxN.

| 15 | QR-B1 | .... |
|----|-------|------|

Diagram 286

Now both White Rooks are in action, unopposed by Black Rooks. Black's choice of moves is greatly limited.

Thus, 15 ... N-Q2 is refuted by 16 R-B7 (*occupation of the open file is transformed into infiltration on the seventh rank*).

As for 15 ... R-B1?, it loses a piece after 16 RxRch, BxR; 17 NxN—or even 16 NxN!

Even 15 ... R-Q1 comes too late; for then White has 16 NxN, BxN; 17 RxRch, QxR; 18 N-N5! attacking the Bishop at his K4. Black cannot then play 18 ... QxN?? (because of 19 R-B8ch with a *back-rank mate*). If 18 ... B-N2; 19 Q-R5! wins because of *double attack* on the King Bishop Pawn and King Rook Pawn. And if 18 ... B-N3; 19 NxKP!, PxN; 20 BxPch with the winning *pin* 21 R-B8.

These variations indicate *the power of White's Rooks on the open files.*

15 ....            NxN
16 QxN!            ....

Keeping a firm grip on the Queen file. Black cannot play 16 ... N-Q2 now, nor can he try 16 ... R-B1??; 17 RxRch, BxR; 18 Q-Q8ch, Q-B1; 19 QxQch, KxQ; 20 R-Q8ch (*double attack*) and White wins a piece.

16 ....            B-N3

A pretty variation is 16 ... N-B3; 17 RxN!, BxR; 18 Q-B3 (*double attack*) threatening mate and therefore winning the Bishop on QB6, with the victorious material advantage of two minor pieces for a Rook.

The text prepares to dispute the Queen file by ... R-Q1.

17 Q-B3!            ....

White constantly seeks new points of invasion. Taking advantage of the power of his Bishops, he creates a weakness in Black's King-side position because of his mating threat.

17 ....            P-B3

Stopping the mate at the cost of weakening his King Pawn, which must now be guarded by the Queen. (17 ... P-B4 is unsatisfactory because of 18 BxPch!)

18 N-Q4!            ....

Diagram 287

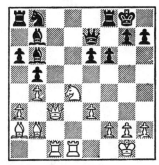

White is relentless in keeping up the pressure. The newly weakened King Pawn is the object of attack, and defending it is impossible.

Thus, if 18 ... B-Q4; 19 N-B5!, Q-N2 (not 19 ... PxN; 20 BxBch winning a Rook because of the *double attack*); 20 RxB!, PxR; 21 BxPch! (*double attack*), QxB; 22 N-K7ch *forking* King and Queen! Or 18 ... B-B1; 19 N-B5! (the

King Pawn is *pinned*), Q-R2; 19 QxB!, RxQ; 20 BxPch, K-B1; 21 RxR mate!

Note that both of these beautiful variations were made possible by the weakening of Black's King Pawn.

18 ....          BxN
19 QxB          ....

Black has eliminated the tactical threats—for the moment—but at what a cost! The black squares in his position are laid bare to invasion; such squares as Q3, QB4 and QB2 are quite vulnerable in Black's camp.

19 ....          N-B3

In reply to this, 20 Q-Q6 is good enough to win. But White finds an even more powerful continuation:

20 Q-B5!          KR-K1

With his Queen tied to the defense of his weak King Pawn, Black cannot play 20 ... QxQ because of 21 BxPch winning a Pawn with an easy endgame win.

21 R-Q6          N-Q1

The only defense to the double threat of 22 RxN or 22 RxP. Thus, by occupying one of the weak black squares, White constricts Black's game still more.

22 Q-Q4!          ....

Threatening the powerful *occu-*pation *of the seventh rank* by 23 R-Q7, and forcing thereby a further retreat by Black.

22 ....          B-B1
23 P-KR4          ....

This move serves several purposes. It creates a loophole for White's King to avoid a possible *back-rank mate;* it threatens, in some cases, a further advance by P-R5 and P-R6, creating still more disorder in Black's Pawn position. It also gives Black a chance to do "something," which soon convinces him that there is nothing he can do!

23 ....          K-R1

Black's King gets off the vulnerable diagonal, but by no means out of the range of White's Bishops.

24 B-N1!          ....

With the nasty threat of 25 Q-K4 (*double attack*) winning Black's Queen Rook because of the mating threat at KR7.

24 ....          QR-N1

This meets the immediate threat, but is of little value in the long run: Black can be forced to create more weaknesses.

25 Q-K4          ....

The mate threat (26 QxRP mate) no longer involves a *double attack,* but it does have the function of forcing a weakening Pawn advance on Black's King-side.

25 ....            **P-B4**

The alternative 25 ... P-N3; 26 Q-KB4 also leaves White with terrific pressure on the long diagonal.

**26 Q-K5**         ....

The constriction of Black's game has reached really pitiable proportions. White's mating threat at KN7 ties down Black's Queen to the defense; and there is also a threat of *discovered attack* by 27 RxN, RxR; 28 QxR.

26 ....            **R-R1**
**27 R-B7!**         **Resigns**

White's lovely Rook move leaves Black without a defense. On 27 . . QxR/B2 there follows 28 RxN!

Diagram 288

with *discovered attack* on the Black Queen, and also threatening the *back-rank mate* 29 RxR mate.

If Black tries 28 ... QxR (Black's Queen is an *overburdened piece*), then 29 QxNP mate.

If 28 ... RxR; 29 QxQ, R-Q8ch and there is no *back-rank mate* because White's 23 P-KR4 has made room for White's King at KR2!

## INFILTRATION

### Benoni Counter Gambit

Berlin, 1913

| White | Black |
|-------|-------|
| J. R. CAPABLANCA | J. MIESES |
| 1 P-Q4 | N-KB3 |
| 2 N-KB3 | P-B4 |

This leads to a cramped game for Black. He is better off to dispute the center by Pawn control (2 ... P-Q4), or by wing control (2 ... P-QN3 and 3 ... B-N2).

3 P-Q5            P-Q3

4 P-B4            P-KN3

Black's King Bishop has no prospects in the way of normal development ( ... P-K3 followed by ... B-K2). He therefore decides to fianchetto the Bishop: at KN2 it will strike along the long diagonal.

| 5 N-B3 | B-N2 |
|--------|------|
| 6 P-K4 | Castles |
| 7 B-K2 | P-K3 |

**8 Castles**          ....

Diagram 289

8 ....            **PxP?**

Here Black violates a basic strategical maxim: *when you have a
constricted position, avoid line-
opening.* The logic of this rule of
thumb is self-explanatory. The
opening of new lines will favor the
player with the better-developed
game; his more mobile forces will
be the first to occupy such lines.

In the present case, the opening
of the King file favors White, as
the more rapid development of his
Queen-side will enable him, if need
be, to muster more force on the
King file than can be summoned
forth by Black. One glance at
Black's crammed Queen-side tells
us at once that it is hopeless for
him to expect his Queen Rook to
play a role in the struggle for occupation of the King file.

The right move is 8 ... P-K4.
True, this blocks the diagonal of
his fianchettoed King Bishop; but

it leads to a rather barricaded position in which Black can maneuver
on interior lines of communication,
with a possibility of having time to
mobilize all his forces.

9 KPxP          N-K1

Why move this piece a second
time when all his Queen-side pieces
are still at home?

10 R-K1!          B-N5
11 N-KN5!          ....

Setting Black a problem which
cannot be solved in a wholly satisfactory manner. If 11 ... B-Q2; 12
B-B4, N-R3; 13 N/N5-K4 and
Black's position is very unwieldy.

11 ....            BxN?

Black's reason for this exchange
is that he weakens White's Pawn
structure. (The resulting doubled
Queen Bishop Pawns are not mutually self-supporting.) But this
weakness is highly theoretical, as
Black has no way of exploiting it.

On the other hand, the disappearance of Black's King Bishop
is a serious matter for him, as all
his King-side Pawns are on white
squares and consequently do not
guard his black squares. These
squares are weak, now that they
are no longer guarded by the King
Bishop.

12 PxB          BxB

This is a rough-and-ready solution of what to do with the remaining Bishop. It is a solution that creates more problems than it solves, for White's recapture immediately gives him *control of the King file.*

**13 QxB            N-N2**

Quite natural: he wants to dispute the King file by ... R-K1.

Diagram 290

White can already *infiltrate on the seventh rank* by playing 14 Q-K7. But first he wishes to create new weaknesses in Black's camp.

**14 N-K4!        ....**

This crafty move has a double function. It prevents the natural developing move 14 ... N-Q2, as Black's Queen Pawn must not be left unguarded. Secondly, the natural-looking 14 ... R-K1 becomes impossible, for then 15 B-N5! (*exploiting the weakness of the black squares*) wins the Exchange through the threat of 16 N-B6ch after Black saves his Queen.

**14 ....          P-B3**

He prevents B-N5, but at the cost of creating a new weakness: his K3 square is no longer guarded by a Pawn.

**15 B-B4!         N-K1**

The only move to save the Queen Pawn.

**16 B-R6!         N-N2**

And not 16 ... R-B2?; 17 N-N5! winning the Exchange (for if 17 ... PxN??; 18 QxNch is ruinous for Black. This is one of the consequences of White's *control of the King file.*)

As a result of White's clever Bishop maneuver, he has gained a whole tempo in comparison to the immediate 15 B-R6.

**17 QR-Q1!        ....**

This Rook is ready to go into action. Black's Queen Rook is still at home.

**17 ....          N-R3**
**18 R-Q3          P-B4**

Trying to break White's grip, he only intensifies it. There is no plausible alternative, for if 18 ... Q-Q2; 19 R-K3, QR-K1; 20 NxPch!, RxN; 21 RxRch, NxR; 22 QxNch, QxQ; 23 RxQch and wins. Again White's *control of the King file* tells the story.

**19 N-N5          ....**

With his last move, Black has definitively bared his black squares to the enemy, and *infiltration* is now the order of the day.

Note that the seductive 19 B-N5? will not do because of 19 ... PxN!; 20 BxQ, PxR followed by the capture of the Bishop, leaving Black with Rook and two minor pieces for the Queen. The moral is that even in the midst of the most refined strategical maneuvers, tactical considerations must never be forgotten.

| 19 .... | N-B2 |
|---|---|

Or 19 ... R-K1; 20 R-K3 with stifling *pressure on the King file*.

**20 Q-K7!** ....

Relentless *infiltration*. Mate is threatened, and Black must lose at least a Pawn.

| 20 .... | QxQ |
|---|---|
| 21 RxQ | N/B2-K1 |

**22 R-R3!** ....

More *infiltration*. (22 RxP is good enough, but not the quickest way.)

| 22 .... | P-B5 |
|---|---|
| 23 BxN | NxB |
| 24 RxRP | .... |

The ideal culmination of White's *infiltration* policy.

| 24 .... | N-B4 |
|---|---|
| 25 R-K6! | .... |

He *infiltrates* on the previously weakened square.

| 25 .... | KR-K1 |
|---|---|
| 26 RxPch | Resigns |

If 26 ... K-B1; 27 R-B7 mate. If 26 ... N-N2; 27 R/R7xNch and mate next move.

In this masterly game, the great Capablanca's *infiltration* moves amount to sheer wizardry.

## CUMULATIVE POSITIONAL PRESSURE

### Nimzoindian Defense

#### Lodz, 1938

| White | Black |
|---|---|
| G. STAHLBERG | V. PETROV |
| 1 P-Q4 | N-KB3 |
| 2 P-QB4 | P-K3 |
| 3 N-QB3 | B-N5 |

By *pinning* the Knight, Black

deprives it of any influence in the struggle for control of the center squares. This struggle, more specifically, involves the control of White's K4 square.

| 4 Q-N3 | N-B3 |
|---|---|

White attacks the *pinning* piece, Black defends it. There is also an interesting threat: 5 … NxP!; 6 QxB??, N-B7ch *forking* King and Queen.

**5 P-K3** ….

Guarding the Queen Pawn and thus parrying the threat.

**5** …. **P-Q4**

Now he is certain of having a firm hold on White's K4 square. Note that both players suffer from an inability to develop the Queen Bishop. In each case, this piece is blocked by its King Pawn.

**6 PxP** ….

This exchange does not make much sense. Black recaptures with the Pawn, and thus obtains a free diagonal for his ailing Bishop.

**6** …. **PxP**
**7 B-N5** ….

*Pinning* Black's Queen Knight and therefore threatening to win a piece with 8 QxB. Black's reply gives his Bishop the needed protection.

**7** …. **Q-K2**
**8 P-QR3** **BxNch**
**9 PxB** **Castles**

[*See Diagram 291*]

**10 BxN?** …

A thoughtless move. White gives

Diagram 291

up the theoretical advantage of the two Bishops and opens the Queen Knight file for Black's Rooks. He also creates a powerful diagonal for Black's Bishop, and *weakens his own white squares* by depriving them of their natural protector: his King Bishop. It would be difficult to find a single move which involves so many drawbacks!

The simple continuation of White's development by 10 N-K2 is preferable by far.

**10** …. **PxB**
**11 N-K2** ….

If instead 11 Q-R4 (to prevent … B-R3), Black has 11 … Q-K5! threatening to win a Rook. Then, after 12 N-B3 there follows 12 … Q-Q6! (threatening *double attack* on King and Rook by 13 … Qx BPch); 13 B-Q2, B-R3 threatening 14 … Q-K7 mate. This forceful *invasion on the white squares* indicates graphically *how these squares have been weakened* by White's faulty exchange on the tenth move.

11 ....            **B-R3**

The formerly hemmed-in Bishop has acquired a magnificent diagonal. Again Black is exploiting *the weakness on the white squares*. Observe that White cannot castle, as his Knight requires protection. Hence White's next move.

12 **Q-B2**        **Q-K5!**

Still operating on the white squares. Black shows splendid judgment in forcing the exchange of Queens, which will enhance his superiority in mobility.

13 **QxQ**         **NxQ**

Diagram 292

Black threatens 14 ... BxN and 15 ... NxQBPch. From move to move, he manages to preserve little threats that maintain his initiative.

In following the ensuing play, you must keep in mind that whereas Black's Bishop is extremely effective, White's Bishop is hemmed in by his own Pawns.

14 **P-B3**        **N-Q3**

15 **P-QR4**       ....

The first step in freeing his Bishop. If instead 15 QR-N1 (to fight for control of the open file), KR-N1; 16 R-N4, B-B5 followed by 17 ... P-QR4! and White must relinquish the open file.

15 ....            **QR-N1**

Taking the open file.

16 **K-B2**        ....

In order to get his King Rook into the game. White remains on the defensive, and must strive to make his pieces mobile.

16 ....            **R-N6**

After this White cannot avoid the loss of a Pawn. The immediate threat is 17 ... BxN; 18 KxB, RxP.
If 17 B-Q2, R-N7 (*pinning* the Bishop); 18 KR-Q1, N-B5; 19 K-K1, NxP! with a winning game. (If 20 BxN, RxNch with *double attack* on King and Bishop.)

17 **B-R3**        **KR-N1!**

Black prefers to maintain the pressure rather than pick up the Pawn with 17 ... BxN; 18 KxB, RxP when 19 KR-QB1! involves Black in serious technical problems.

18 **KR-K1**       ....

If 18 BxN, PxB and Black has complete control of the open

Queen Knight file, continuing with ... R-N7 and leaving White in a virtually paralyzed state.

18 ....          **B-B5!**

In order to play ... P-QR4! preventing White from trying to close the Queen Knight file by means of B-N4.

19 **B-N4**          ....

He forestalls ... P-QR4 and closes the Queen Knight file. But the departure of the Bishop from QR3 allows a further penetration by Black. Move by move his pressure becomes more intense.

19 ....          **R-N7**

Now the Knight is *pinned*, with a further diminution of White's mobility.

20 **P-R5**          ....

White still wants to fight for the open file; but he cannot play 20 QR-N1? because of 20 ... RxR; 21 RxR, P-QR4 and the *pin* nets Black a piece.

20 ....          **N-N4**

Another strengthening of the pressure. Note how efficiently Black continues to maneuver on the white squares.

White is still unable to dispute the open file. For if 21 QR-N1?, RxR; 22 RxR, BxN; 23 KxB, Nx BPch and wins (*fork* and *pin*).

Diagram 293

21 **QR-B1**          **P-KB4!**

A new threat: 22 ... P-B5! when the *pinned* Knight cannot capture.

If then 23 PxP, R-K1 winning a piece because of the *pin* on the Knight.

Or if 23 P-K4, NxQP!; 24 PxN, R/N1xB winning easily.

22 **P-B4**          ....

A further weakening of his white squares which permits a dangerous invasion. But 22 P-N3 is answered by 23 ... P-N4 renewing the threat.

22 ....          **N-Q3!**

And White is still unable to fight for the open file! Thus if 23 QR-N1?, N-K5ch (another white square!); 24 K-B3 (or 24 K-B1), N-Q7ch (*Knight fork*) winning a whole Rook.

If White tries 23 BxN, he finds that after 23 ... PxB he is virtually without moves. Black can simply play 24 ... R-R7 and 25 ... R/N1-N7 ganging up on the hapless *pinned* Knight.

**23 K-B3**          ....

He *unpins* the Knight. But by now the pressure is too strong, and there is no hope of salvation.

**23 ....**          **N-K5**

Now White can only mark time. Black has all the play.

**24 R-QR1**          **P-KR3!**

Planning the final attack. One possibility is 25 P-R4 (to take the sting out of Black's intended ... P-N4), R-K1; 26 QR-B1, R-K3; 27 QR-R1, R-N3; 28 P-R5, BxNch; 29 RxB, R-N6 mate.

**25 P-R3**          ....

An amusing alternative is 25 N-N3, R-KB7 mate!

**25 ....**          **P-N4!**
**26 PxP**           **PxP**
**27 P-R4**          ....

Or 27 P-N4, PxPch; 28 PxP, K-N2!; 25 QR-B1, R-KR1 and White is helpless against the coming 26 ... R-R7. The tie-up of White's forces is truly pathetic.

**27 ....**          **BxNch**
  **Resigns**

For after 28 RxB, P-N5ch White loses a Rook. The way in which Black's pieces co-operated to reduce White to immobility make a fine study in the art of increasing pressure until the enemy reaches the breaking point.

## CENTRALIZATION

### Queen's Indian Defense

Lucerne, 1949

| White | Black |
|-------|-------|
| H. MUELLER | H. KRAMER |
| 1 P-Q4 | N-KB3 |
| 2 P-QB4 | P-K3 |
| 3 N-KB3 | P-QN3 |
| 4 P-KN3 | B-N2 |
| 5 B-N2 | B-K2 |

For the time being, Black is operating with the idea of controlling the center by the action of his pieces: his Knight at KB3 and his Bishop at QN2 are bearing down on his K5 square.

To counteract this pressure—at least to some extent—White has fianchettoed his King Bishop. The subsequent struggle for control of the center will involve the question of who is to dominate the diagonal on which the two opposing Bishops are located.

| 6 Castles | Castles |
|-----------|---------|
| 7 P-N3 | .... |

White's Queen Pawn controls White's K5 square. By fianchetto-ing his Queen Bishop as well, White hopes to strengthen his grip on that square, and on the long diagonal on which the Queen Bishop will be located.

7 ....          P-B4!

Diagram 294

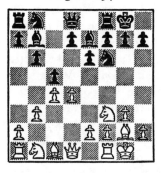

A sharp struggle for control of the center is in progress. Black's last move is in effect a flank thrust against White's control of the K5 square by his Queen Pawn.

**8 N-B3          P-Q4!**

Black's last two moves have a specific aim in view: he hopes to neutralize the whole Pawn center by removing most of the Pawns from there. In that case, all the center squares will become accessible to his pieces.

9 BPxP          NxP
10 NxN           BxN
11 B-N2          B-KB3

Note that both Black Bishops are placed somewhat more aggressively than their White colleagues. Black's slight pressure in the center persists. It may not be enough to win, but to seize the initiative at so early a stage represents a distinct triumph for Black.

12 Q-Q2          PxP
13 BxP           N-B3
14 BxB           QxB

And still Black's slight initiative persists. With the center squares accessible to his pieces, the struggle takes on a new form: who will be the first to post his Rooks effectively on the Queen file and Queen Bishop file? The placement of White's Queen on the Queen file is unfortunate in this connection, as the Queen will be a convenient target for Black's Rooks. White will lose further time getting his Queen out of danger.

15 KR-B1         QR-B1
16 N-K1          BxB

White is unlucky. The simplifying exchanges consistently fail to achieve their purpose: easing White's difficulties.

If he now continues 17 NxB, then 17 ... KR-Q1 is a troublesome move to meet, for example 18 Q-B3??, R-Q8ch! (White's Rook at QB1 is an *overburdened piece*) and Black wins at least a Rook. Or 18 Q-K1, N-Q5! (primarily

threatening the *Knight fork* 19 ...
N-B7) and the magnificent centralization of Black's Knight will
decide the game in his favor.

**17 KxB          KR-Q1**
**18 N-Q3          ....**

White might try 18 Q-B3 to provoke 18 ... N-Q5? which allows
19 QxR! so that if 19 ... RxQ; 20
RxRch with a *back-rank mate* to
follow.

**18 ....          Q-Q5**

This *centralization* of the Queen
intensifies the *pin* on White's
Knight and makes his position
even more difficult.

**19 Q-K1          ....**

*Unpinning* his Knight.

**19 ....          P-KR3**

Creating a loophole for his King
and thus ruling out *back-rank mat-*
*ing* possibilities. This is always a
useful precaution in such situations; see for example the note to
White's eighteenth move.

**20 R-B4          ....**

He strives with might and main
to drive away the *centralized*
Queen.

**20 ....          Q-Q4ch**

The Queen transfers to an
equally useful center square, the
reply 21 P-K4? being out of the

question because of 21 .... QxN.

**21 K-N1          N-Q5!**

Powerful *centralization* with a
flock of threats, such as 22 ... N-B7
(*Knight fork*) winning the Exchange, or 22 ... RxR or 22 ...
NxKPch winning a Pawn.

**22 RxR          ....**

Yielding the *open file* to Black;
but if he tries to hold the file, we
get this pretty conclusion: 22 QR-
B1, RxR; 23 RxR, Q-K5!! (more
*centralization!*). White cannot
meet the threat of 24 ... NxKPch.
For example: 24 K-B1??, Q-R8
mate! Or 24 N-B1, N-B6ch (*fork*
and *pin!*); 25 K-R1, QxR! and
wins.
Note how the scope of a *central-*
*ized* piece radiates in all directions.

**22 ....          RxR**
**23 R-B1          ....**

Black was threatening the *fork*
... N-B7; and in any event, White
cannot renounce the open file for
good.

**23 ....          RxR!**

Simple and strong. White must
not reply 24 QxR?? because of 24
... NxKPch *forking* King and
Queen.

**24 NxR          ....**

[*See Diagram 295*]

Diagram 295

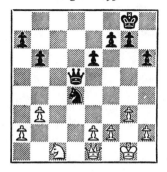

24 ....        Q-B3!!

An amazingly powerful move, considering the drastically simplified character of the position.

The threat is 25 ... QxN!; 26 QxQ, NxPch (*Knight fork*) and wins. White of course cannot play 25 K-B1?? in view of 25 ... Q-R8 mate.

25 N-Q3        Q-K5!!

Now the threat is simply 26 ... NxKPch; 27 K-B1, NxPch with two Pawns ahead and an easy win.

White cannot play 26 N-B1, for then 26 ... N-B6ch (*fork* and *pin*) wins White's Queen.

If 26 P-B3, QxN!; 27 PxQ, Nx BPch followed by 28 ... NxQ and the King and Pawn ending is won for Black. And 26 P-K3?? allows the terrible *fork* 26 ... N-B6ch.

In short, White has no move to ward off the threatened loss of material. He cannot contend with Black's *centralized* forces.

26 Q-Q1        NxKPch
27 K-B1        N-B6!

*Double attack!* He threatens 28 ... Q-R8 mate and 28 ... NxQ.

28 P-B3        Q-K6
  Resigns

He must play 29 Q-B2, when his position falls apart after 29 ... QxPch, etc.

One of the most convincing examples in all chess literature of the power of *centralization*. The game will repay repeated study, for there is much to learn from the way in which Black nullifies White's control of the center, and then achieves domination in that vital sphere for his own pieces.

## POWERFUL PAWN CENTER

### French Defense

Maehrisch-Ostrau, 1923

| White | Black |
|-------|-------|
| E. BOGOLYUBOV | R. RETI |
| 1 P-K4 | P-K3 |
| 2 P-Q4 | P-Q4 |
| 3 N-QB3 | N-KB3 |
| 4 P-K5 | KN-Q2 |

By driving away the Knight, White deprives Black's King-side of one of its most reliable guards, and thereby creates attacking chances for himself. On the other hand, Black, despite the passive appearance of his position, can react powerfully in the center with ... P-QB4 and, possibly, ... P-KB3. The upshot of such counteraction is that both White's Queen Pawn and King Pawn disappear, and Black assumes the initiative by reason of his *powerful Pawn center.*

**5 Q-N4**          . . . .

Immediately utilizing the absence of Black's King Knight from KB3. As we know, however, early Queen moves are apt to result in retreat and loss of time.

**5 . . . .          P-QB4**

The indicated counterplay, which menaces White's Queen Pawn directly and his King Pawn indirectly.

**6 N-N5**          . . . .

These brutal but naïve attacking moves have an air of futility about them.

**6 . . . .          PxP!**

With the interesting point that if 7 N-Q6ch, BxN; 8 QxNP?, BxP and wins—another indication of the shaky state of White's center.

| 7 N-KB3 | N-QB3 |
|---------|-------|
| 8 N-Q6ch | BxN |
| 9 QxNP | BxP! |
| 10 NxB | Q-B3! |

Saves the Rook and forces the exchange of Queens.

**11 QxQ          NxQ**

The end of White's attack. All he has to show for it is a Pawn minus—which he can regain with a bit of trouble.

**12 B-QN5**          . . . .

This pin is necessary to regain the Pawn.

| 12 . . . . | B-Q2 |
|-----------|------|
| 13 N-B3 | N-K5! |
| 14 Castles | P-B3! |

Threatening to hold the Pawn with ... P-K4.

| 15 | BxN | PxB |
|----|-----|-----|
| 16 | NxP | P-QB4 |
| 17 | N-K2 | K-B2 |

Diagram 296

It is now time to take stock of White's attack and its consequences. The attack was a mere flash in the pan, being brushed off with ease by Black. The White center Pawns have disappeared, and Black is left with a *compact Pawn center*. In due course he will be able to obtain a passed Pawn. Furthermore, he has open lines for his Rooks, and his King is actively posted in the center, ready to co-operate in a *centralized Pawn advance*.

White has no prospects, and is reduced to passivity.

| 18 | P-KB3 | N-Q3 |
|----|-------|------|
| 19 | P-QN3 | P-K4 |

The *Pawn center* begins to take on a formidable appearance.

| 20 | B-R3 | QR-QB1 |
|----|------|--------|
| 21 | QR-Q1 | P-Q5 |

Note that the placement of the Black center Pawns on black squares has given his Bishop much greater scope than it had, say, on move 12.

| 22 | N-B1 | N-B4! |
|----|------|-------|

Played with a double object: (1) to post the Knight aggressively at K6—there is a direct *forking* threat now to win the Exchange—and (2) to *unpin* the Queen Bishop Pawn so that ... P-B5 becomes possible.

| 23 | R-B2 | N-K6 |
|----|------|------|

Black is able to occupy this useful outpost thanks to White's eighteenth move, which renounced control of his K3 square by the King Bishop Pawn.

| 24 | R-K1 | P-B5! |
|----|------|-------|

Diagram 297

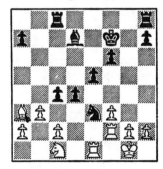

From this point on, White never has a tranquil moment. The immediate threat is 25 ... PxP; 26 BPxP, N-B7 (*Knight fork*) winning the Exchange.

**25 P-QN4**      ....

No better is 25 PxP, RxP; 26 R/K1-K2, KR-QB1 and Black wins *the backward Pawn on the open Queen Bishop file.*

**25 ....          B-R5!**

Now the Bishop takes a hand in the proceedings. White cannot respond 26 P-B3? for then the deadly *Knight fork* 26 ... N-B7 is decisive.

**26 R/K1-K2      N-Q8!**

White has been reduced to complete passivity, as he is stifled by the *powerful center Pawns,* which rob his pieces of accessible squares. The following elegant Knight maneuvers accentuate Black's advantage.

**27 R-B1         N-B6!**
**28 R/Q2-B2      ....**

And not 28 R-Q2?? losing a piece because of the terrible *Knight fork* 28 ... N-N8.

**28 ....         N-N8!**
**29 B-N2         P-B6!**

If now 30 B-R1, N-Q7; 31 R-K1, BxP and White can resign: his Bishop is nailed in permanently, and Black has *two connected passed Pawns.*

**30 N-N3         BxN**
**31 RPxB         ....**

If 31 RxN?, BxRP; 32 R-R1, PxB and White is lost. Or if 31 BPxB, P-B7; 32 B-B1, P-Q6 and *the two connected passed Pawns* win at once, there being no defense to the threat of 33 ... P-Q7; 34 BxP, NxB; 35 RxN, P-B8(Q).

**31 ....         N-Q7**
**32 R-K1         KR-Q1**
**33 B-B1         P-Q6!**

Forcing *a passed Pawn.*

If now 34 BxN, PxB; 35 RxQP, PxP; 36 RxR, RxR and White is helpless against 37 ... R-Q8 forcing *the promotion of the passed Pawn.* This is the ultimate destiny of *the powerful Pawn center.*

**34 PxP          RxP**
**35 BxN          ....**

He cannot permit ... NxNP.

**35 ....         RxB!**

If now 36 RxR, PxR; 37 R-Q1, R-B8 and *the passed Pawn becomes a Queen.* Note the *pinning* technique here and in the note to Black's move 33.

**36 R-R1         K-K3!**

So that if 37 RxP?, RxR; 38 KxR, P-B7 and *the passed Pawn becomes a Queen.*

**37 K-B1         RxRch**
**38 KxR          P-B7**
**39 R-QB1        K-Q4**
**40 K-K3         R-B6ch!**
**41 K-Q2         K-Q5!**

The *centralized* position of Black's King pays off. For if 42 RxP, RxRch; 43 KxR, K-K6; 44 K-B3, K-B7 and the massacre of the King-side Pawns gives Black an easy win.

| 42 P-R4 | R-Q6ch! |
| Resigns | |

White has had enough. If 43 KxP, R-B6ch; 44 K-Q2, RxR; 45 KxR and Black wins the King and Pawn ending by 45 ... K-B6 or 45 ... K-K6.

Or if 43 K-K2, K-B6 followed by 44 ... R-Q1 and 45 ... K-N7, when White must give up his Rook for *the passed Pawn*.

An ideally effective example of the strength and consequences of *the powerful Pawn center*. Reti demonstrated its advantages with almost mathematical exactitude.


## BREAKING OUT OF A CONSTRICTED POSITION

### Caro-Kann Defense

Zurich, 1949

| White | Black |
| M. Blau | P. Leepin |

| 1 P-K4 | P-QB3 |
| 2 P-Q4 | P-Q4 |
| 3 PxP | PxP |
| 4 P-QB4 | N-KB3 |
| 5 N-QB3 | P-K3 |

Black wants to be sure to retain a Pawn at Q4 in order to command his K5 square. His last move is directed toward that objective, but it has the familiar drawback of constricting the scope of his Queen Bishop.

| 6 B-N5 | B-K2 |
| 7 R-B1 | Castles |
| 8 N-B3 | N-K5 |

Black's game is still cramped, and he offers an exchange of pieces in order to ease his position.

| 9 BxB | QxB |

Now Black's prospects appear more favorable. His Queen has been developed, his King Knight has an aggressive post. On 10 PxP he interpolates 10 ... NxN with a fair game. Or 10 NxN, PxN; 11 N-Q2, P-B4 with a fighting game in which both sides have chances.

| 10 P-B5!? | .... |

White's last move leads to a game highly critical for both players. Black's game is seriously constricted. This is especially true of his Bishop, which has virtually no scope. Worse yet, Black does not

Diagram 298

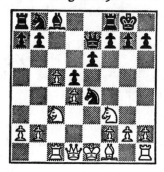

seem able to free himself with ...
P-K4.

10 ....                    **P-QN3!**

Black makes immediate efforts
to break the chain of Pawns which
White hopes to maintain. That is
to say, White's advanced Pawn on
QB5 requires the support of a
Pawn on QN4, in turn supported
by one on QR3. To avoid total
encirclement, Black must fight
the establishment of such a Pawn
chain.

11 **P-QN4**          **P-QR4!**

Still carrying out the idea explained in the previous note.

12 **P-QR3**          **RPxP**
13 **RPxP**           **PxP**

Now White has an interesting
problem: which way to recapture.
14 QPxP looks inviting, as it assures him two connected passed
Pawns. But these Pawns would be
vulnerable to counterattack, for

example 14 ... N-R3! Now 15 P-
N5? loses a Pawn, while 15 BxN,
BxB leaves White with a wretched
position, castling being impossible.

So, after 14 QPxP, N-R3!; 15
Q-N3 seems proper, but then 15 ...
R-N1! is much too strong. And 15
Q-R4 is refuted by 15 ... B-Q2!
winning at least a Pawn in reply
to 16 P-B6 or 16 B-N5.

Diagram 299

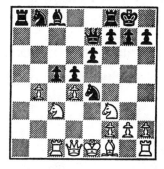

14 **NPxP**             ....

This does not permit the counterattacking opportunities mentioned
in the previous note, and still leaves
Black with a very crowded position, ... P-K4 being impossible.
But actually, Black has a brilliant
emancipation plan at his disposal.

14 ....                    **NxN!**
15 **RxN**                **P-K4!!**

Black's play is of the highest
order. The first fine point is that
after 16 NxP? Black wins the
*pinned* Knight with 16 ... P-B3.

16 **PxP**                **N-B3!**

Continuing in the same enterprising vein. White dare not play 17 QxP??, R-Q8ch; 18 K-Q2, R-Q1 (*pinning* and winning the Queen) or 18 K-K2, B-R3ch; 19 K-K3, N-N5 with equally disastrous effect for White.

17 B-K2          . . . .

White discreetly steers for safety: he wants to castle, but Black continues his disquieting tactic.

17 . . . .          P-Q5!

Now the point is that if 18 NxP?, NxN; 19 QxN, R-R8ch followed by 20 . . . R-Q1 with an easy win for Black.

18 QR-B1          R-Q1!

Even now White is not prepared to castle, for example: 19 Castles?, P-Q6!; 20 BxP, B-R3; 21 N-K1, N-N5; 22 R-B3, RxB!; 23 NxR, R-Q1 and the *pin* yields Black two minor pieces for a Rook. This is a fine example of *pinning* technique.

19 Q-Q2          P-Q6!
20 B-Q1          R-R4!

All this time, be it noted, Black has been operating nonchalantly with a Pawn down. But now the extra Pawn must be returned.

21 Castles        RxP
22 R-B3           RxR
23 QxR            B-N2
24 B-R4           Q-N5!

White has defended rather well, but he still has to contend with the far-advanced passed Pawn. The game winds up with surprising suddenness—surprising if you are not familiar with the power of the passed Pawn.

25 QxQ            NxQ
26 R-N1?          . . . .

Relying too much on the *pin*. 26 N-Q2 (*blockading the passed Pawn*) would be much more to the point.

26 . . . .          BxN

Diagram 300

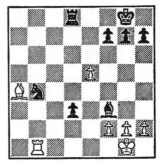

27 PxB           . . . .

The weakening of his Pawn position results in a very curious mating net. However, if 27 RxN, B-K7!; 28 R-N1, P-Q7; 29 B-Q1, R-QB1! and the deadly threat of 30 . . . R-B8 (*Pawn promotion!*) is decisive.

27 . . . .          N-Q4

Threatening to win quickly with

the terrible *fork* 28 ... N-B6, for example 29 R-R1, NxB (the simplest way); 30 RxN, P-Q7 and White must give up his Rook for the Pawn (31 R-R1, etc.). Again *the Pawn promotion* theme appears.

**28 R-QB1        P-Q7**

The *passed Pawn* is now only one square away from queening!

**29 R-B6        ....**

If 29 R-Q1, N-B6 wins on the spot.

**29 ....        P-N4!**

A farsighted move. He creates a loophole for his King, so that he can move his Rook without having to worry about a *back-rank mate*.

**30 B-Q1        R-K1**
**31 P-B4        ....**

Despair.

**31 ....        NxP**
**32 P-R4        RxP!**
**    Resigns**

There is nothing to be done against ... R-K8ch (*double attack* plus *promotion* motif).

While this game is highly instructive all the way, it is particularly so in the early-middle-game stage in which Black forcibly breaks out of a seriously constricted position.

# The

# LAWS OF CHESS

## OFFICIAL CODE

Compiled by the Fédération Internationale des Échecs

1. DEFINITION AND OBJECT.
    i. Chess is played by two persons on a square called the Chess Board and divided into 64 squares colored light and dark alternately. Each person shall play with a series of Sixteen men, one series to be light colored and called White, and the other series to be dark colored and called Black.
    ii. The object of the play is to checkmate the Opponent's King and the Player who checkmates thereby wins the game.
    *The meaning of the technical terms used in this law will be found in 3, 4 (iv), 10 (i).*

2. THE CHESS BOARD.
    i. The Chess Board shall be so placed between the two persons that the corner square nearest to each at his right hand side shall be light colored.
    ii. Each sequence of eight adjoining squares in a straight line from one player to the other is termed a file.
    iii. Each sequence of eight squares at right angles to the files is termed a rank.
        Each straight sequence of squares of the same color from edge to edge of the chess board and touching at angles only, and at an angle of 45 degrees with a rank or file is termed a diagonal.

3. DESCRIPTION OF THE MEN.
    The men in each of the two series are:—

(Printed symbols)

| NAMES | WHITE | BLACK |
|---|---|---|
| A KING | ♔ | ♚ |
| A QUEEN | ♕ | ♛ |
| TWO ROOKS | ♖ | ♜ |
| TWO BISHOPS | ♗ | ♝ |
| TWO KNIGHTS | ♘ | ♞ |
| EIGHT PAWNS | ♙ | ♟ |

4. INITIAL POSITION OF THE MEN.

i. The men shall be arranged on the chess board before the commencement of a game as shown in the diagram below:—

*Black*

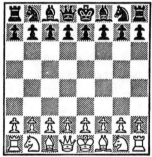

*White*

ii. The first move in a game shall be made with a White man.

iii. The persons shall play alternately, one move at a time.

iv. The person whose turn it is to move is termed the Player and the other is termed the Opponent.

*These terms "Player" and "Opponent" come into force as soon as the right to the first move has been determined.*

5. NOTATION.

i. Only the two most widely used systems of recording chess moves, namely, the Descriptive and the Algebraic, are recognized by the F.I.D.E.

ii. Affiliated Units can select either of these two systems for their use.

The Descriptive System is as follows:

The men (except the Knight) are designated by their initials and the Knight by Kt or N.

The Bishop, Knight and Rook from the Kings' side of the chess board are, if necessary, further designated by prefixing the letter K and the corresponding men on the Queens' side by prefixing the letter Q.

The eight files counting consecutively from left to right on the side of the chess board initially occupied by the White men are designated the QR, QKt, QB, Q, K, KB, KKt and KR files respectively.

The eight ranks are numbered for the White men 1 to 8 from the side of the chess board initially occupied by them, and inversely for the Black men 1 to 8 from the side of the chess board initially occupied by them.

A move shall be recorded by the letter designating the man moved followed by a hyphen and the letter or letters and number designating the file and rank respectively of the square to which the man has been moved. For instance, Q-KB4 means the Q is moved to the fourth square in the file of the King's Bishop. When two men of the same series and denomination can be moved legally to the same square, the letter or letters and number designating the file and number of the square which the moved man occupied shall be added in brackets to the letter designating the man moved. For instance R(KKt2)-Kt4 means the R on the second square of the KKt file is moved to the fourth square of the same file.

*If an opposing man occupy the square to which a man is moved, the designation of such opposing man shall be substituted for the designation of the square, preceded by the symbol for capture, but the latter designation, stated as from the Player's side of the chess board, shall be added in brackets if otherwise the record could be interpreted as applying to more than one opposing man.*

## Abbreviations

Castles KR or O-O = Castles with the KR (Short Castling).

Castles QR or O-O-O = Castles with the QR (Long Castling).

X = Captures.

Ch. = Check.

Mate = Check and Mate.

The Algebraic System.

The men (except the Pawns, which are not specially indicated) are designated by the same letters as in the Descriptive system.

The eight files counting from the side of the board initially occupied by the White men and from left to right are lettered consecutively a to h.

The eight ranks counting from the same side of the board are numbered consecutively 1 to 8.

Each square is therefore named by the combination in the following order of the letter of the file and the number of the rank in which it occurs.

A move shall be recorded by the designation of the man moved (not being a Pawn) followed by the designations respectively of the square it occupied and then the square to which it has been moved, but in abbreviated notation mention of the first-named square may be omitted unless thereby the record becomes capable of interpretation as applying to more than one man. For instance, Bc1-f4 means the Bishop on square c1 is moved to square f4 and in abbreviated notation is recorded as Bf4. A move of a Pawn shall be recorded by the combination in the following order of the letter of the file and the number of the rank in which the square to which it has been moved occurs. For instance, e7-e5 means the Pawn on square e7 is moved to square e5 and in abbreviated notation is recorded e5.

*If either of two Pawns can be moved to the square named, the letter designating the file which the moved Pawn previously occupied shall precede in brackets that of the square to which it has been moved.*

### Abbreviations

O-O = Castles with the KR (Short Castling).
O-O-O = Castles with the QR (Long Castling).
: or X = Captures.
+ = Check.
:+ = Captures and Checks.
X = Check and Mate.
:X = Captures and Checkmates.

*Commentary Signs, common to both systems of notation*
! = Good move.
? = Inferior move.

6. CURRENT EXPRESSIONS.

    *Man.*—A term applicable to each King, Queen, Rook, Bishop, Knight and Pawn.

    *Piece.*—A term applicable to each man except a Pawn.

    *Pinned Man.*—A man that occupies a square between the King of the same color and an opposing piece that would otherwise be giving check to the King, or a man the movement of which would expose to capture a piece of a higher value than the capturing man.

    *Discovered Check.*—Check given to the Opponent's King when the line of action of the checking piece is opened by the movement of another man of the same color.

    *Double Check.*—Check given by the man moved in addition to the discovered check from another piece.

    *An Exchange.*—The exchange by capture of *identical* men, or of men of practically the same theoretical value.

    *To Win or to Lose the "Exchange."*—To exchange by capture a Bishop or Knight for a Rook is to win, and of a Rook for Bishop or Knight is to lose, the Exchange.

7. MOVEMENTS OF THE MEN IN GENERAL.

    i. *and* ii. The move of a man shall be to an unoccupied square or to a square occupied by an opposing man.

    iii. The move of a man shall not cause such man to pass over any occupied square, except in the case of a move of a Knight.

    iv. A legal move of a man to a square occupied by an opposing man requires the removal of that opposing man by the Player from the chess board.

8. MOVEMENTS OF THE INDIVIDUAL MEN.

    The King can be moved to a square adjoining the square he occupies *except* in the case of Castling, which is a combined move of the K and the R, but counts as one move, in which first the K, occupying his own square, is placed on one of the two nearest squares of the same color as his own in the same rank and then the R, towards which the K has been moved, is placed on the next square on the further side of the moved K. Castling is not permitted (*a*) when either the K or R has been moved previously; (*b*) when any square between the K and the R is occupied by a man; (*c*) if the K be in check; or (*d*) if Castling would cause the K to pass over, or occupy any square on which he would be in check. (See 9.)

Subject to the limitations imposed by Rule 7: A Queen can be moved to a square, being one of those forming the file, or the rank, or the one or two diagonals to all of which the square the Queen occupies is common.

A Rook can be moved to a square, being one of those forming the file, or the rank, to both of which the square the R occupies is common.

The Bishop can be moved to a square, being one of those forming the one or two diagonals to which the square the B occupies is common.

The Knight can be moved like a R one square and then like a B one square, which final square must not adjoin the square from which the Knight is moved, such movements constituting one move.

A Pawn, when not making a capture, can be moved forward on the file one or two squares on its first move, and afterwards one square only at a time.

A capture with a Pawn can be made when the opposing man occupies the adjoining square forward of either of the diagonals to which the square occupied by the capturing pawn is common.

*En Passant.*—A Pawn which has been moved two squares on its first move is liable to be captured on the following move by a Player's Pawn that could have captured it if it had moved only one square, precisely as though it had so moved.

*Promotion.*—Each Pawn that is moved to a square on the eighth rank must be exchanged for a Q, R, B or Kt of the same series without regard to the number of such pieces already on the board.

9. CHECK.

   i. *and* ii. The King is in "check" if so placed that an opposing man (whether pinned or not) could capture him.

   *Note.*—It is customary, but not obligatory, for the Player to advise the Opponent of this fact by saying "check."

   iii. *and* iv. The K must not be moved to a square on which he would be in "check" or to any one of the squares adjacent to the square occupied by the opposing K.

   v. A checked King must be moved out of check, or the checking man captured, or the check parried by the interposition of another man in the next move after the one giving check. (See 10 (i).)

   vi. A Player who makes a move which does not fulfil the conditions in (v) must retract that move and make another move which does so comply, and, if possible, with the man he has touched in making the retracted move.

10. CHECKMATE.

    i. Checkmate is a check from which the King cannot be relieved by any of the moves prescribed in 9 (v) and ends the game.

    ii. The fact of having announced erroneously a checkmate in an indefinite or stated number of moves shall not affect the after-course of the game.

11. THE MOVE.

    The choice of playing the first game with the White men or the Black men shall be determined by lot, or by agreement, and in a match of two or more games the two persons shall play with the two series alternately, irrespective of the results of the games, but games annulled according to 12 shall not be reckoned in applying this rule.

12. ANNULLED GAMES.

    i. If in the course of or *immediately* after a game it be proved that the initial position of the men on the board was incorrect, or the chess board wrongly placed initially, the game shall be annulled.

    ii. If in the course of a game the number or position of the men be altered illegally the position immediately before the alteration occurred must be reinstated and the game resumed therefrom.

    iii. If this position cannot be ascertained the game shall be annulled and there shall be a re-play.

13. COMPLETION OF MOVE.

    A move is complete:

    (*a*) In moving a man from one square to another, when the Player has removed his hand from the man.

    (*b*) In capturing, when the captured man has been removed from the board and the Player has removed his hand from the man making the capture.

    (*c*) In Castling, when the Player has removed his hand from the Rook.

    (*d*) In promoting a Pawn, when the Player has replaced the Pawn by the selected piece and removed his hand from the latter. *For sealed move see* 21.

14. ADJUSTMENT OF THE MEN.

    i. The Player may adjust one or more of his men on their respective squares after giving previous notice of his intention so to do.

(*Note.*—It is customary to use the expression "I adjust.")

ii. The Player shall not adjust the Opponent's men, or the Opponent the Player's men. The Opponent, however, shall adjust the position of his men on the board if requested by the Player.

iii. If the men be disarranged accidentally, the timing clocks, if in use (see 20), must be stopped immediately and the position reinstated, and, if a Tournament game, under the direction of the controlling official in charge thereof. If, moreover, it be proved either in the course of the game, or *immediately* after it is finished, that the position has been incorrectly set-up, the game shall be resumed from the correct position.

## 15. Touching Men.

If the Player touch

(*a*) One of his own men he must move it.

(*b*) One of the Opponent's men he must take it.

(*c*) One of his own men and one of the Opponent's men, he must take the latter with the former, if such capture be a legal move. If not, the Opponent may require either that the Player shall move his man touched, or take with any one of his men at the Player's option with which the capture can be effected legally, the Opponent's man touched.

   If none of the moves indicated in *a, b, c* can be made legally, no penalty can be exacted.

(*d*) Several of his own men, the Opponent has the right to name which of those men the Player shall move. If none of these men can be moved legally no penalty can be exacted.

(*e*) Several of the Opponent's men, the Opponent has the right to name which man shall be taken. If none of these men can be taken no penalty can be exacted.

## 16. Drawn Games.

The Game is drawn

(*a*) When the Player cannot make a legal move and the King is not in check. This King is then said to be stalemated.

(*b*) If the Player prove he can subject the Opponent's King to an endless series of checks.

(*c*) By recurrence of position when the same position occurs three times in the game, and the same person is Player on each occasion, and if such Player claim the draw before the position is altered by further play, otherwise no claim can be sustained. (For the purpose of this Clause there shall be no distinction between the King and Queen's Rooks and Knights, or between the original pieces and pieces of the same denomination and color obtained through the promotion of Pawns.)

(d) By Mutual agreement, but only after 30 moves have been made with the Black men.

(e) The game shall be declared drawn if the Player prove that 50 moves have been made on each side without checkmate having been given and without any man having been captured or Pawn moved.

(f) Either the Player or the Opponent may at any period of the game demand that the other shall checkmate him in 50 moves, subject to the conditions attached in (e). If checkmate is not given in 50 moves, the game shall be declared drawn. Nevertheless, the count of 50 moves shall begin again after each capture of any man and after each movement of a Pawn. Exception shall be made for certain positions where theoretically more than 50 moves are necessary to force a checkmate and in this case a number of moves double the number established by theory as being necessary for this object shall be allowed in lieu of the 50. The draw must be claimed by either the Player or the Opponent immediately the stipulated number of moves in Conditions (e) and/or (f) of the particular case is completed without checkmate being given, and not at any later period.

17. ILLEGAL MOVES.

If a Player make an illegal move and the Opponent draw attention to the fact before touching any of his own men, the illegal move must be retracted, and the game shall be continued as follows:—

(a) When a capture has not been made, the Player shall make a legal move with the man he moved illegally, but if no such legal move can be made no penalty can be exacted.

(b) If a capture has been made, the Player must either take the Opponent's man by a legal move or make a legal move with his own man touched, at the option of the Opponent, but if no such legal move can be made no penalty can be exacted.

(c) When the illegal move is a sealed move and the mistake cannot be rectified with absolute certainty by the official in charge of the game, it shall be scored as lost by the Player who sealed the illegal move.

(*d*) If in the course of a game it is proved that an illegal move has been made and not retracted, the position existing immediately before the illegal move was made shall be reinstated and the game shall be continued from that position. If the position cannot be reinstated the game shall be annulled.

## 18. PENALTIES.

i. The Opponent can exact a penalty for an infraction of these laws only if he has not touched one of his own men after the infraction occurred.

ii. Castling cannot be exacted as a penalty move.

iii. If the Opponent names as penalty a move which is illegal, his right to exact a penalty for the illegality committed by the Player shall be abrogated.

iv. Before enforcing any penalty the position which existed before the illegality occurred shall be reinstated.

## 19. GAMES FORFEITED.

The game shall be declared forfeited by the Player or the Opponent:

i. Who wilfully upsets the board or disarranges the men.

ii. Who refuses to resume an adjourned game within a reasonable time and in accordance with the usual regulations of Tournaments and matches.

iii. Who refuses to comply with a legal requirement under these laws.

iv. Who in the course of the game refuses to obey the rules and conform to the arrangements made for the conduct of the game.

v. Who whether present or absent exceeds any time limit fixed for the consideration of his moves.

*Note.*—Except when unavoidably prevented the competitors in a Tournament shall conform to the directions of the officials in charge.

## 20. THE USE OF THE CLOCK.

i. If the game be played with a time limit, the following rules shall apply:—

(*a*) Each competitor shall make at least 30 moves in the first two hours of his own time, 45 moves by the end of the first three similar hours, and a proportionate number of moves by the end of each successive similar hour.

(*b*) This time limit may be modified in the regulations framed for any match or Tournament.

(*c*) When it is proved there has been a mistake not caused by negligence in the recording of the time occupied the mistake shall be rectified.

(*d*) The player is forbidden to stop his clock before completing his move except in the cases detailed in this Law.

(*e*) When there are grounds for a claim under this Law the two clocks shall be stopped and as soon as the official in charge of the Tournament has given his decision in respect to the claim shall, if necessary, be set going again by him.

ii. If the Player exceed the time allowed for the consideration of his moves, the official in charge shall declare without making any exception the game lost by the Player (even if he and the Opponent object.)

iii. If the Opponent's clock be allowed to go on, the person who notices the occurrence may not inform the Player or the Opponent but shall inform the official in charge, who shall take the necessary steps to deal with the occurrence.

iv. If a competitor in a match or a Tournament be absent at the time fixed for commencement or resumption of play, his clock shall be set going as soon as he becomes the Player, and the time which elapses until he has made his move shall count as time for the consideration of his move.

v. The competitor who without valid reason arrives at the place of meeting more than one hour late loses the game.

vi. If both competitors without valid reason arrive at the place of meeting more than an hour late the game shall be declared lost by both.

## 21. Adjourned Games.

i. When a game played with or without time limit is adjourned the Player at the moment of adjournment has the right to record his move in writing.

ii. The Player must record the move himself and place it in an envelope, which he shall then seal. After affixing his signature he shall hand the envelope at once to the official in charge of the Tournament. The Player's clock, if one be in use, shall not be stopped until the record of the move is sealed.

iii. So long as the game stands adjourned neither the Player nor the Opponent shall be allowed access to the envelope containing the sealed move.

iv. At the adjournment it shall be the duty of the Player and the Opponent to make sure that a correct record of the position as well as the time indicated as elapsed by each of the two clocks, if in use, has been recorded on the envelope.

v. On resumption of the game it shall be the duty of the Opponent to reinstate the position on the board, set the clocks to the correct times, open the envelope, make the sealed move on the board, and finally set the Player's clock in motion.

*The Player is regarded as having completed his move by sealing it and becomes the Opponent referred to in paragraph v.*

vi. The envelope containing the sealed move shall not be opened in the absence of the Player, but the official in charge shall set the Player's clock in motion at the time fixed for resumption of the game.

*In paragraph vi the Player is he whose turn it is to move after the execution of the sealed move.*

vii. If the position or (in the case of a game played under the time limit) the times that have elapsed at the adjournment cannot be correctly ascertained, the game shall be annulled.

viii. If the position be reinstated incorrectly all the subsequent moves, if any, shall be annulled and the game resumed from the correct position. If the correct position cannot be ascertained, the game shall be annulled.

## 22. GAMES AT ODDS.

i. In a set of games, a person may give odds in all the games to the other person by giving up the right to move first.

ii. The person who receives the odds of two or more moves must make them all at the beginning of a game in his first turn to play.

iii. If the odds consist of several moves they shall count for that number of moves in all calculation of time-limit. Similarly the first move of the person who gives the odds shall count as the same number of moves as those made by the receiver of the odds.

iv. The person who receives odds of two or more moves must not move any man beyond his fourth rank until the other person has made one move.

v. The person who gives the odds of a man or men shall have the right to move first unless such right to move is also granted.

vi. If the odds of a Pawn be given, or of a Pawn and one or more moves, the King's Bishop's Pawn shall be the Pawn removed from the board.

vii. At odds of a Rook, or a Bishop, or a Knight, the piece given is usually, and in the absence of an agreement to the contrary shall be, the Queen's piece.

viii. The person who gives the odds of a Rook may Castle as though this Rook were on the board, on the side from which the Rook has been removed, subject to the condition that this Rook's square is not occupied by any other man of either series.

## 23. RECORDING OF GAMES.

i. Each competitor in a match or Tournament shall record all the moves in his games in a clear and intelligible manner.

ii. In case of discrepancy between the number of moves recorded in any game by the two competitors they may stop the clocks while they are engaged in rectifying the mistake. In order to avail themselves of this right each competitor must have recorded his last move.

iii. The winner of a game shall give to the official in charge a correct and legible record of the game immediately on completion, and in the case of a drawn game, both players shall give in such record.

## 24. SUBMISSION OF DISPUTES.

i. A dispute on a question of fact may be submitted by agreement of the Player and Opponent to the decision of a disinterested spectator, in which case his decision shall be binding without right of appeal.

ii. Any question of a special nature in connection with a game, and not provided for in these Laws, or any disagreement between a Player and his Opponent as to the interpretation, or application of any of these Rules shall be submitted without delay (*a*) to an Umpire whose decision shall be given at once; (*b*) if the game is being played in a Tournament, to the governing Committee.

In both cases the game shall be adjourned until the decision is given, which decision shall be binding without right of appeal.

## 25. DECISION OF F.I.D.E.

The Bureau of the F.I.D.E. shall have the right to give an official, final and binding decision in any case referred to it of general doubt as to the interpretation or application of any of these Laws.

## ANNEXE

CONDUCT OF PLAYER AND OPPONENT.

i. Written or printed notes (except the record of moves made) dealing with or having any bearing on a game in progress shall not be referred to or utilized by the Player or his Opponent, and neither of them shall have recourse to any extraneous advice or information.

ii. No analysis of games shall be allowed in the Tournament Rooms.

iii. Neither Player nor Opponent shall make any comments on any of the moves in the game in progress between them.

iv. Neither Player nor Opponent shall touch or point to any square on the board for the purpose of facilitating reckoning possible moves.

v. A legal move shall not be retracted.

vi. A move shall be made by transferring the man touched directly towards the square to be occupied, and the man must be quitted immediately it has been placed on that square.

In Castling the King shall first be moved and afterwards the Rook.

In promoting a Pawn the Player shall immediately remove the Pawn from the Board and place the substituted piece on the vacated square.

In Capturing, the Player shall immediately remove the captured man from the board.

vii. No comments of any kind, or suggestions as to drawing or abandoning the game shall be added to a sealed move.

viii. The Player who perceives that his Opponent's clock is going should call his attention to the fact.

ix. Neither Player nor Opponent shall in any way whatsoever distract the attention of, or cause annoyance to, the other.

## CERTIFICATE

The Undersigned, instructed by the General Assembly of the F.I.D.E. for the publication of Laws, declares the present text to agree with the final draft approved by the General Assembly of the VIth Congress of Venice.

(Signed)    A. RUEB,
*President.*

THE HAGUE,
31*st March*, 1931.

# INDEX OF RULES

# INDEX